GOOD
START

GOOD START

*A Guidebook for New Faculty
in Liberal Arts Colleges*

Gerald W. Gibson
Roanoke College

Anker Publishing Company, Inc.
Bolton, MA

Good Start

A Guidebook for New Faculty in Liberal Arts Colleges

ISBN 0-9627042-3-7

Composition by Deerfoot Studios.
Cover design by Barbanel Design, Inc.
Cover photo and effects by James Wehtje.
Printing and binding by Goodway Graphics.

Anker Publishing Company, Inc.
176 Ballville Road
P.O. Box 249
Bolton, MA 01740-0249

DEDICATION

Good Start is dedicated with warm affection
and deep appreciation
to colleagues from the days of my own start as
a young professor in a venerable liberal arts college:
Carl J. Likes and Edward E. Towell,
who had the confidence — or courage — to select me as an
unseasoned co-worker;
Maggie Pennington, Norman Chamberlain, Jr., Julian Harrison,
and James Anderson,
who served as mentors and friends during a time when I needed both;
and Gary C. Faber,
with whom I shared an office, and who is an important part
of some cherished memories of days as a faculty member.

ABOUT THE AUTHOR

Gerald W. Gibson is Vice President-Dean of the College and Professor of Chemistry at Roanoke College, Salem, Virginia. He received his B.S. degree (1959) in chemistry from Wofford College, and his Ph.D. degree (1963) from the University of Tennessee. He received a certificate (1983) from the Institute for Educational Management at Harvard University.

Gibson chaired the chemistry department at the College of Charleston for fourteen years, and served there as associate provost. In those positions, and as vice president-dean of the college at Roanoke College, he has had extensive experience in hiring new faculty and in designing faculty development programs, both at the departmental and institutional level. The faculty development program at Roanoke, which begins with two terms of First-Year Faculty Sessions, has been marked by greatly expanded faculty scholarly activity, coupled with significantly improved student response to teaching. Gibson has made presentations at national and regional conferences on faculty evaluation, faculty orientation, the orientation of new deans, academic budgeting, curriculum, and costs of operating academic departments.

He has publications in chemistry, in poetry, and in higher education. His books include *Mastering Chemistry* (1975), *Mastering Organic Chemistry* (1979), and *Mastering Chemistry Problems* (1988) (with Gary C. Faber). His poems, several of which have won awards, have appeared in the *Cape Rock Journal*, *The Cresset*, *Patches of Carolina Sunshine*, and other publications.

Contents

Foreword

We all know that college professors learn the content of their academic specialties in one of the graduate departments of our leading universities. But where do they learn to teach their subjects—design courses, prepare exams, advise students? Who informs them what is involved in the fullness of a faculty role—being a good colleague, understanding the mission and heritage of their academic profession, or the place of their institution in the over 3,000 colleges and universities in the country. Certainly not in graduate school. Indeed, most faculty members learn these important matters the same way most people learn about sex—through gossip, trial and error, and individual experimentation.

Gerald Gibson now offers a better way. *Good Start* provides a great deal of useful information to young professors and those who would become professors. He writes about selecting a college, securing a position, and getting oriented to the new job. He demystifies and offers valuable suggestions about teaching, scholarship, service, and tenure. He focuses on working within the academic organization, managing time and stress, and maintaining effectiveness. In short, he discusses everything a new faculty member needs to know about being a college professor that graduate school did not teach.

The book is based on Gibson's over twenty-five years of experience as a professor, department chair, and academic dean. He has recruited many faculty members and observed first-hand what happened to them as they entered and developed in the profession. It is remarkable what this sensitive, observant, caring, and thoughtful individual has been able to distill from this rich laboratory of personal experience.

But there is more. This book transcends personal experience and draws on the abundant scholarship about higher education that too often remains unknown to faculty members—even mature ones. This includes surveys of students and faculty, student learning styles, research on student ratings of teaching, histories of liberal education, and more. All of these topics are discussed in clear, succinct, jargon-free prose that is useful to neophytes. Indeed, the ideas for this volume arose as Gibson was designing and operating an actual faculty orientation program. Perhaps that is why his ideas and suggestions are so practical.

The book is filled with information about many topics of import to new faculty members. It also contains thoughtful advice for getting a career in college teaching off to a good start. The feel of the book, though, is mostly that of an extended conversation with a mentor, and the conversation takes a decidedly avuncular tone. Although no book can have the last word on any of the subjects covered, it manages to open the conversation about a myriad of academic topics and to launch the conversation on a sophisticated plane.

This book is particularly timely, because today we have the rare opportunity to recast the American professoriate. A large number of faculty retirements is imminent and the largest infusion of new professors in many decades will be trained, recruited, and nurtured. This is the perfect time to assure that tomorrow's instructors know and care about more than their specialities. They need to know about students—their motivations, the ways they learn, and their meaningful relations with teachers; about working within an academic organization—being a good colleague, building a vital department, and contributing to college-wide programs; and about developing a life-long agenda of personal and professional growth.

There are indications that some graduate universities are starting to give greater attention to teaching and encouraging graduate students to get supervised experience in the classroom. But their contribution to this effort remains limited. A larger share of the responsibility to help faculty members develop fully is borne by colleges and universities, especially those emphasizing undergraduate education. But most responsibility rests with the individual faculty member; *Good Start* is their ideal resource. This should be read by every new faculty member and should be a staple of every college's faculty orientation program. As Gibson says, "Small differences at the start make for large differences later on."

Jerry G. Gaff
Association of American Colleges

Preface

When my college teaching career began, I recall showing up for duty all brimming with enthusiasm, optimism, and expectation—only to discover that no one had thought to assign me an office. Upon looking back, I see in that humbling experience something of a metaphor for how new faculty in American colleges have typically been treated over the decades. If we judge from the attention traditionally given to their preparation for professorial work, both in the graduate schools and on the campuses where they begin, the evidence is not reassuring. Trained thoroughly as specialists in their disciplines, they tend to come to campus otherwise naive about what it means to be a faculty member.

Good Start is intended to ready new faculty for the important work they have taken on. It is addressed directly to the new professor, and its counsel is based on a mix of personal experience and research findings. The idea for the book came from recognition, after years of hiring faculty and observing their progress, that success as teacher-scholar-citizen can trace quite clearly to the start of the career, and that all too often colleges allow that start to be happenstance and halting. Much of the content and organization of *Good Start* comes directly from "First-Year Faculty Sessions," a faculty orientation program which I introduced at Roanoke College in 1987.

The majority of the manuscript was written during a residency at the Institute for Educational Management at Harvard University in the summer of 1990. I express gratitude to Arthur Levine, Educational Chairman of IEM; to Sharon McDade, IEM Program Director in 1990; and to Tacy San Antonio, Senior Program Coordinator, for their invaluable assistance in arranging the residency, which gave me access to the Harvard libraries and a pleasant working environment for the project. Thanks is also due President David M. Gring of Roanoke College, and to the Roanoke College Staff Development Fund for financial assistance during that summer.

A number of colleagues have helped shape *Good Start* by providing encouragement, astute insights and very helpful critiques, including suggestions for the addition of material that I believe adds considerably to the value the book will bring for new faculty readers. Fellow deans to whom I owe thanks include David Deal of Whitman College, James Lott of Mary Baldwin College, Mike

Marty of Drake University, Dan Maultsby of Wofford College, Elizabeth McKinsey of Carleton College, Jeanne Neff of Susquehannah University, Richard Pfau of Emory and Henry College, Conrad Stanitski of Mount Union College, and William Wilson of Virginia Wesleyan College. Good commentary and advice was contributed as well by two directors of faculty development, Mary Deane Sorcinelli of the University of Massachusetts-Amherst, and Kenneth Zaborski of St. Norbert College. Two "graduates" of Roanoke's First-Year Faculty Sessions, Hans Zorn and Gerald McDermott, also furnished very thorough and helpful reviews of the chapters on managing stress and time, and the liberal arts tradition, respectively.

Not originally part of the manuscript, "Becoming a Patriot: The Liberal Arts Tradition," was a chapter added as a result of participating in the excellent seminars provided by the Christian A. Johnson Leadership Program during the summer of 1991. I express deep appreciation to Nicholas Farnham, director of that program, and to Adam Yarmolinsky, provost of the University of Maryland-Baltimore County and seminar leader, for the inspiration supplied by the Troutbeck experience.

A very special debt of gratitude is owed to Jean Rosendahl, administrative assistant to the dean at Roanoke College. She has been a constant support from inception to publication, and without her help the project could not possibly have been completed with such dispatch.

Finally, I want to acknowledge the contribution both to the book and to my own satisfaction that has come from working with new faculty at Roanoke College. They have helped renew my optimism, and to feel again something of the enthusiasm that comes with starting out in the best career I know about.

Gerald W. Gibson
Salem, Virginia
April 1992

Who Needs a Guide?

In my experience, the world's happiest man is a young professor building bookcases...

Wallace Stegner
Crossing to Safety

*A*dam Newprof imagined that Christopher Columbus must have felt something like this when he first spotted land on the horizon. Cruising down the interstate in his new compact car, Adam saw up ahead his first stand of palmetto palms, and he knew the coast couldn't be far away now. He could almost smell the salt air.

The image of the College of Port St. Julian campus was still clear in his mind, although it had been six months since his interview visit. They had liked him at the college, had in fact offered him a position on the spot. And he had liked the college. It would come, he felt assured, as close to his dream of the place where he wanted to teach as anything he could imagine short of Benjamin College, his alma mater. The College of Port St. Julian was a small and historic liberal arts college. Its antebellum buildings and arched porter's lodge entrance were connected around the perimeter of a city block by ancient brick-and-stucco walls topped in stretches by wrought iron fencework. Large, moss-draped live oaks shaded its enclosed campus, and azalea bushes and ferns grew in cool clumps against outside walls.

He didn't know exactly how many students were enrolled, but certainly a minuscule number compared to the enormous swarm of undergraduates at the state university where he had completed his doctorate. At the university, in the chemistry department where he had studied, lecture sections often numbered over three hundred, and it was rare that an undergraduate had an actual conversation with a professor. It would be different at the College of Port St. Julian.

He looked forward to working with the students. In college he had been a lab assistant for three years, and in graduate school he had taught recitation sections and assisted in undergraduate labs for two more years. He felt master of chemistry, his discipline. He could talk about thermodynamics and organic synthesis and kinetics and aqueous solutions and much, much more. He was ready to be a teacher. He had lived on a campus for eight years, and he expected no real surprises. He knew exactly how it would feel, what approaches he would take, what wisdom he wanted especially to impart, and what satisfaction it would bring. He could see the lights going on in students' eyes, and it was that payoff more than any salary that motivated him. Teaching at the College of Port St. Julian would be like coming home.

Adam's foot pressed harder on the accelerator, bringing the palmettos, the salt air, and the venerable classrooms closer with every turn of the tires.

Those of us who have selected college teaching as a career can recall a moment something like the one that Adam Newprof experienced as he drove down the interstate to Port St. Julian. Those who have just moved to a new campus may have had a similar experience only last week.

Adam is about to start a new phase of his life, what promises to be a career of perhaps thirty-five years. Like a student enrolled in a new course, the start will matter more than he realizes. Just as the first few weeks can determine whether a student winds up passing, failing, or excelling in a course, the first few years can determine how successful the career of a new faculty member will be. Speeches, especially commencement speeches, often use the metaphor of the finish line, but it strikes me that we ought to talk much more often about how things are begun, for it is at the start that directions are set. In his book *Chaos*, James Gleick reports the attempts by Edward Lorenz of MIT in the 1960s to predict the weather by computer modeling. Out of those frustrated efforts came the recognition that initial conditions, how things are started off, can be critical to how a vast variety of things turn out:

> In weather…this translates into what is only half-jokingly known as the Butterfly Effect—the notion that a butterfly stirring the air today in Peking can transform storm systems next month in New York.…The Butterfly Effect acquired a technical name: sensitive dependence on initial conditions.[1]

Initial conditions can be just as critical to the teacher with a new appointment to the faculty of the College of Port St. Julian, or anywhere else. The person whose teaching style develops merely out of imitation and avoidance tends to take a very different "teaching trajectory" over the years than the person who invests the little extra time at the beginning to find out what research says works well and poorly. The new faculty member who determines at the outset to stay at the cutting edge of his or her discipline is apt to be, twenty years

---

[1] James Gleick, *Chaos: Making a New Science* (New York, NY: Viking Press, 1987), pp. 8, 23.

later, a still-lively and engaging teacher-scholar; the one who keeps postponing until next term getting back into the library or laboratory is likely to realize too far down the career path that mastery has atrophied—and mobility been lost—along the way. Small differences at the start make for large differences later on.

This book is intended for those who have chosen college teaching as a profession, but for whom it is not yet either second nature or old hat. It is for those who are living in apartments in university towns and finishing dissertations; and for those who are beginning to scan *The Chronicle of Higher Education* and the disciplinary publications on the lookout for notices of openings for assistant professors; and for those who are traveling over the country for interviews at urban colleges and in little hamlets where The College is the center of things; and for those who are packing U-Hauls with the accumulation of graduate school to trek across three states to that college where everything looked just right on the visit. It is intended for those who are building bookcases and thinking, even in the exhilaration of setting up their first office, that in less than a week there will be real classes to teach to real students, and that there is still a lot of reading and planning to do.

That's not to say that professors who have taught for a while already won't find anything of use here. They might, and I hope they will. What they find of value is, however, more likely to be of the I'm-skeptical-but-let-me-give-it-a-try or it's-good-to-have-what-I've-been-doing-confirmed variety than of the okay-if-that's-what-works-I'll-try-it variety. Moreover, experienced faculty members, even those whose experience is relatively brief, will have a harder time taking advice than true novices. So the reader I'm picturing is too new to the profession to be either overly smug or jaded and is still open to ideas of how it all might be done.

Good Start is also aimed primarily at faculty who have chosen the *liberal arts* college as the vineyard for their labor. America is a land of immensely varied settings for college education. Prospective professors, like prospective students, will find many possible environments in which to work. There are private, public, selective, open-door, church-related, military, all-male, all-female, historically black, pre-professional, well-endowed, financially struggling, urban, and rural colleges and universities. The greatest divider is, however, the primary mission of the institution. And whatever the other labels, the most significant factor affecting the day-to-day professional life of the faculty member is whether the primary mission of the college is to educate the whole person. From a practical standpoint, the great separation is between the large university with a principally research mission and the liberal arts college with a teaching mission.[2] Because the liberal arts college environment, with its

---

[2] We may include with the liberal arts colleges those institutions commonly referred to as "comprehensive" colleges. These tend to have broader curricula and to have larger enrollments than most liberal arts colleges, but they are scarcely distinguishable from the latter; both have teaching as a primary mission.

emphasis on whole-person education, is so distinctively different, it seems wiser to attempt a guide specifically for faculty planning a career in that setting.

I have an admitted bias in writing for liberal arts college faculty. It was in that type of college that I did my undergraduate work, began my own teaching career, came to chair a department, and now serve as vice president and dean. It is an environment that I know well, and while acknowledging the excellence of many universities, I believe it is in the liberal arts colleges that the very best *undergraduate* teaching is likely to be found and the very best *undergraduate* education is likely to be obtained.

Recognizing that even incipient faculty members expect anyone offering advice to have established credentials, let me point out that most of what is offered here comes from having done the work of a faculty member for seventeen years, having supervised the work of faculty members in a department for fourteen years, and having recruited faculty members and participated in their development for twenty-four. As circumstances turned out, I have been in two institutions that grew rapidly, and as department chair, associate provost, and dean had the responsibility for sustained faculty recruitment over a long period. I have observed close-up what actually has happened with scores of new faculty members as they entered and aged in the profession, and have learned to identify some things that work and some that don't, and to spot the pitfalls and moments of opportunity. I don't presume to claim expertise, but I do claim experience. There will be references in footnotes throughout the book, but the guidance is offered chiefly out of experience. You may even find me waxing avuncular now and again, for which I ask your indulgence in advance.

If we may return again now to Adam Newprof as he drives toward the College of Port St. Julian and the realization of his dream of becoming a college teacher, you do not get the impression that he thinks he needs a guide of any kind. Oh, he may have a few butterflies as he dwells on the first-day entrance to the classroom, or when he allows himself to wonder what off-the-wall questions he may have thrown at him by precocious students. But you can see that he starts with a certain confident assumption that he knows what he's doing. Of course, he'll need to learn the other faculty members and the staff and who to see for what, but he expects no real surprises. He's going into familiar territory. He'll just be stepping from one side of the desk to the other. And he will step with assurance because he knows his subject thoroughly, and he has thought considerably about how he wants to teach it. A guide? For what? This isn't a jungle he's driving toward, but a college of good reputation and long tradition in one of the country's oldest cities, a college not greatly different from the one that issued his Bachelor of Science diploma with its *magna cum laude* and Phi Beta Kappa seals. Not only is this not a foreign territory, it is surely the place on earth where he wants to be for the rest of a long career. No guide needed here.

What Adam Newprof has not reckoned with is an inevitable gap between expectation and reality. He *expects* the teaching profession to be what he saw as an undergraduate. He sees himself in the role of Professor Paradigm, his mentor through four years at Benjamin College and a person beloved by chemistry majors who made problem-solving look easy, who always had a ready word of wisdom, and who always knew when you needed a smidgin of personal encouragement. He knows about the paper grading, of course; his own father was a high school teacher, and Adam used to watch him ply the red pencil after supper. So the grading is acknowledged, even if not factored prominently into Adam's picture. And from his stint as a graduate assistant, he recognizes that another less pleasant piece of the picture is the debating with "grade grubbers," the students who want to argue about how many points the teacher has taken off for this or that error. He understands that not all of the teaching day is spent opening eyes and being adored. Adam believes, in fact, that he is more realistic about teaching than the typical beginning faculty member. He believes, too, that he has profited from a protracted analysis of the teaching to which he has been subjected from first grade through his doctoral program. He will *never*, for example, as old Dr. Caustic used to do, ridicule the student who has an inane question to ask, or the one whose valiant try at an answer is maddeningly absurd. And he will always be available to and patient with students who come by his office for extra help, as Professor Paradigm was.

Adam Newprof does, very likely, have an edge over many faculty members who are just starting out. The unreckoned reality into which he is blithely driving down the interstate is not a reality he has any reason to know about. He has learned perfectly well from his own experience. But that's the point. What he has learned about the college teaching profession thus far has come (a) from his time observing seasoned teachers, and (b) from the fairly limited taste of teaching that comes from working as a graduate assistant. He has yet to live the complete life of a college faculty member. He has never put together a course from scratch, never attended a faculty meeting, never served on a college committee, never aspired to tenure or promotion, and never tried to squeeze into one day or week the multitude and variety of tasks that must be managed by every faculty member.

In short, he has been thinking about his career as that of *teacher*. It will be much more than that. He will discover that what he *saw* was only a *piece* of Professor Paradigm's world.

I hasten to underscore my lack of intent to discourage anyone who has chosen the career of teacher or to take some of the shine off what I truly believe to be the finest of all vocations. I point out the expectation gap because I believe it makes good sense to accept the *full* role of faculty member from the outset. Not to do so invites later frustration and even cynicism. There are faculty members who have worked on a college campus for twenty years, and who go home muttering at the end of the day about all the intrusions into their teaching.

They feel this way because they have never come to accept that there is not in America any such career as "college teaching"—not pure teaching. There is no formally established full-time position in any college that calls for someone simply to lecture and assign readings and answer student questions and grade papers and go home. "Teaching" is the name given to what is really a slightly different career, the *faculty* career. Teaching is part of a package. To teach, one must become a faculty member, and accepting that assignment means accepting responsibility not only for what goes on in the classroom and laboratory and studio and gymnasium, but also for the conditions in which teaching and learning take place.

This guide deals, then, with all the principal duties of a faculty member. New members of the profession will soon discover the connection between what committees do and the conditions for learning. They will soon wrestle with the question of their own personal scholarship and whether it matters to the atmosphere in which students are called on to be scholars. They will early on have to decide how to juggle two classes, a laboratory, a help session, two telephone calls that need to be returned, a visit from a representative of a textbook company, finishing up a set of papers that *must* be returned first period tomorrow, a department meeting, and at least one meal with their families— all within one twenty-four hour period. This guide is written in full recognition of what a typical day—and career—for a typical faculty member in a typical liberal arts college is like. It is my hope that it will help conscientious and committed teachers to claim the profession—the *actual* profession—as their own.

Finally, a word about the best use of *Good Start*. Chapters 2 and 3 deal with selecting a college and getting hired there. They may not be of particular interest to those who have already passed those mileposts. Chapter 4 offers suggestions about getting oriented to a new college, and so will be of the most value to those who are just beginning work (or are about to) at their chosen institution. Chapter 5 ("Becoming a Patriot: The Liberal Arts Tradition") provides a review of the history of the liberal arts ideal and is meant to equip the new faculty member to represent the tradition with enthusiasm and authority. Chapters 6 ("Good Teaching"), 7 ("What about Scholarship?"), 8 ("Citizenship and Service"), and 9 ("The Individual in the Organization") all need to be read as early in the game as possible; they deal with issues and strategies that every teacher should be alert to and thoughtful about from day one. Chapter 10 ("Taking Charge of Your Life: The Management of Time and Stress"), addresses coping skills that should be acquired as soon as possible. Chapters 11 ("Tenure and Promotion") and 12 ("Staying Good") can be delayed until all the bookcases are built and the books unpacked and syllabi are ready. They can even wait for a Christmas holiday.

Chapters 5 through 11 are designed for use in a faculty orientation program. At the end of each chapter are questions suitable for group discussion. They are aimed at moving from general principles and suggestions to specifics of the individual college where the good start will—or will not—take place. It was, in fact, through designing and operating a faculty orientation program called "First-Year Faculty Sessions" that the idea for this book arose.

I hope that this guidebook, whether read alone or discussed as part of a college-sponsored faculty orientation program, will assist the Adam and Eve Newprofs to get off to the good start that will propel them through extraordinarily productive and satisfying careers in college teaching.

Selecting the Right College

In the United States today, we have approximately 2,100 baccalaureate-granting colleges and universities, each with its own unique history, traditions, and special sense of worth.

Ernest L. Boyer
College

*L*ying on his taut khaki blanket in the Bachelor Officers' Quarters, Adam Newprof found it hard to believe that in less than two months he would be leaving Edgewood Arsenal for good, and a month after that he would be, instead of Lieutenant Newprof, Assistant Professor Newprof. His nearly two years in the Army had been a better experience than he had expected, but he was eager to have it behind him now and to get started with his life as a teacher.

It was back at Benjamin College that he had fallen into the track that took him in due course into a two-year Army stint. He had to choose between taking physical education or military science courses. Never having really been the athletic type, he had chosen military science which meant that he had to become an ROTC cadet and be commissioned upon graduation. The Army did not have a reputation for giving people a lot of breaks nor of assigning people according to their obvious strengths, but in Adam's case they must have slipped up. First they deferred his reporting to active duty until he had completed his graduate work in chemistry and then they assigned him to the Chemical Research and Development Labs at Edgewood Arsenal. He knew a lot of lieutenants with worse stories.

It was also back at Benjamin that some seed had, unbeknownst to him at the time, been planted, which eventually sprouted into a notion that he might become a teacher. It had then grown into full-leafed certainty that he never wanted to do anything else. When he had left Athenstown for the state university and graduate school, he pictured himself as a research chemist for some large company like DuPont or Eastman. But somewhere about halfway through his four years there, he began thinking more and more about Professor Paradigm (or "Doc," as the students often called him) back at Benjamin College, and about Professor Scribe, too, who had taught him creative writing. It was funny; Paradigm and Scribe didn't even get along with each other, he had discovered later. But each had influenced him in a profound way. He had learned from each of them important lessons that went well beyond the very different subjects they taught. Both were teachers who clearly cared about their students, who invested themselves wholeheartedly in their teaching, who spoke with a certain reverence about liberal education, and who were positioned to wield great influence, even power, in the lives of countless young people. He liked that prospect more and more. By the end of his doctoral program, there was no question but that he would be a teacher.

Being in the Army made it a little complicated to search for an opening as a faculty member. He was beginning his second year at Edgewood when another lieutenant who worked in the labs said one Friday, " Hadn't you better get some applications in the mail, if you want a job next year? They're not going to come looking for you, you know." Adam thought about what he should do over the weekend, then on Monday went upstairs to the base library and pulled the *Higher Education Directory* off the reference shelf. Sitting at a table, he chewed on a pencil. It was a pretty daunting tome. In it were listed what Adam assumed were all the colleges and universities in the country, hundreds of them, maybe a couple of thousand. How should he proceed?

He closed his eyes and tried to imagine himself on a campus somewhere. The scene came swiftly—it was Professor Paradigm's cluttered office at Benjamin College. He could even smell the aroma of Doc's pipe tobacco mixed with the musty smell of aging books that crammed the shelves above the office desk. Adam kept in touch with Doc Paradigm, so he knew that there was no opening for him on the Benjamin faculty. He also knew that he wanted to find a place as much like Benjamin College as possible. The four years at the university had been great ones for him. He had been well prepared for graduate study, had greatly enjoyed research, had relished the camaraderie of the chemistry graduate students, and had distinguished himself in the course work. But he had also seen the immense lecture halls, observed the avoidance of undergraduates by busy professors, and had taken note of the publish-or-perish pressure on his research director. If he were choosing where to spend a career, it would have to be on a small liberal arts college campus. He opened his eyes again.

That part was settled. But to which of the hundreds of liberal arts colleges in the directory should he write? As he thumbed through the volume, he noted that it was organized by state. What appealed to him was going back home. It struck him that he didn't even know the names of all the colleges in his home state. Why not begin the search there? To get a sense of what the directory was like, why not read the section on Benjamin College, then see what other possibilities the state held that might come close to that description? Wouldn't it be great to go back and make a contribution to the very state where he had grown up and been educated, and where his family still lived? His forefinger slid slowly down a page, looking for colleges that might be glad to hear from an idealistic native son who wanted to come home.

The Prospects for Choice

It is a splendid circumstance indeed when there is an exact match between faculty member and institution. When that happens, faculty member and institution alike profit. The faculty member enjoys coming to work, and that work tends to be more enthusiastically and effectively done. The faculty member is more likely to identify with the institution, and to feel his or her own fortunes intimately connected with those of the college as a whole. A sense of "match" is affected by many things large and small: whether salaries allow an acceptable standard of living, how agreeable a setting the campus provides for spending one's working day, whether it is possible to learn the names of all one's students by mid term, and even whether or not there is a football team. But mostly "match" is a matter of congruence between individual and institutional values, and of complementarity between what the individual faculty member has to offer and what the college needs, and vice versa. It is, yes, very much like finding a mate for marriage. I suspect that there is computer software out there somewhere that helps prospective faculty members with that kind of match-making; if there isn't yet, there will be soon.

However it is done, anyone who is approximately where Adam Newprof was when he picked up the *Higher Education Directory* is well advised to place the highest possible premium on match with institution. That is not meant to imply, nor is the title of this chapter, that finding match (or "fit," as it is often called in student admissions and retention work) is a simple matter, like selecting an automobile that has all the accessories you were looking for and is precisely the right color. How close the first-time professor comes to the perfect institutional match will depend not only on finding a college with all the characteristics one can think to list as important, but also exactly which of those colleges, if any, have an opening at the right time for someone with his or her credentials.

While it pains us perhaps to concede the fact, college teaching, like every service, is subject to what the economists call market forces. There is supply and there is demand, and the two are virtually never in balance. In the latter half of the twentieth century, academe has seen some pronounced bouncing about of the supply/demand graphs for college faculty. Throughout most of the 1960s demand outpaced supply, and, as Bowen and Sosa put it:

> Shortages of faculty were widely proclaimed, faculty salaries increased markedly, and there was talk of a "golden age" for academics.[1]

A decade later the picture had changed drastically. The 1970s were a sad time during which Ph.D.s were literally, in some cases, painting houses and pumping gas. What had happened? Just that the laws of supply and demand worked as they're supposed to. When demand for faculty went up, salaries went up, and more students decided on college teaching as a career. Graduate schools responded to *that* demand for graduate preparation, and the supply of Ph.D.s rose sharply—about 200% between 1960 and 1970,[2] while demand for new faculty rose more modestly. The resulting glut allowed many colleges to hire faculty in the 1970s with credentials far better than any those colleges could have dreamed of previously—and it left many young Ph.D.s coming out of the pipeline with no options, creating what some have called a generation of "itinerant scholars," who could hope for little better than a series of short-term visiting appointments. The imbalance also created many unhappy tenure-track faculty, for sagging faculty salaries soon reflected the shift.[3] Faculty families experienced a decade of decreased standard of living unprecedented since the Great Depression, as the consumer price index outstripped faculty salary increases for eight successive years.[4] Bitter professors could not in good conscience encourage their students to consider the teaching profession. The word was out. Graduate school enrollments fell quickly, and the number of doctorates awarded remained essentially constant from 1972 through the 1980s.

Those of us whose job it was to recruit new faculty in the 1980s can testify that, while the period was not a "golden age" for those seeking positions in college teaching, there were signals of a supply/demand shift back toward the demand side. Even early in the decade there were well-known shortages of faculty in certain disciplines, such as business or computer science, but there was also a "shrinking pool" phenomenon that provided an omen of things to come in other areas as well. Floods of applications still came in for positions in the humanities and most of the social sciences, but it was common to advertise

---

[1] William G. Bowen and Julie Ann Sosa, *Prospects for Faculty in the Arts & Sciences*, (Princeton, NJ: Princeton University Press, 1989), p. 3.

[2] *National Research Council Survey of Earned Doctorates*, survey results published annually.

[3] The picture of the 1970s is perhaps oversimplified by describing it strictly in market terms. Student demand actually increased during the 1970s by about 35% nationally, but demand for faculty increased less than that, as American colleges struggled with financial difficulties. Federal dollars for education were reduced during the Vietnam era, and, of even larger effect, the country weathered double-digit inflation during this decade. Many colleges responded not merely by holding down faculty salaries, but also by increasing student-faculty ratios.

[4] American Association of University Professors, *Academe*, (March-April 1991), Table I: p. 10.

for, say, mathematicians or chemists and get just a handful of responses, whereas at any point in the 1970s there would have been a pool of a hundred applicants or more for every position. Applicant pools were definitely smaller, and the odds were going up that the aspiring young faculty member would get an acceptable offer somewhere.

New faculty looking for a good institutional match in the 1990s and beyond should have a far better chance of succeeding. Just how much of a "seller's market" they will find as the decade goes along depends on which projections one accepts, but it seems clear that demand will outstrip supply. Looking at things from the "buyer's" perspective (i.e., the perspective of colleges hoping to hire good faculty), the most pessimistic prospect is for retirements and competition from business to drain off doctoral disciplinarians and leave classrooms staffed, at best, with marginally qualified faculty. Even the more optimistic (again, from the buyer's point of view) investigators of the supply and demand conditions in academe project an imbalance quite favorable for new faculty who want some choice in the matter of the college where their careers are to start. Bowen and Sosa made this forecast in 1989:

> When we combine projections of supply with projections of demand, we find no compelling reason to expect major changes in academic labor markets within the next few years. But we do project some significant increase in demand relative to supply as early as 1992-97—and then far more dramatic changes beginning in 1997-2002. All of our models project demand to exceed supply from that point on.[5]

Forecasts rest on assumptions about conditions, and these can surely change. Following the publication of Bowen and Sosa's study and projections, the national economic picture changed sharply. 1990-91 was a time of economic recession and increased unemployment. Shortfalls in state revenues led to cutbacks in faculty positions and increased student-faculty ratios at public colleges and universities. In the early 1990s, as this book is written, it is difficult to know how much reality will diverge from the forecasts.

But even with demographic and economic uncertainties, for faculty interested in liberal arts and comprehensive college positions, the prospects seem especially favorable (and, conversely for the hiring colleges, unfavorable), and most favorable of all for those disciplines in which there were so many "itinerant scholars" during the 1970s. In the more selective liberal arts and comprehensive colleges (the Carnegie "Liberal Arts I" and "Comprehensive I" groups)[6] Bowen and Sosa project between 1987-92 and 1997-2002 an increase

---

[5] William G. Bowen and Julie Ann Sosa, *Prospects for Faculty in the Arts & Sciences* (Princeton, NJ: Princeton University Press, 1989), pp. 13-14.

[6] We are using here what has come to be a common method of classifying institutions of higher education, that introduced by the Carnegie Foundation for the Advancement of Teaching. In the Liberal Arts I category are the "highly selective institutions...primarily undergraduate colleges

of over 100% in demand for faculty, compared to a 57% increase at selective research institutions.[7] As they point out:

> A surprising conclusion is that the projected imbalances are particularly severe for the humanities and social sciences. For at least a decade, beginning in 1997, three out of four models imply that there will be only seven candidates for every ten positions in these fields.[8]

"Seven candidates for every ten positions" promises young scholars like Adam Newprof, who are rather clear on the kind of college they're seeking, the best prospect for a near-perfect institutional match that seekers of faculty positions have seen in many, many years.

What Matters?

Some mention was made above of factors, from salaries to football, that might contribute to a sense of match between faculty member and college. Adam Newprof has begun to think more systematically about just which factors matter enough for him personally to warrant adding them to his mental list. It isn't a bad idea to take time to go further than Adam has. There is something about the discipline of writing things down that helps the thought processes, and a good beginning point in a search for the ideal teaching position is simply to write down a list of factors that you are convinced will contribute significantly to your satisfaction with the college where you accept an appointment. There could be any number of these, but let me mention a few that have a good chance of proving to be key for nearly everyone.

For Adam Newprof, geography is an important consideration as it often is for others. In Adam's case, he has a strong desire to return to his home state. He grew up in a southern state, went to college there, knows its people and customs, and wants to contribute to its future progress. There may be a sizable element of sentimentality contributing to that desire, but geographical location is high up on his list as he looks for a match. Other people will have a very different interest in geography. Some will have some state or region or city that holds a special appeal for them, and the very fact that moving there offers an opportunity for them to get away from familiar territory and into a kind of geographic adventure puts it on their "match list." I have known faculty members, for example, who have chosen a college because it was located on the coast, where they could sail a boat, and others who wanted to live in

---

that award more than half of their baccalaureate degrees in arts and science fields." In the Liberal Arts II category are "primarily undergraduate colleges that are less selective and award more than half of their degrees in liberal arts fields." Definitions of all of the institutional categories may be found in the reference from which these quotes were taken: Ernest L. Boyer, *A Classification of Institutions of Higher Education* (Princeton, NJ: Princeton University Press, 1987).

[7] Bowen and Sosa, pp. 142-143.

[8] Bowen and Sosa, p. 14.

the mountains because "mountains so often provide inspiration when you drive home at the end of a long day on the campus." There is obviously no right or wrong preference with regard to geography. Fortunately, predilections about such subjects tend to be as varied as the geographic possibilities, but it is only sensible to take fully into account the locale of the college.

Included in the geographic caveat should be consideration of whether the college is in an urban, suburban, or rural setting. If you are someone who hates the subway and city noises, and who wants a campus not to be sliced up by busy streets, then clearly you should think twice about selecting an urban college. Conversely, if you find it important to have access to theater, opera, symphony, and zoos, or if you crave Armenian food once a month and need a wide choice in department store shopping, then you will want to find a college not too far off the beaten track.

It is, however, worth noting that one should not make hasty judgments about what locale just won't do. If you talk with faculty hired during the academic depression of the 1970s, you will often discover people who have come to love places to which they wouldn't have moved on a bet except that the one job offer they got was there.

Adam Newprof has chosen private education over public education as he begins his job search. In truth, he hasn't reflected very explicitly on what differences might exist between the two types. He remembers Benjamin College, knows it was affiliated with the Methodist Church rather than the state, and has sort of concluded that a private college is better for him because of that fact. From a student standpoint, there is really no distinction to be made between public and private education; from a faculty and administration standpoint there are distinctions. The student meets degree requirements set by the faculty, takes courses taught by the faculty in a curriculum designed by the faculty, and is graded by the faculty—and faculty in state-supported colleges and universities get their degrees from the same mix of institutions that graduate the faculty of private institutions. Thus the educational experience of the student depends hardly at all on the public or private status of the college.[9] For faculty who are prone to agonize over delays in getting things done, a public college will probably prove to be a more frustrating working environment than will a private institution. Public colleges are accountable to state legislatures, and usually to a state commission on higher education as well, and so have not only the local institutional bureaucracy, but also bureaucracies of the state, to deal with. Especially in personnel matters, faculty can find the requirements of the remote bureaucracies onerous, although

[9] One is beginning to see disconcerting instances of state legislatures setting competency levels for students in certain basic skills, or setting expectations for results of "outcomes assessment" for state colleges and universities. There is surely potential for this kind of practice to have impact on the educational experience of students in public institutions. At this point such impact seems minimal.

some private institutions have created what will seem to most faculty members processes and regulations equally as burdensome. I have worked in both private and public institutions, and certainly find the former work environment to be generally preferable. That said, I would have to acknowledge that there are many issues of greater import and impact for the individual faculty member than the constraints or intrusions of a state bureaucracy.

As I admitted in Chapter 1 with Adam Newprof, I have stronger feelings about the distinction to be made between the liberal arts college and the research university as a place for educating undergraduates. If Adam decides to write down an explicit list of institutional match items, this will come high on that list, and he will be more conscious of why it is there. I would place it similarly. We will, however, look at those distinctions in greater detail in later chapters of this book; moreover, this is being written primarily for faculty who have already decided that it is in the liberal arts setting that they want to teach, so I won't linger overly long here to elaborate on differences.

To say "liberal arts" in this age is, regrettably, to use a phrase that has become blurred indeed in its meaning.[10] Surveys have established what associations the public makes with the phrase,[11] and the results are disconcerting. For example, "art" (i.e., fine arts) and music are the subjects most often linked in the public mind to the liberal arts, and there is a general belief that a liberal arts education is not considered "good training...for graduate school." Music was one of the original seven *artes liberales*—but as Plato used the word "music," it was considered one of the four *mathematical* arts![12] And liberal arts colleges compare very favorably indeed with the research universities in the per capita production of doctoral students.[13] The former error—what subjects are properly associated with a liberal arts program—we will not fret over here; the latter misperception is more worrisome, although we shall not belabor it now either. For purposes of this book, let us move away from the edge of the definitional morass and think more practically.

---

[10] It may well be that this situation is no worse now than it has long been. See: Bruce A. Kimball, *Orators & Philosophers* (New York, NY: Teachers College Press, 1986).

[11] Jan Krukowski Associates, Inc., with Kane, Parsons & Associates, *Attitudes About the Liberal Arts* (New York, NY: Jan Krukowski Associates, Inc., 1987).

[12] As a reminder, the original seven liberal arts consisted of the language-related *trivium* (grammar, rhetoric, and logic) and the mathematical *quadrivium* (arithmetic, geometry, astronomy, and music). There appears never to have been unqualified agreement, even among the ancient Greeks, as to the precise content of these subjects. This kind of debate will become very familiar when the new faculty member has lived on a campus for a year or more! For an excellent treatment of the history of the liberal arts see Reference 10.

[13] See, for example, David Davis-Van Atta, Sam C. Carrier, and Frank Frankfort, *Educating America's Scientists: The Role of the Research Colleges* (Oberlin, Ohio: Oberlin College, 1985). In this report for the conference on "The Future of Science at Liberal Arts Colleges," the authors cite National Academy of Sciences data, noting that the per capita doctoral productivity ratio for 48 "leading liberal arts colleges" was 8.22%, compared with 7.84% for the Ivy League universities, 6.92% for the NAS top-rated 20 universities, and 4.27% for the Big 10 universities (p. 29).

In ancient Rome, education labeled *liberalis* was education appropriate for a *liber*, or free citizen. From the practical standpoint of selecting a college, we will use the term "liberal arts college" in something of the same sense, to refer to the colleges that by their mission statement give first priority to the broad education of the whole person (citizen). In these colleges, in the ideal at least, curricula are designed purposefully to accomplish precise educational goals consistent with such a mission statement; the primary responsibility of the faculty is to assure this kind of liberal education; and undergraduate teaching is the focus of the college.

To give a quick summary of some differences that faculty see in the two workplaces, liberal arts college and research university, consider these results of a survey conducted by the Carnegie Foundation for the Advancement of Teaching and reported in *Change*.[14] At liberal arts colleges, significantly more faculty:

+ find the quality of life and the sense of community to be "excellent" or "good"

+ see their relationships with undergraduates as being strong

+ see themselves as having strong ties to their departments and college

+ are positive about their profession

+ report a greater enthusiasm about their work now than when they began their careers

+ say the institution is well managed

+ feel they have significant influence in shaping policies

+ find their teaching loads too heavy and their salaries too low.

These are all things—except for the last item on the list!—that would confirm to Adam Newprof, if he read the *Change* article, the rightness of his keen interest in finding a place "like Benjamin College." Adam understands why the university setting is attractive to a number of his former graduate school colleagues. Those going into university teaching will find teaching loads lower. Their research laboratories and libraries will be the best. They will be paid salaries that are maybe 25% higher than those choosing the liberal arts campus. But to Adam, those circumstances that he believes will matter most over a lifetime are most likely to be found at Benjamin College, or some place very much like it.

---

[14] Carnegie Foundation for the Advancement of Teaching, "Are Liberal Arts Colleges Really Different?", *Change*, (March/April 1990), pp. 42-44.

Mission: Ideals, Values and Traditions

Here and there I have alluded to the "mission" of a college, and I have even implied that there might be something like a uniform mission statement that stamps every liberal arts college as part of a matched set and sets them apart from all other institutions of higher learning. If that impression has been given, let me hasten to amend it. Not only is there no such uniform mission statement today, there has not been one in history, even though there have been serious attempts at pinning down a definition for American liberal arts colleges in the twentieth century, to get everyone to "sign up," as it were. A notable illustrative attempt was that of the Commission on Liberal Education, which adopted a statement on "The Nature and Purpose of Liberal Education" in 1943. Bruce Kimball sums up the gist of what was intended to be a definitive declaration:

> On the side of "Nature," they included physical, intellectual, aesthetic, spiritual, and moral training through a curriculum of social and natural sciences, arts, classics, philosophy, language, and literature, all of which together had the "Purpose" of promoting individual freedom and fulfillment as well as social responsibility along with the "skills and abilities...to use intelligently and with a sense of workmanship some of the principal tools and techniques of the arts and sciences."[15]

The most confidently offered definition can, however, realize early frustration when there is at issue deeply held intellectual convictions, not to mention the very business of institutions that must temper idealism with pragmatism. So it was with the CLE report. Kimball goes on to point out that "despite the 'enthusiasm' with which many educational leaders...greeted the report, members of the Commission themselves...were soon advancing their own plans for liberal education and talking as though nothing had been resolved."

To the new or prospective faculty enthusiast of the liberal arts college: be not dismayed. This account from the 1940s captures one reality about liberal arts education, but it misses others that count for more. There is no universal, invariable canon to which all liberal arts colleges subscribe and, the allure of erasing ambiguity notwithstanding, there will be none. The hundreds of liberal arts colleges across America are, however, much like the members of a single race. Anthropologists will point out that "race" is a somewhat elusive concept, that we can find greater differences between two individual members of the same race than between two individuals from different races. Similarly, however lacking in fungibility, the liberal arts colleges do: (a) tend toward mission statements that hold up the ideal of broad education for the whole person, along with in-depth concentration in some single discipline;

---

[15] Reference 10, pp. 203-204. Kimball's chapter VI, "Confrontation in America of the Oratorical and Philosophical Traditions," is an excellent treatment of the history of the debate in America over the nature and purposes of liberal education, and the factors which influenced that debate.

and (b) provide a workplace for faculty and a learning environment for students that is marked by personal relationships and a sense of community.

That still leaves a lot of room for plurality. You, as a new faculty member who plans a career on the liberal arts college campus, still have decisions to make. Indeed, one of the bonus attractions of opting for a liberal arts setting is the strikingly varied assortment of settings there are to choose from. While not suggesting at all that the large universities present prospective faculty with monotonous uniformity—Stanford is not Duke is not Ohio State—, I am convinced that the liberal arts colleges offer more pronounced diversity of educational environment.

It may be useful to point out how a college comes to have a specific mission statement and how that statement is connected to the work of the faculty and the education of the student. We will take a closer look at institutional governance in Chapter 8, but at this point we will note merely that the ultimate authority over a college is not its faculty nor even its administration, but its board of trustees. Wording of the mission statement may be drafted by the faculty, but it is the board that has the final say. In theory, the mission statement itself is fairly concise and broadly stated, but its words are chosen with extreme care for they are intended to provide the foundation—the philosophical underpinnings—for all that the college does. As an example, consider this "Statement of Purpose"[16] for Roanoke College:

> Roanoke College is dedicated to educating men and women in high standards of scholarship and in creativity in the arts and sciences. It seeks to give students a broad understanding of their own and other cultures and competency in a field of specialization. It also recognizes a responsibility to serve its community.
>
> The College believes that it can serve a free society by developing in students a capacity for responsible leadership. It seeks to achieve this purpose through the intellectual, emotional, spiritual, and practical aspects of a liberal arts education. It strives to provide its students with the knowledge, skills, and adaptability needed for the successful pursuit of their careers.
>
> Roanoke is a small college with a concerned and dedicated faculty, nurturing sensitivity, maturity, and a lifelong love of learning. It honors its Christian heritage and its founding by Lutherans in 1842, while welcoming and reflecting a variety of religious traditions.[17]

In these three short paragraphs, the college has laid out in broad, clear strokes several things: what its fundamental business is; what it sees as the principal outcomes of education at Roanoke; and what its historical roots and traditions are.

---

[16] Sundry titles other than "Mission Statement" will be found in the literature of the colleges, "Statement of Purpose" being the most common alternative.

[17] 1990 catalog, Roanoke College, Salem, Virginia.

Some mission statements are substantially longer than this one, and a few may be shorter. The language can often be flowery, erudite, poetic, and occasionally even unabashedly promotional. Some make quite specific reference to location.

Saint Mary is a Catholic, liberal arts college sponsored by the Sisters of Charity of Leavenworth.[18]

Our effort to nurture these ideals is aided by a splendid setting in the Blue Ridge foothills...[19]

The distinctive language suggests the multiplicity of "history, traditions, and special sense of worth" that Boyer alluded to in the quote that began this chapter. Even a hasty inspection at random of college catalogs unearths evidence of the great diversity of liberal arts colleges:

Simpson College is a church-related, undergraduate, coeducational, residential, Midwestern liberal arts college dedicated to higher education excellence in Iowa, the region, the nation and the world...[20]

LeMoyne-Owen is a viable, visible, and constructive regional black college that provides in its academic programs, well-educated graduates for leadership positions in this community and beyond; it is a significant contributor in teaching, research and community service related to breaking the cycle of poverty in Memphis and Shelby County...[21]

For more than a century, Mills College has offered women an education of the highest quality. Our curriculum has evolved over the years, but our basic purpose remains the same...[22]

Whatever the style, all mission statements are attempting to accomplish the same thing; i.e., to define for the reader what the college is and what it is committed to doing. Faculty are sometimes heard grousing, however, that the mission statement of their institution "is so wide you could drive a Mack truck through it," meaning that its terseness and lack of precise language leave open too many opportunities for interpretation. What does it mean, for instance, to say that the business of the college is "educating men and women in high standards of scholarship and in creativity in the arts and sciences"? What are "high standards" and what kind of "creativity" is being suggested?

For a mission statement to lead to anything practical and concrete, something more is needed. It falls to the faculty to construct detailed goals based on

[18] 1990 catalog, Saint Mary College, Leavenworth, Kansas.

[19] 1990 catalog, Ferrum College, Ferrum, Virginia.

[20] 1990 catalog, Simpson College, Indianola, Iowa.

[21] 1990 catalog, LeMoyne-Owen College, Memphis, Tennessee.

[22] 1990 catalog, Mills College, Oakland, California.

the curriculum, objectives based on these goals, and methods of assessing the extent to which goals and objectives are being achieved. During the 1980s regional accrediting agencies and, for public institutions, state legislatures and commissions of higher education as well, began to place much more emphasis on planning and assessment. College and university faculty are much more likely in the 1990s to have moved beyond the mission statement, and to have translated it into goals and objectives more precise in nature and subject to assessment. It is, in turn, out of these goals and objectives that curricula and programs flow.

Mission statements are a good starting point in considering how well a college matches your values and interests. Veteran faculty members may tell you that no one pays attention to the mission statement, that it's mostly PR. It is true that few faculty and administrators have the statement framed and hanging on the office wall, and that not every goal that is adopted is checked thoroughly for grounding in the college mission. It should be kept in mind that no community is totally faithful to the ideals that are intended to ground it, including a college community. That has been true since Moses brought down the stone tablets from Mount Sinai. And what portion of American citizens can recite the Declaration of Independence or the Bill of Rights? No, the value of a mission statement is not that it constrains, but that it tends to keep us on track over time. Physicists tell us that a great singer does not actually ever hold a pure note, but repeatedly veers off ever so slightly on either side and returns. Perhaps that's a helpful analogy for faculty using mission statements. At a given moment in its history, a college may have, for example, a curriculum that is not totally faithful to every word of the statement, but chances are that future changes will pull contents and requirements back again.

Student Selectivity

You won't find on Adam Newprof's institutional match list, if he writes one up, anything about how selective his prospective college is with regard to recruiting students to teach. He knows that the people with whom he attended Benjamin College (the only college to which he applied) were on the whole more interested in the academic side of college than were the people in his freshman recitation sections at the state university. But then the latter were grouped by ability, and he tended to get a lot of jocks who were on athletic scholarships and who probably weren't typical of the whole university student body. The truth is that Adam has sampled only two institutions. Out of his limited experience, he unconsciously presumed that students who get admitted to an accredited college are "college material," and that, except for those at notoriously elitist places like Harvard, Yale, and Wellesley, college students are pretty much the same everywhere.

You may know already that he is wrong in making such an assumption. The colleges in this country, where there is longstanding popular commitment to universal education, differ widely in their admissions standards, and also in the academic readiness and record of their student bodies. It is generally understood in America at the end of the twentieth century that the doors of occupational opportunity are closed to those who lack a baccalaureate degree. In reality it is too often the case that even holders of the baccalaureate degree must settle for employment that offers minimal challenge and interest. The structure and expectations of American higher education have shifted in response to the increasing percentage of high school graduates who apply for college admission. States have erected whole systems of colleges and universities that assure access to students across the admissions standard spectrum, and private colleges no longer cater to the intellectual elite or pre-professional aristocrats.

Add to this equation the vicissitudes of student demographics over the past several decades, and one appreciates even better the move toward tiering, or stratification, of colleges and universities on the basis of student selectivity. Birth rates have varied during this century, the most famous birth cohort surely being the "baby-boomers" of the post-World War II era. That cohort naturally enough began to reach college age in the mid-1960s, and they added in unprecedented numbers to the demand for college admission. College and university enrollments rose by about 160% between 1963 and 1983, at a rate of about 387,000 additional students per year! Little wonder that the campuses became scenes of frenzied building activity during the 1960s. But by the 1980s the boom was over. There has been a slow, but steady decline in total numbers of enrolled college students since that time, and a return to the level of 1983 is not projected before 2007 (see Graphs 2.1 and 2.2[23]).

Numbers of student applications will, of course, be affected by large national demographic trends, but they are often affected far more, particularly in the private liberal arts colleges, by circumstances nearer home. In a time of decline nationally in traditional college-age students, the 18- to 24-year-old group, not every college feels the same pinch. Those with national reputations or in large population centers may be able to preserve admissions standards; those with lower profiles or in regions that are remote or economically depressed are likely to suffer disproportionately and to have a much harder time preserving their standards. Whatever the particular pieces of the equation look like for a particular institution, every college is inclined to settle into a kind of "student quality niche" with which it is, if not totally satisfied, at least prepared to live. Every year, as it admits a new class, comparisons are made with some recognized quality range, and when a given class falls outside that range, strategies are devised to recruit a new class for next year that falls within it. In a period like 1990-1996, admissions officers expect to see a

---

[23] *High School Graduates: Projections by State, 1986 to 2004* (Boulder, CO: Western Interstate Commission for Higher Education, 1987). Note: Figures for 1986-87 and years thereafter are projections made by WICHE.

"trickle-down" theory operating, as the demographics produce a smaller national pool of high school graduates. As competition becomes fiercer, the more selective colleges and universities are lowering their standards for admission, thus taking students who would previously have been in the customary application pool for the institutions in the next-lower tier—which are in turn lowering their admissions requirements and taking applicants from colleges in the third-down tier, and so on. Graph 2.1 (using data from Bowen and Sosa, p. 42) shows trends and projections for college and university enrollments from 1986 to 2004, from which you may infer something about the relative difficulty of holding standards intact from year to year. Some advantage in this kind of competition accrues to colleges that are best able to increase offers of financial aid. Over the decade of the 1980s and into the early 90s, government support for college students has declined, and much of the aid available is in the form of loans rather than grants.[24] Many colleges have reacted in a kind of Robin Hoodish way, using funds from increased tuition charged to "full-pay" students who can afford it to offer tuition assistance to less affluent students. Despite such strategies, which have been major contributors to tuition growth, colleges without large scholarship endowments have found themselves struggling to keep their place in the selectivity tiers.

If someone had made Adam Newprof privy to the information in graphs 2.1 and 2.2, and if he had had time to study their implications, there is little question that student selectivity would be a matter of some import to him. He loves learning. He wants to open up the minds of students. He wants to see lights go on in students' eyes. He isn't looking for a campus of Einsteins, and he accepts that some students will be more able and serious than others, wherever he goes. But if he has a choice, he would pick a campus where by-and-large students were reasonably able to think clearly and to express themselves reasonably well and were in good control of the algebra they would need to work freshman chemistry problems. It will make a difference in the pleasure he takes in teaching if very many students fall below those expectations. It isn't high school teaching after all, but college teaching that he wants to make his career.

Similarly, for you as a new faculty member, how selective your college is in admitting students will have considerable influence on the satisfaction you derive from teaching. For what you will be able to achieve as a teacher is more than a question of your brilliance as a teacher; teaching presumes students with the ability and inclination to learn what you expect to teach. You should enter the teaching ranks with great devotion to your calling, but realism is also in order. In the Lake Wobegon of humorist Garrison Keillor, "all the children are above average." Few colleges can make that claim for their students, as former Harvard dean Henry Rosovsky suggests:

---

[24] For a good overview of the student financial aid situation, see Carol Francis, "Student Aid: Is it Working Like It Is Supposed To?," *Change*, (July/August 1990), pp. 35-43.

Graph 2.1
College Enrollment Trends and Projections

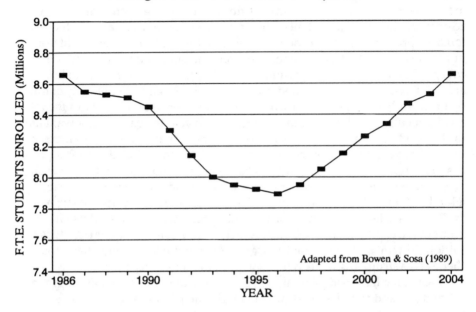

Adapted from Bowen & Sosa (1989)

Graph 2.2
High School Graduate Trends

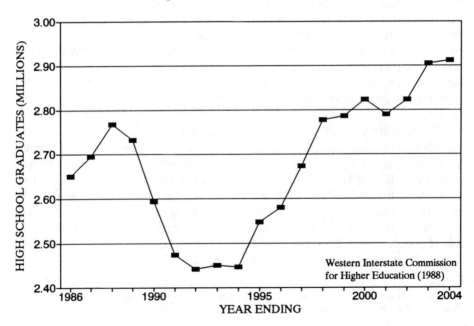

Western Interstate Commission
for Higher Education (1988)

Of the over 3,000 colleges and universities in this country, only 175 are considered selective, and that leaves a lot of "unselective choice."[25]

Not everyone can teach at Harvard or Princeton, and, indeed, many aspiring (and veteran) faculty members find a calling in the education of high risk students whose preparation for college may be poor, but whose only hope of escaping lives of desperation and poverty lies in getting a college degree. Student selectivity may not be summed up by statistics on SAT scores or class rank alone. By the implications of their mission statements, numerous colleges clearly do not aspire to skimming off the intellectual cream. Teaching can be just as satisfying for faculty in these colleges as for those in an Ivy League setting—indeed, they may gain something extra from being at a place with a special mission.

For Adam Newprof, and for many incipient faculty, the expectation is that most of the young faces looking back at him during a lecture are inherently competent to do the kind of college work that they, the new faculty members, were called on to do as undergraduates. The important points for you to keep in mind are: (a) that student bodies vary in readiness for college as the institutions vary in selectivity; and (b) you need to guard against the kind of expectation gap that can come from not determining ahead of time what traditions a prospective college has in this regard. It is a factor that will make a difference in how you feel about coming to work in the morning.

Working Conditions

As he looks forward to life as a faculty member, Adam Newprof hasn't had any phrases like "coming to work in the morning" flit through his mind. Unquestionably a significant, although not primary, motive in making a choice for teaching was to insure for himself a daily life free of the routine, the intrusion, the stress of what everyone called the "rat race." Teaching, he knew from living so long on a campus and watching professors like Doc Paradigm and Professor Scribe, was not like other work. "Coming to work in the morning" was the kind of expression one would use in a job, and Adam would never have thought of the profession he was entering as a job. Unless you're very atypical, you will empathize with Adam. One of the attractions you find in the profession of college teaching is that it promises a daily life as independent and interesting and flexible and as different from, say, the corporate life as can be imagined. And so it does.

But no life, not even the life of a college teacher, can claim total immunity from impact by the circumstances under which it is lived. You will find some colleges that simply have created better climates for doing the work of a faculty member than others. You will judge the state of working conditions on

[25] Henry Rosovsky, *The University: An Owner's Manual* (New York, NY: W.W. Norton, 1990), p. 60.

your first campus primarily on the basis of (a) how able you feel to do work of satisfying quality there, (b) how valued you feel there, (c) how much support it provides for your day-to-day work as a teacher-scholar, and (d) how pleasant it is working with the people there. Let's look at each of these factors.

As a group, people who have chosen teaching set as high standards for themselves as any I can think of. Their hallmark is conscientiousness. You will find among faculty, to be sure, some exceptions to this rule, but I have found that number to be exceedingly small. So the expression "satisfying quality" used in (a) above, when applied to you, is quite likely to mean something high up on the quality scale. Various factors can come into play here, from having the kind of maps you need to having students who are highly motivated, but a chief factor, one that you will hear much talk about in any faculty lounge on any day, is teaching load. At this juncture, standing on the verge of a teaching career to which you feel a strong calling, if you're anything like Adam Newprof, this is another phrase that you might find strange or even disagreeable. If teaching is a calling, how have those who practice it come to use terms like "load" in characterizing it? A glib rejoinder might be that there can be too much of anything, even chocolate cake. A more analytical answer would be that one's teaching load is, as was suggested in Chapter 1, only one part of a larger set of obligations as a faculty member, and that what is set as the officially required amount of teaching should leave enough time to meet your full range of responsibilities. When the amount of teaching required of you exceeds the amount you can do without neglecting something else you need to do, the word "load" becomes more accurate. At any rate, it is a term you will hear often, and it is worthwhile being informed about it.

Just how a given college expresses its formal teaching load will be a matter of local preference and tradition. It is probably most often expressed in terms of semester hours (or in some cases quarter hours), terms with which you will be familiar from your student days. If the load is said to be twelve hours per term, it means the faculty member is expected to teach each week enough courses to add up to twelve semester hours of credit for a student enrolled in them. That will make eminent sense to those whose disciplines are English or History or Sociology, but, if your subject is Art or Biology or Physical Education, it will hit you right away that you are being required to put in more class hours to meet your load than are your colleagues whose classroom teaching consists of lecture only. Laboratories, for example, typically carry only one hour of credit (or in some places no separate credit at all). Adam Newprof, should he be given a teaching load of twelve hours, will actually be teaching something like fifteen or eighteen clock hours per week, because each four-semester-hour chemistry course with a lab that meets once a week will require him to give six hours of his time, three in lecture and three more in lab. Similarly, faculty members whose duties call for teaching studio or physical education classes will have to commit to additional clock hours in order to make the semester hours come out right. Of course, it is common, though by no means a universal practice, for a college administration to take this "hidden" responsibility into account, and to amend the basic definition of teaching load by using contact hours, the number of hours per week that a teacher is in formal contact with students, instead of semester hours as the measure of "load." At a few colleges other factors, notably the total number of students being taught and the number of course preparations, are taken into account; both add to the time it takes to do the total job of teaching. The basic issue here, whatever the local currency, is that you should select your college with a clear sense of how much classroom time you are committing to, for that is time you won't have available for conferences with students, grading papers, and all the rest.

What can you expect to find? For four-year baccalaureate colleges, the range of actual teaching loads is surprisingly wide, judging from Graph 2.3. The mode is obviously the 9-12 hour range (this is clock hours), with 47% of all faculty reporting that they spend that amount of time in scheduled teaching per week. Thirty-three percent report, however, that they teach more than twelve hours per week, and about 20% report teaching loads below nine hours.[26] Unfortunately, these Higher Education Research Institute (HERI) study[27] data blur an important line, that between nine and twelve hours. During the 1980s there has been some movement, even in the liberal arts colleges, from the long-typical 12-hour load to a more moderate load of 9 hours. It would be informative to know what the partition is currently with regard to nine-hour and twelve-hour loads.

In any case, a fuller picture of time taken for teaching emerges only when we look beyond the hours spent in contact with students in classroom, laboratory, studio, or gymnasium. Popular public conviction notwithstanding, the mode of nine-twelve hours does not, of course, mean that a professor "works only nine to twelve hours per week." The same study cited that produced the figures on hours of scheduled teaching revealed that a greater piece of the iceberg was under the water than was above it. The mode for "time preparing for teaching" was again nine-twelve hours—but over half (53%) reported that they spent more than twelve additional hours in preparation, and more than a third (34%) said they spent above sixteen (see Graph 2.4). You yourself will obviously have a great deal to do with how much "hidden" time you spend in preparing lectures and grading papers; there is no official requirement in this regard.

[26] Care should be taken in interpreting these figures. Some faculty responding in this study (see reference 29) have positions split between teaching and administration, and no distinction is made between required loads and voluntary overloads taught for extra pay.

[27] Alexander W. Astin, William S. Korn, and Eric L. Dey, *The American College Teacher, National Norms for the 1989-90 HERI Faculty Survey* (Los Angeles, CA: Higher Education Research Institute, 1991).

Graph 2.3
Time in Scheduled Teaching

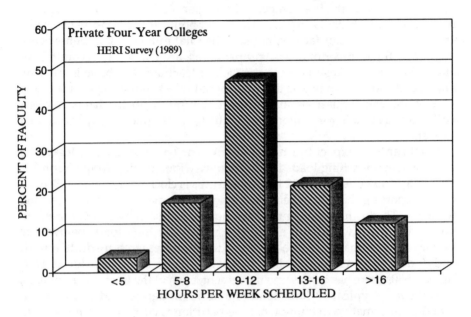

Private Four-Year Colleges

HERI Survey (1989)

PERCENT OF FACULTY

HOURS PER WEEK SCHEDULED

Graph 2.4
Time Preparing for Teaching

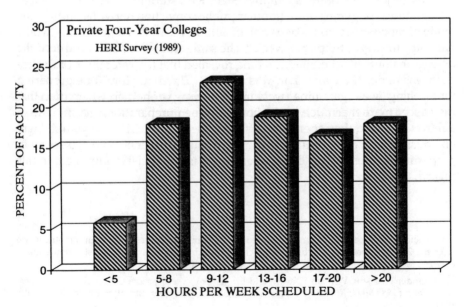

Private Four-Year Colleges

HERI Survey (1989)

PERCENT OF FACULTY

HOURS PER WEEK SCHEDULED

Also affecting the time demanded to meet your teaching obligations and ambitions will be the degree of support for teaching that the college is able to provide. Is secretarial help available for typing tests and course materials? Are adequate audio-visual aids, maps, computers, and instructional equipment furnished? Are student assistants provided where such assistance is appropriate? Is there support for curriculum development? Is time provided for first-time preparation of courses? Is there adequate staffing for assuring good teaching in special programs, such as honors and general education programs, and in the majors as well? The answers to these questions give clues not only to how efficiently and effectively you will be able to teach, but also to the place of teaching in institutional priorities.

Adam Newprof has not, at this point in his search for the right college for him, thought much about salary. He has never been much motivated by materialistic concerns, naive as that might be. And he never heard Doc Paradigm or Professor Scribe or Dr. Publisher, his research director at the university, talk about money at all, and so he assumes that they made enough to have a decent standard of living. Even though other factors may well outweigh income when options for positions are being pondered, it is nonetheless sensible not to take salary for granted. Its magnitude will determine whether you become distracted from your work by worry over having sufficient resources to support a family or maintain a reasonable standard of living. Its symbolic importance, especially for extremely conscientious people, should also not be overlooked, for you will be inclined to infer from it how much you are valued by the administration of the college. What can you expect there?

What a college can afford to pay will depend, naturally, on its financial vigor. The range is wide indeed. Further, there are such disparities in the cost of living from one region of the country to another, that comparing faculty salaries between two areas in America can be almost as misleading as comparing salaries in dollars with salaries in lire! This latter consideration will become even more important when one has an equity investment in a home in one part of the country and is thinking of moving to another, where that equity may buy either a much larger house or one much smaller. Some average salaries of assistant professors in different groups of baccalaureate colleges in 1991-92 are given in Table 2.1.[28]

The Higher Education Research Institute faculty survey of 1989-90 gives an idea of what the distribution of salaries were for that year in all baccalaureate colleges, looking at faculty in all ranks. About 27% of all faculty reported nine-month salaries between $22,500 and $29,250, and another 27% reported a range of $30,000-$36,750. Twenty-eight percent reported earning $37,500 or more, 13% $45,000 or more, and 18% less than $22,500. (See reference 27). Care must be taken when comparing salaries between institutions, for salary is not

[28] Data taken from AAUP, *Academe*, (March-April 1992), Table 4, p. 19.

Table 2.1
Assistant Professor Salaries in Baccalaureate Colleges

Baccalaureate College Group	Average Assistant Professor Salary (9-months)
All Baccalaureate Colleges	$31,500
Church-related	$29,580
Public	$32,580
Independent	$33,370
South Atlantic	$30,550
Middle Atlantic	$34,000
New England	$34,530
East North Central	$30,710
West North Central	$30,150
East South Central	$28,090
West South Central	$30,800
Mountain	$30,270
Pacific	$32,970

From *Academe* (March-April 1992)

Graph 2.5
Change in Buying Power of Faculty Salaries

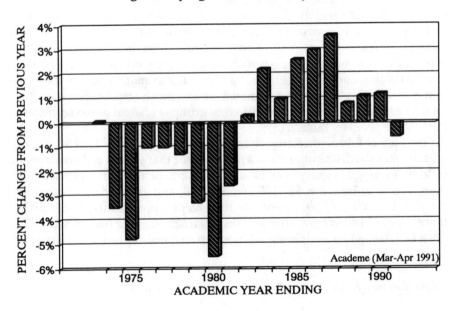

Academe (Mar-Apr 1991)

the same as compensation; the latter includes fringe benefits such as retirement contributions and health insurance. You'll want to be sure you are not comparing apples with oranges.

The effect of supply and demand on faculty salaries in the 1970s and 1980s was mentioned earlier in this chapter. That history is depicted rather vividly in Graph 2.5, where the difference between nominal salary increases and consumer price index (CPI) increases are chronicled for the academic years 1972-73 through 1990-91. For those looking ahead in the early 1990s to a college teaching career, there is certainly more financial incentive than there was earlier. Faculty salaries gained steadily in real buying power for nine years, 1981-82 through 1989-90. In 1990-91 there was a slight (0.6%) decrease again, and one cannot predict with certainty what the trend over the 1990s will be. Writing in *Academe*, economist Ronald Ehrenberg puts it this way:

> The future of academic salaries will depend upon the interplay of short-run and long-run forces....Focusing on the short run leaves one pessimistic about the future of academic salaries. However, focusing on fundamental long-run forces leaves one more optimistic....To the extent that ...projections [of faculty shortages] are accurate, academic institutions will be forced to increase faculty salaries in an effort to attract and retain faculty. Market forces suggest, then, that once we get past the recession and the ...short-run fiscal problems that it has created for public institutions, the future for academic salaries is likely to be brighter.[29]

Given the current projections for excess demand for faculty, the prospects appear to remain relatively bright well into the next century. It is well, however, to keep in mind that, although the academy is not an industry manufacturing widgets, it is vulnerable to many of the vagaries that affect other enterprises in our society. Things can change down the line. But for now, the financial future for college faculty appears brighter than it has been since the 1960s. From that standpoint, if you are deciding for a career in the academy in the early 1990s, you have picked a good time to go into teaching.

In discussing above how able you might feel to do "work of satisfying quality," we looked only at teaching load. That is a more obvious consideration than another factor that deserves mention, i.e., what you can expect in the way of support for your personal scholarship and professional development. We will spend a chapter on the topic of scholarship later on, but for now let me simply underscore that continuing active scholarship will prove important, no matter what the college, to your sense of professional competence, your ability to serve as mentor for young scholars in your classes, and your mobility in your profession. You will want to know what kind of support for research, travel to disciplinary meetings, and enrollment in workshops a college interested in hiring you is prepared to make. Some colleges have a quite extensive

---

[29] Ronald G. Ehrenberg, "The Future of Academic Salaries: Will the 1990s Be a Bust Like the 1970s or a Boom Like the 1980s?", *Academe*, (March-April 1991), p. 11.

collection of support programs for professional activities: released time for research, internal grants to provide research budgets, funds for travel to professional conferences, and sabbaticals. Other colleges take the position that the faculty member's personal research is his or her own affair, to be invested in to whatever extent that faculty member is inclined and able. While at the latter, little or nothing is generally expected from anyone in the way of public evidence of scholarship (e.g., publications or presentations), I will argue in Chapter 7 that personal scholarship is a vital part of a good start for anyone looking toward a full career in academe and so will urge here that you make careful inquiry about this kind of support before deciding which campus offers you opportunity for the best beginning.

Finally, you will want to know how your working conditions might be influenced by the people with whom you will be in daily contact. When you visit the campus, take time to get acquainted with as many of the faculty and staff as possible. Are they pleasant people, or will they set your teeth on edge every morning? Will they be contentious or cooperative? Are they dedicated and able? Most important will, of course, be your potential departmental colleagues, for you will spend most of your time with them, should you take this job. Will you and they be compatible? Are they open to new ideas? Will they be the kind of people you can sit down and drink coffee with and enjoy it? Can you expect to have stimulating discussions with them? If you find a place where you get all the answers you hoped for to these questions—you've probably erred in answering them! You won't find a place with perfect people. You should, however, reflect more than superficially on what kind of difference they will make to your work day.

Getting the Information You Need

We left Adam Newprof scanning the *Higher Education Directory* in search of colleges that might be a match for an idealistic young man hopeful of coming home to teach. What he will do in the next few days is to write letters of inquiry to chemistry departments at the colleges he picks from the directory, sending them his curriculum vitae, telling them something about himself, and asking about an opening. He will also be inspecting every week the "Academic Positions" section of *Chemical & Engineering News* to see which colleges are advertising for organic chemists, his specialty, and sending his vitae and a request for application materials to those that are in, or at least very near, his home state, since geography is important to him. But this is just the commencement of what will turn out to be, if he does it well, a research project with high stakes. How will he get all the information he needs to answer the questions about values, student selectivity, salaries, and all the rest? How will you proceed with your own research project?

Table 2.2 is offered as a concise synopsis of information that will be valuable to the person who is about to begin that project, with likely sources for each type of question.

Table 2.2
Sources of Information
Useful in Locating and Deciding On Positions

Type of Information	Source
The factors important to you as you seek an institutional match	• Your own list, reflecting your own priorities
Names and addresses of colleges in a given state or geographic region	• *Higher Education Directory*
Names and addresses of liberal arts colleges	• *Higher Education Directory* • Council of Independent Colleges
Positions open in your discipline and speciality	• *Chronicle of Higher Education* • Various disciplinary publications
College mission statements and related statements of institutional ideal, values and traditions	• Individual college catalogs • Faculty handbooks • Other college publications • Conversations with college faculty and administrators
Institutional goals and objectives	• College publications
Student selectivity and ability	• College publications • College admissions or dean's office • Various commercial college guides
Salaries	• AAUP's *Academe*, March/April issue • College department or dean's office
Teaching loads	• College department or dean's office • This book for comparative data
Support for teaching	• College department or dean's office
Support for scholarship and professional development	• College department or dean's office
Characteristics of potential colleagues	• Conversations with people on campus

3

Getting Selected:
Vitae, Interviews and Negotiations

His resolve is not to seem, but to be, the best.
Aeschylus
The Seven Against Thebes

*I*t was nothing like he had expected. Nothing. The president looked up and greeted him with a broad smile.

"Come in! Come in!"

Adam Newprof found himself in the doorway of a vast room with twelve-foot ceilings and wide, heart-pine flooring. Tall undraped windows spilled floods of sunlight in from the east side, but on the south shadows of live oaks wafted against the antique glass. There was nothing elegant about it, very little furniture: a grouping of three chairs under the east-wall windows, a large, paper-stacked bookcase against the west wall to Adam's right, and in the very center of the room, facing the north wall, a massive desk covered totally with more sheaves of paper and a big, open ledger book. A long electrical cord dangled a bare light bulb over the middle of the desk, and the light glinted off the president's green plastic eyeshade. Yes, eyeshade. He was wearing an eyeshade, and garters on his shirt sleeves as well, looking like an aging accountant or perhaps a crusty dealer in a casino somewhere. The face was Irish and slightly flushed under a thick shock of pure-white hair.

"President Fitzgeorge, I'd like you to meet Dr. Adam Newprof," the dean was saying.

Adam, recovering quickly from surprise at this appearance of a president's office, strode across the heart-pine boards and shook the outstretched hand offered by the president of the College of Port St. Julian. "It's a pleasure to meet you, President Fitzgeorge."

"Pleasure's all mine, sir. Yes indeed. Come on over and let's have a chat." Fitzgeorge pulled off the eye-shade and waved toward the three chairs under the windows.

They sat, the president, Dean Pennington, and Newprof, and Adam was vaguely aware of a tension in his muscles. This was his first interview trip, and he thought it had gone fine so far, but Fitzgeorge's judgment would be what finally counted. He wanted to appear relaxed, as if this interview stuff was old hat to him, but inside he felt like the Port St. Julian harbor had looked earlier—unsettled and choppy. There was a brief moment of silence which Dean Pennington broke with:

"Well, Dr. Fitzgeorge, we've had a good visit so far. Dr. Newprof spent the morning with Professor Venable and Professor Noble in the chemistry department, and we had a nice lunch at the St. Julian Hotel down by the harbor." She turned and smiled at Newprof. "I think he looks good, Mr. President."

Adam felt awkward, remembering how he used to feel as a child when adults talked to his parents about him as if he weren't there. It was a reminder that this wasn't just a visit; the dean and president were inspecting him.

"Well, let's just chat a little bit," Fitzgeorge said. "You grew up in the upstate, I understand?"

"Sure did," Newprof answered. "Athenstown."

"Well, we won't hold that against you." He spoke with the distinctive St. Juliano accent. The president laughed, and the dean and Adam joined in. "So tell me, Dr. Newprof, what's your impression of the College?"

"I like what I've seen," Adam replied, wanting to choose the right words. "I know it has a long tradition for academic quality. And it reminds me a lot of Benjamin College, where I graduated." It did. It was a place with real character, antebellum buildings, lots of trees, musty rooms, not much around that was new and shiny, an attractive setting, even smaller than Benjamin. Ted Venable even reminded him strongly of Doc Paradigm.

"Good college, Benjamin is." The old man nodded. "What about the department? Think you could teach with Professor Noble and Professor Venable? Got what you need to get the job done down there?"

"Yes sir. Yes, to both questions." The total truth would have been that he liked Noble and Venable a great deal, and that the department needed to spend a *lot* of money to equip itself to teach modern chemistry. That part had been a mild shock. Still, he figured that with time he could help correct the situation.

"Good. Good." Fitzgeorge's white head nodded again. "Tell me how you feel about teaching. Why do you want to do it?"

"Well," Adam smiled, relaxing a little as he launched into a subject dear to his heart. "I guess I think I know how to get chemistry across to students, maybe even get them to enjoy it. I want to try my hand at it anyway. And I'm a little bit of an evangelist when it comes to a liberal education. I'm a strong believer in seeing that society has as many citizens as possible with a broad understanding of things, who know something about language and history and culture, who can solve problems, who have encountered the perennial questions. I guess I think if I'm a teacher, I'll be in a good place at a good time in people's lives to help make that happen." He paused, thinking the speech sounded a little stuffy, and maybe slightly conceited.

"And so you will, my boy," the president said. "So you will." Then: "You know Kenneth Scribe?"

Adam grinned and relaxed some more. "Sure I do! Professor Scribe is a great guy. He taught me creative writing, and that turned out to be the best course I took in college. I always go by to visit him when I'm in Athenstown."

"Well, I know him, too. Known him well for years. Listen, why did a chemistry major take creative writing?"

"Isn't that the kind of thing that *ought* to happen at a liberal arts college?" Adam was on a favorite subject now. "Shouldn't students be taking all sorts of things, as many different things as they can?"

Fitzgeorge didn't answer that. Instead he said, " We really didn't need this interview from my side, Dr. Newprof, because if Ken Scribe says you're okay, you're okay. And I'm sure not hearing anything to change my mind. So let's get to the bottom line. If you want to teach at the College of Port St. Julian, you have a job starting in September. We're not rich here, but tell you what I'll do, I'll pay you the top of the range for assistant professors and come up with a thousand dollars to get you started in a research project to boot. Does that sound all right?"

Adam Newprof's interview with President Fitzgeorge is not, as you can gather, a typical one. Getting from one's initial survey of possible colleges, through the application stage, through the interview step, and into a job offer is usually a longer process than Adam has found it to be. The time invested can turn out to be truly substantial. And each phase is a sieve, sifting out some options and leaving others. The obvious objective at each stage of the process is to make as certain as you can that the options that prove worth keeping are kept. The whole experience should be seen as an adventure rather than an ordeal, but there are likely to be times before you sign a contract when you are feeling more anxious than adventuresome and more exhausted than exhilarated. I use "adventure" here to mean not a lark but a quest. While the search for the right college position should not produce ulcers, it should be approached with thoughtfulness and prudence. The sieves don't do their work whimsically. What you give them to work with is decisive. In this chapter we will look at what can make a difference.

Applying for an Opening

The first clues you provide to a college of interest will be in the inquiry you make about an opening. If you are "writing blind," i.e., without knowing whether there is an opening, as Adam Newprof did with several colleges from his match list, your first correspondence may be nothing more than a short letter. If you have found a notice of an open position in the *Chronicle of Higher Education,* in a publication of your discipline, or perhaps in an announcement posted in your graduate department, you may be sending a letter plus other materials requested in the notice. In either case, the letter will start to paint some kind of picture of you as a potential faculty member. I have read literally thousands of letters of inquiry and application by now, and I have seen candidates winnowed out of serious consideration at this earliest of stages because their letters spoke more than they realized about their suitability for the institution. There is no one magic formula for the letter, and what appeals to some readers will not appeal to others, but I offer here a brief list of points I believe will stand a candidate in the best stead in the vast majority of searches.

+ Write with care. The letter should show that you take the inquiry or application seriously. Choose your words carefully.

+ Keep the length reasonable. The letter should be long enough to say what needs saying, but short enough not to lose the reader or make you sound like a windbag. A page or a page-and-a-half will usually suffice.

+ The tone should show confidence, but not arrogance. Whatever may work in the business world, saying, "You will not be able to do better than me. I'll help put your department on the map," will *not* add points to your application for a teaching position.

+ Write for the specific college, not a generic form letter. This can be very important. Take time to learn about the institution, and let the letter reflect that knowledge. It gives evidence of your interest. If you know alumni or faculty from the college, mention their names. In many cases, simply mentioning the name of the college in the body of the letter can pull your inquiry out of a pack of routine form letters from other candidates!

+ Make the basis of your interest in the position very clear. Your motives and values should come through. You are helping the institution establish from its side whether a match is probable; say why you think there is a match between your interest and the position. If responding to a notice, point out explicitly how your training fits their position as advertised, using key words that appeared in the notice. If you have genuine commitment to liberal learning, and the college mission emphasizes that, express your commitment.

✦ Write well. Remember the rules of grammar and style—and don't forget that spelling counts! Get a friend to read the letter and critique it. A well-written letter can move you up several notches on a search list.

✦ Type it. This may seem an unnecessary reminder, but in nearly every search that I have seen—including presidential searches!—at least one or two handwritten letters have come in. A handwritten letter suggests an indifference you don't intend, and is most unlikely to be taken seriously. In a day of wordprocessors, it is easy to produce a neat letter.

The greatest amount of information that you will supply will be through your curriculum vitae, or resumé. Whatever credentials, experience, and achievements readers at the college find there will certainly be the most critical contributions to your portrait as a candidate. Even if you are making a blind inquiry, it can give you at least a time advantage to send it along with the letter. If you are responding to a position notice, you will almost certainly be including a vitae with your initial letter. There is no universal format for vitae, but, as with letters, how you do it can influence greatly the attractiveness of your candidacy. What is included is, up to a point, a matter of personal choice. There are, however, certain types of information that colleges will expect to see in the vitae. What appears below is an outline of the typical ingredients, with the starred (*) items being those that are customarily expected. If undecided about an item such as hobbies, include it; too much information is nearly always better than too little, and what readers care about and can't find can matter.

✦ Personal information
    Name (*)
    Address, home and office (*)
    Date of birth
    Place of birth
    Marital status
    Hobbies
    Church affiliation

✦ Educational history
    Degrees (*)
    Institutions awarding degrees (*)
    Dates of degrees (*)

Institutions attended without getting degrees
Areas of specialty and sub-specialty (*)

✦ Honors and awards
Latinate honors at graduation (*)
Honor societies to which you have been elected (*)
Scholarships and fellowships which you have received (*)

✦ Work history
Places you have held positions (*)
Positions held by exact title (*)
Beginning and ending dates of employment (*)
Brief description of principal duties in each position

✦ Publications
Full citation in accepted form of all papers or books which you
have authored or co-authored (*)

✦ Presentations
Full citation in accepted form of all papers presented at
professional meetings (*)

✦ References
Names, addresses, and telephone numbers of at least three people
who have agreed to comment on your ability, qualifications,
character, and suitability for this position (*)

The visual impact of the vitae will be important. Organize everything in a logical manner, using headings that stand out boldly, and separating sections from one another by ample space. Avoid prose; put that in the letter. Aim for ease of reading; readers will have a stack of vitae, and they will appreciate one that stands out as being clear and concise. Remember that your resumé will be read not only by people from your discipline, but by administrators as well; clarity and succinctness will be especially appreciated by them, for they probably have stacks of vitae from other searches to review as well.

There are placement firms that faculty candidates can hire to help them with the entire process, and that will prepare a printed vitae with your photograph on it for you to mail off. There may be a time soon when this approach becomes standard, but my own reaction to a vitae that is too "slick" is not the best. Wordprocessors make it possible for the applicant to produce a vitae in perfectly good form.

You may discover, no matter how well you put together your vitae, that some colleges request that you fill out application forms. Don't be offended by this and don't take short cuts. This may seem like so much red tape, but the fact is that every college has an established search process, and institutions serious about affirmative action especially will often be keeping certain kinds of statistical data. Moreover, a college earnest in its desire to find faculty who fit the institution will want to have answers to some specific kinds of questions that are most easily obtained by an application form. In church-related colleges, the values espoused by a candidate may be even more important than his or her academic credentials. It is not uncommon for those applying for their first faculty position to be surprised at how probing such questions can be and even to take exception to them. I would say simply that if you find a questionnaire unacceptably offensive, you should cross that college off your application list. Otherwise it can only help to provide as complete responses to forms and questions asked on them as you possibly can. To clip a vitae to an application blank form and return it, or to write in "green Martian" (as I actually had someone do in one search) when asked about one's race,[1] can, rightly or wrongly, suggest an obdurate personality at a time when you're trying to convey your rightness as a new member of the campus community.

The Search Process

It seems improbable that President Fitzgeorge and his colleagues at the College of Port St. Julian have followed the steps colleges more commonly use in a search. It may help for you to see the process from the campus perspective. An overall search process will look something like this:

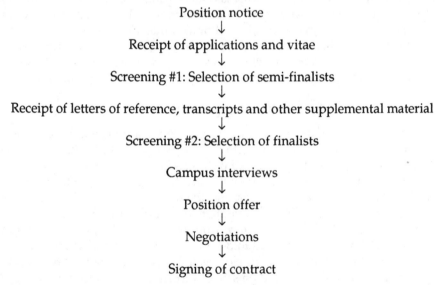

Position notice
↓
Receipt of applications and vitae
↓
Screening #1: Selection of semi-finalists
↓
Receipt of letters of reference, transcripts and other supplemental material
↓
Screening #2: Selection of finalists
↓
Campus interviews
↓
Position offer
↓
Negotiations
↓
Signing of contract

The exact details will, of course, vary considerably from campus to campus. The search will be conducted by the office of the dean or the academic vice

---

[1] Questions about race on application forms are normally optional. Those institutions including them are usually keeping affirmative action statistics, and may even have that part of the form returned to a separate affirmative action office.

president in some colleges; more often the academic department will be responsible. In some cases, particularly when the application pool is not large, the two screening steps may be collapsed into a single screening from which finalists are selected. When both steps are included, the department and dean will keep as semi-finalists those applicants who appear from their paper credentials to fit the advertised position reasonably well. That judgment usually comes from having all department members and the dean evaluate dossiers (mostly containing letters and vitae at this point) independently, then looking for accord among evaluators. Semi-finalists will be asked to have transcripts, probably both undergraduate and graduate, sent to the college; to have references written; to complete and return application forms; and to provide any supplemental materials the college may wish to see. As these new materials come in, they are added to the dossiers, and a second screening of them by department members and dean produces a small group of finalist names. These will be invited to come to campus for an interview. If funds are available, a college will usually want to bring in at least three finalists before making a decision about an offer.

For some disciplines, it is also common to insert another step, interviews at meetings, after the receipt of the applications. Employment clearing houses are operated by a number of professional organizations that hold annual national meetings. These provide a convenient and inexpensive way for departments doing searches to hold preliminary interviews with a larger number of candidates than can be brought to campus. This interviewing seldom can involve more than one or two departmental representatives, so this step supplies notes from them to go into dossiers before screening proceeds.

The Campus Visit

In a typical search, the first chance the people on campus will have to compare their picture of a candidate with the real person will be when he or she comes for a campus visit. By this point the candidate has passed through the sieve of the application phase, and knows that the impression made by the letter, the vitae, the application forms, and the responses from references have been positive enough to elicit an invitation to visit the campus.

In Adam Newprof's case, he knew from what Dr. Noble, the department chair, and Dean Pennington had told him, that his letter and vitae had produced a lot of interest. His *magna cum laude* graduation, his membership in Phi Beta Kappa, and his graduate school record told them that he was the kind of person who would hold students to high standards, something the college prided itself in. The interest he expressed in his letter in teaching at a small, liberal arts college in his home state had made points with them too. But they appeared to have been most swayed by his references. At lunch, both Dean Pennington and Dr. Noble had talked, without getting specific as to who had said what, about the high praise his letters of reference had contained. "I don't see many like that," Dean Pennington had told him, and Adam had blushed over his she-crab soup. Only President Fitzgeorge had named names; his confidence in Professor Scribe's approval of Newprof had supplied the clincher.

But Adam had not known ahead of time how he would be received. For someone preparing for his first interview, he had been understandably nervous, not exactly certain how he should dress or whom he would meet or how acceptably he would answer questions put to him. He wasn't sure beforehand that the College of Port St. Julian would be the college for him, but from what he had learned about it up to now, there was a good chance it might be. He had no intention of faking anything, but he did want to make the best possible impression.

The kind of things Adam was nervous about do matter, including how one dresses for the interview. However we would like it to be, one's appearance influences people. It is important, certainly, to dress neatly. There is no "uniform," but men should wear a coat and tie, and women should choose clothes that look tidy and professional. For men, dark colored coats are best. Plaids, kelly green, and sneakers of any color should be avoided at all costs (I have seen all of these). Ties should be conservative, and should be coordinated with jacket and pants. Sedate colors work well for women interviewees also, but they can use prints and brighter colors also without getting a negative reaction. It is understood at most colleges that your appearance at the interview is not necessarily indicative of how you will dress every day once you've moved to campus, but interviewers will, however unconsciously, be biased for good or ill by how you look, and they will, moreover, make inferences about your attitude towards the place and position from your appearance. Dress for the day with some care.

The most critical judgments about you will not, of course, come from your apparel, but from the impression you make in conversations. Just who will be included in the interview is a matter of campus choice and custom, but there is a key group that you can depend on spending time with. Most of your time will be spent with department members, the faculty in the department that has advertised the opening. If the department is small, you can expect to have individual conversations with each of them. If it is larger, you will certainly have one or more private conversations with the department chair, but other meetings may be with small groups of faculty. You will probably have an opportunity to talk to student majors in the department, a group from whom you can gain valuable insights about both the department and the college community. If there is time, you may also meet with faculty from outside the department, or even with members of the Faculty Personnel Committee. The dean, as the chief academic officer, and the person who must approve any recommendation about hiring from the department, will probably spend at least an hour with you. In many colleges, the president, too, will be in the interview schedule, but because presidents of today spend so much time off campus, it is difficult to make this a rigid requirement. If you do meet with the president, the conversation will likely be relatively brief, though not perfunctory. Visits to some places may permit time for talking to other members of the administrative staff, such as the associate or assistant dean, the dean of students, the registrar, or the chaplain.

In all these conversations you will be doing more than trying to make a good impression. This is not, after all, just a PR game. You might think of the purpose of the interview as two-fold: (1) to allow a sense to develop as to whether you are the right person for the position and college; (2) to develop a sense as to whether this position and college are right for you.

Purpose (1) is not a euphemistic way of urging a counterfeit presentation of yourself with a view to getting a job offer, but a very sensible aim for the candidate; if the real candidate is not right for the institution, the institution will not turn out to be right for the candidate once hired. Purpose (2) will require that you stay alert throughout the interview, asking as many questions as you need to, observing, and collecting written information and literature for later study. The attitude that will serve you best is one of polite forthrightness. As with letter-writing, one should aim for confidence without arrogance, courtesy without obsequiousness. An experienced interviewer will be looking for a good listener, who is not simply trying to sell him- or herself, but sincerely working at learning about the college and expectations for the position.

You should think prior to the visit about some of the questions you need answers to, and you should not be shy about asking them. It is not unusual for a first-time applicant not to know enough to ask many questions, and certainly questions should not be forced. It is, however, indicative of good preparation for your new profession to have identified items that those already in the profession know to be important. A number of key issues that can get cleared up quickly on the interview are listed back in Chapter 2 (Table 2.2), but a new summary, including these with additions, are suggested below.

- ✦ College mission statement
- ✦ Standing goals of the college
- ✦ Curriculum goals
- ✦ Long-range plan for the college, with progress reports
- ✦ Student selectivity data
- ✦ Teaching load information
- ✦ Programs of support for teaching
- ✦ Availability of secretarial assistance
- ✦ Availability of student assistants
- ✦ Information about student evaluations of teaching
- ✦ Programs of support for scholarship and professional development
- ✦ Travel funds available to faculty
- ✦ Expectations for tenure and promotion
- ✦ Information about student retention

- ✦ Information about the quality of student campus life
- ✦ Salary information, including comparative data
- ✦ College support for moving expenses
- ✦ Faculty orientation programs
- ✦ Sense of community on campus
- ✦ Employee benefit information
- ✦ Cost of living and cost of homes in the area

Your conversations in the department will naturally center on the position itself, the activities in the department, and a range of associated issues. You will want them to give you a close look at physical facilities, including the classrooms where you will teach; faculty offices, including the one that will be assigned to you as a new faculty member; instructional equipment, particularly if the position is in the sciences, fine arts, or physical education; and the library. In the case of the library, you will want to tour that building and review the holdings in your discipline, including periodical subscriptions. If you want to build time for exercise into your work week, department members can show you the gymnasium and discuss what accommodations the new faculty member can expect there. Departmental conversations will also take you into other obvious topics: student quality, class sizes, departmental and college governance, departmental arrangements for secretarial support, the use of student assistants, and the state of departmental morale (ask about this one, if no one mentions it).

When you meet with the dean, the conversation is apt to be much more institutional in scope and even philosophical in tone. For someone coming straight from a doctoral program, it is much easier to know what to talk about with fellow disciplinarians in the department than to know what subjects are within a dean's purview. As the chief academic officer, the dean is ultimately responsible for all academic programs and personnel and is the supervisor of the department chairs. It is more likely that the dean will be interested in questions of institutional fit, and in what a candidate will contribute to the overall development and vigor of the faculty and the strength of the campus community, than in such esoteric concerns as the times of classes you would teach. From your side, you are much more likely to get from the dean than from the department chair a vision of where the college is headed, and a sense of where institutional values and priorities lie. The dean can also usually provide institutional data that might be of interest to you. Questions about student selectivity, financial stability, enrollments, and trends over time should be asked during this time in the dean's office. It is also here that you will get the clearest picture of expectations for tenure and promotion of faculty. If you find anything you learn from the dean to be at apparent odds with what you learn in the department, try to get that cleared up before leaving campus; it may be a simple misunderstanding, but you need the facts.

A formal presentation to a group of faculty and students is a valuable means for your ability as a teacher to be demonstrated, and many interview schedules will call for such a presentation. You will be alerted ahead of time about this, but some invitations to interview come with relatively short notice, so it is prudent during your season of search to have ready a presentation based on some aspect of your doctoral dissertation work. It may well be that a given host department will ask for a lecture to an introductory (or other) class in the discipline instead, and you should be prepared for that possibility as well. In either event, you will be talking about a subject familiar to you, and you should relax and concentrate on your presentation. If the audience does contain both faculty and students, speak primarily to the students and pitch the presentation at their level, leading them from definitions, principles, axioms, and premises to the points that you wish them to take away. In other words, teach. Choose lucidity over profundity. What will most impress both faculty and students far more than your store of knowledge is your ability to communicate and develop ideas with clarity.

Negotiating

The exchange between Adam Newprof and President Fitzgeorge ends with the beginning of the negotiating phase of the search process. Newprof is getting, from the sound of it, a this-is-our-best offer. Fitzgeorge has proposed a salary at the top of the assistant professor range, meaning that the board of trustees has authorized this as the highest salary any assistant professor, new or otherwise, can be paid. That's unusual. He has also thrown in an offer of $1,000 as a research budget, not a grand sum, but not routine either, especially at a small college like this. Just the fact that it was the president, rather than the department chair or the dean, who is making the offer, is significant. Fitzgeorge hopes that Adam will find this proposition so attractive that there can be only one answer. It is generally not judicious to accept any offer, even a most attractive one, on the spot. Adam is going to ask for a week to think this one over.

A majority of faculty who get to this point in the process begin to feel like a tourist in a Tiajuana shop. They experience a pronounced disquiet at the prospect of haggling, a practice that may well seem beneath the dignity of people entering a respected profession. Negotiating the terms of appointment is nonetheless a very practical and consequential step for the new faculty member. If an offer has been made by a college, you can be sure that they want you on their faculty and are anxious to have you say yes to their invitation. You are unlikely ever again to be in such a favorable circumstance for shaping your conditions of employment. What I am urging is not wanton or recreational bargaining. College deans and presidents are no more merchants than you are a tourist, and their tolerance for hard bargaining is not unlimited, so you will want to negotiate realistically.

What is realistic with regard to salary you can judge only if you have comparative data, so it is good neither to make demands nor to accept an offer without first having done your homework. In Table 2.2, the March/April issue of the AAUP's *Academe* is suggested as a source for data on salaries. This issue is devoted entirely to information about faculty salaries and compensation (i.e., salary plus employee benefits), including accounts and analyses of trends over time. In it you will find listed (with near certainty) all the colleges where you are interviewing, with an indication of the average salaries and compensation each pays to its faculty in each academic rank. A code also appears which indicates how salaries at this college compare with all salaries nationally. Obviously, this is just the sort of information that can assist you in deciding whether the initial salary offer is reasonable or not. If it is, you should not feel obliged to bargain. But if it is not, a counteroffer can be made with more confidence.

If no one has mentioned it at the point of the offer, you should ask also about moving expenses. Moves across country can be costly, and many colleges are prepared to help with that expense.

President Fitzgeorge has offered Adam Newprof funding for research as part of his appointment package. Among liberal arts colleges, this kind of support is seldom automatic, but it can frequently be obtained. In those colleges where commitment to a scholarly faculty is high, you will almost surely find a comprehensive assortment of programs established to provide encouragement to all faculty in their research efforts, and that will include first-year faculty. But even where there are not strong traditions of research in the faculty, a department or dean seeking to attract new faculty of high quality will respond as favorably as financial circumstances will permit to your request for research start-up funds.

There may be less latitude when one attempts to negotiate a teaching load lighter than that required of veteran faculty. Faculty as a group have a very well developed sense of what is fair, and more senior faculty tend to look askance at relaxation of formal expectations for teaching, recognizing perhaps that the fewer students first-year faculty teach the more students other faculty will teach. Nonetheless, colleges are beginning to appreciate the importance of reducing somewhat the formal expectations of new faculty for scheduled teaching, acknowledging that those just starting out spend far more hours on time preparing for teaching (see Chapter 2) than do more experienced faculty, and providing a rational basis for loads being reduced for first-year faculty on equity grounds. Psychologist Roger Baldwin argues that colleges should make reduced loads for the "novice professor" standard policy.[2] You won't know

---

[2] Roger G. Baldwin, "Faculty Career Stages and Implications for Professional Development," in Jack H. Schuster, Daniel W. Wheeler, and Associates, *Enhancing Faculty Careers* (San Francisco, CA: Jossey-Bass, 1990), pp. 20-40.

the possibilities until you ask and, given the extraordinary amount of time that you will need to invest in preparing courses in your first year of teaching, asking is very much in order.

Getting Oriented:
The Lay of the Land

It was like the spectacle which greeted the eyes of Moses from the summit of Pisgah, and in the warm glow of their feelings, they cried out, "It is the promised land!"

William Hickling Prescott
The Conquest of Mexico [1843]

*H*e had a desk now, and yesterday two sweating men with very strong Juliano accents had brought in what was unmistakenly a home-made bookcase that had been in storage somewhere. He had unpacked some of his books from graduate school and shelved them, but there was still one more box to go. He sat in the cane-backed swivel chair and dumped paper clips into a little tray built into the front of his desk drawer, beside another little compartment containing rubber bands and refills for the antique stapler on top of the used desk. In the two-drawer file cabinet behind him were arranged neatly a drawer-and-a-half of manila file folders filled with collections of things from graduate courses, library searches at the university, graph paper, scribblings relating to his doctoral research, and a miscellany of other materials collected back at Benjamin and during the Army tour. He had hung a calendar on the wall over the work table and tacked up a small bulletin board above his desk. He had earlier this morning skewered to the bulletin board with map tacks a hand-drawn schedule for the semester that would start on Monday. Adam Newprof was starting to feel, well, professorial.

As if on cue: "Well, good morning, Professor Newprof. You feeling good this morning?" It was Tommy Venable, his office mate.

"Good morning, Tommy." There was the slightest pause between "morning" and "Tommy." Adam still felt strange calling a man nearly thirty years his senior by his first name. "I'm just fine. Almost through unpacking. Hope I'm not crowding you up too much."

He had not expected to have to share an office with anyone, but that's how it had turned out. Tommy's desk faced the doorway, at right angles to the wall across the room from Adam. The office was large enough for two, but Tommy Venable had been there for twenty-three years, and had accumulated quite a bit of stuff.

"No indeed! Glad to have the company." Tommy tossed two envelopes onto his own desk, then looked over his shoulder as he hung up his light blue cotton cord coat on a hanger behind the door. "You need anything? Anything I can help with?"

"Well, you might tell me how to get something for the analytical lab. I studied the situation down there yesterday afternoon, and I could use one more cabinet. I want to be able to put away the pH meters and the Spectronic 20s when they're not in use."

"A cabinet? You just need to talk to old Sam MacDougal."

"Sam...?"

"MacDougal. Yeah, he's sort of the chief fixer-upper around here. Just go down to the shop right after lunch, maybe, and you can catch him. Mac makes half the furniture at the college. Probably made that bookcase the boys brought in for you." Tommy sat down and picked up one of the envelopes. "I stopped and picked up the mail I forgot to pick up yesterday."

"Where do we get mail?" Adam asked him.

Venable jerked a thumb toward the wall behind Adam. "In there in the faculty lounge. Over beside the window there are mailboxes for all the faculty. You ought to have a box in there with your name on it by now. Have you checked?"

"No, but I think I'll do that now."

The faculty lounge had been cut off from a larger room, the remainder of which had become Tommy Venable's office some years in the past. Both rooms opened into the dark hallway that ran from front to back of the ground floor of the Main Building. Their walls, except for the drywall partition, were two feet thick, made of concrete two hundred years old. Ground floors in Port St. Julian were much like basements in other parts of the country, so the faculty lounge had that basement look and feel, with only the small window through two-foot concrete to let in outside light. The furniture was shabby, but homey looking, a naugahyde couch and a half-dozen chairs. Somebody had been smoking a cigar.

"Hey. You must be the new chemistry professor." A small, wiry man not too far from his own age pushed out of an overstuffed chair and put down a letter he had been reading. "I'm Carlisle Ravenel. I teach biology."

Adam grasped the proffered hand. "I'm Adam Newprof. Good to meet you."

Ravenel appeared quite friendly, but nervous. "You—uh—you settled in?"

"Pretty much. In with Tommy Venable."

"Mm. Listen—you want to go get a cup of coffee?"

Newprof's face lit up. "I'm dying for some coffee. Haven't bought a coffee pot yet. Where do you go for coffee around here?"

"Now there's a sensible question for a new faculty member to ask. Come on, I'll take you to the College Street Café. Not much atmosphere, but outstanding coffee."

The café was only a block away. It had booths along one wall and stools at the counter on the other. The dominant smell was bacon grease. Ravenel led Newprof to the booth just inside the door. A smiling middle-aged Greek with curly greying hair and a matching moustache was at their table with two cups of coffee before they had been seated half a minute.

"Morning, Professor Ravenel!" The greeting was hearty and genuine. "You bring us a new customer this morning?"

Carlisle Ravenel did the introductions: "Mr. Makropolos, this is Dr. Newprof, a new chemistry professor at the college. Just moved here."

"Hey, welcome to the greatest city in the South—in the world! And the greatest college! Tell you what. Coffee's on the house this morning."

"Thanks, Mr. Makropolos."

"Call me Pete. Everybody calls me Pete. The professor here's being formal today. Anyway—you drink up. Then come on back for lunch. Can't ever have too many customers."

They chatted over the black coffee. Ravenel remained nervous, but after a time Adam realized that this was just his manner. He had joined the biology faculty only two years ago, but he was an alumnus of the College of Port St. Julian. Adam was enjoying getting acquainted with him. They were halfway through the second cup when Ravenel asked with an enigmatic grin:

"What do you think about our dean?" He was watching Newprof's face closely.

"Dean Pennington? Well, I haven't spent all that much time with her, but—I guess so far, so good. She was a gracious enough host when I came for the interview. Why?"

Carlisle Ravenel looked around the café. "Well, there are people on the faculty who would be just as happy if she found another college to do her deaning. Tommy mention that to you?"

Adam shook his head.

"She's pushing for a lot more research and publishing and stuff than most of the College of Port St. Julian faculty want to do. You know, she came here from Davidson, and that's a lot more high-powered place than this is. Vernon Becker from math says we're becoming a publish-or-perish kind of place, and we were hired to teach. He spent half his time in the faculty lounge last year trying to get some organized resistance going. Vern also says," Carlisle looked around again, "that she was forced to leave the Davidson faculty because of some kind of affair with another professor whose wife had a private detective get the goods on them. Vern is going to get all the details, and see what he can do with them."

This had been a good morning for him, but now Adam Newprof found himself feeling uneasy. He had liked Dean Pennington, and all this talk about publish-or-perish and private detectives—well, it wasn't very reassuring.

The Start of the Start

Adam Newprof is starting out this week his life as a faculty member. Up until now all has been theories and ideals; now he will live the life for real. He is very aware that he has some learning to do himself. This is his third day on campus, and he didn't even have an office until yesterday. He is beginning to be able to find things in the chemistry labs and stockroom, but he has just discovered where his mailbox is, and he hasn't the vaguest idea where to look for the shop Venable mentioned. He has met only maybe ten faculty members other than Tommy Venable and Charles Noble. On the one hand he has been made to feel most welcome; on the other he still feels very much the new guy on the block, almost like a trespasser. It is hard to call Venable and Noble, both of whom are so much older, Tommy and Charles. Port St. Julian itself is still a foreign city for him—its narrow old streets, edged with palmettoes and live oaks, running across the peninsula at all kinds of odd angles, many of them unpredictably one-way—and driving the two miles from his apartment to the campus is not yet a totally natural or certain migration. The architecture, too, is different from anything he has seen before, block after block of houses with their ends turned to the street and the front of each facing the back of its neighbor. Moreover, the native Julianoes speak a distinctive low-country dialect that he has yet to master. He likes the place, but he is not yet at home.

This is "the start of the start." Next year at this time Newprof will be an experienced hand, but for now he is in an intense learning mode, getting the lay of the new land.

Reporting for work on the first day is a time of at least mild trepidation for all but the most supremely confident. Indeed, if you find yourself feeling too calm on that day, you may well need to ask whether you are in the kind of appropriate "learning mode" that will facilitate your adjustment to a new environment. You will, of course, have things other than the new campus and position on your mind. Having just moved, you will have moving boxes still unpacked; there will be a visit to the Department of Motor Vehicles to make soon; there may be family responsibilities, perhaps getting children ready for the opening of the public schools; and you will have other assorted personal duties as well. A new place to live, a new place to work, myriad things to get done—it all makes for a pretty crowded mental landscape.

You will doubtless spend considerable time on that first day getting information from your department chair and whatever other departmental colleagues are around. They will see that you know where your office is, and will presumably offer assistance in getting things moved into it. They will also be your first source of answers to many nuts-and-bolts kinds of questions that will arise as you assemble your office materials and start to think about course syllabi. In addition, the dean, associate or assistant deans, and the secretary or assistant to the dean will be prepared to provide information and help, as will other staff on campus. In the first week there will seem to be an endless number of things to find out about; as the first year goes along, the number will diminish, but some things you will learn only by making mistakes. This approach to getting started is somewhat happenstance and disorganized, but it is often the way one makes the transition into a department and college.

Other colleges, recognizing how much more quickly and surely new faculty can become knowledgeable and acculturated, have designed first-year faculty orientation programs. Typically, these will have an early period of extensive orientation, when new faculty become acquainted with a set of things that are best learned at the very beginning, before the first day of class. This orientation may be a single session, or it may be more. I have found that a year-long program has many benefits. Although each year there are some shifts and amendments, the most effective and practical format has come from looking at the needs of first-year faculty in three phases, and fashioning a program that fits those phases:

Phase	*Need to know or do*	*Program*
Entry	Sense of place	**Retreat (one day)**
	How to get things done	The College Past & Present
	Key people	The Students of the College
	How to get support for teaching	The Faculty of the College
	How the faculty conducts business	Library Support for Faculty
	Basic responsibilities	Faculty Governance
	How faculty are evaluated	Evaluation at the College
		Tenure & Promotion
		Nuts & Bolts
		Campus Historic Tour
Settling In	Identity & details of programs	**Fall-Term Sessions (weekly)**
	Wider circle of faculty & staff	The General Education
		Curriculum

	What makes for good teaching	The Effective Teacher (3 sessions)
	How to approach scholarship	The Teacher-Scholar
	The heritage of the college	The Church Connection
	College financial operations	The Financial Front
	Answers to arising questions	The Individual in the Organization
		The Honors Program
		Directors' Showcase
Consolidation	Profit from reflection	**Spring-Term Sessions (monthly)**
	Plan for the future	Looking Back on the Fall Term
		The Management of Stress and Time
		Staying Good
		Winding up the First Year

This kind of program is not, of course, merely a means of feeding information to new faculty; there are benefits far beyond that aim. Run by the dean's office and using numerous presenters from the faculty and staff, it brings together on a regular basis all new faculty, gets them acquainted with a broad spectrum of people from across campus, provides balance against the centripetal pull of the department, and provides a natural peer group for them during a period of adjustment. It has been very rewarding to see the friendships that have sprung up across departments as a result of these sessions, and I would argue that the sense of overall college community is enhanced as well. We have each year, during the sessions "Looking Back on the Fall Term" and "Winding up the First Year," preceded the meetings with a survey of the group, and used the results of the survey to guide discussion about what is going well and less well. Out of these two sessions have come some very clear perceptions of where new faculty concerns are and what aspects of the college they find particularly satisfying. It has also proved an effective and objective way to monitor trends in campus morale by asking observers who have, one would expect, a minimum of bias.[1]

The People

The College of Port St. Julian is a place of charm. Its Main Building dates from the late Eighteenth Century, and although it sits now in the center of a city, there are live oaks all around it draped with Spanish moss and palmetto palms peering over window sills, so that the feel is distinctively rustic inside its walls. How pleasant a place the college turns out to be for Adam Newprof

---

[1] The reliability of this kind of survey will, of course, depend on a number of factors, the first being how large the new group of faculty is. Several years of surveying reveals that with groups of about ten each year regular patterns to responses are quite obvious.

will, however, depend far more on the people there than the charm of its setting.

When you report to your new campus, you will have an impression of the sort of professional home it is going to be. That impression is presumably good at the outset, and will inevitably be prominently, if not primarily, shaped by the quality of the accommodations and equipment available for your use. The physical environment is assuredly important to one's satisfaction in any workplace, but over the long haul it is always the people who have the most profound influence on how much you look forward to coming to work in the morning. That will be no less true of a new college where you have gone to teach than of a corporation.

You should not be passive about the need to get to know as many people as possible as soon as possible. It will have practical consequences as you do your work, for there will be times when you will need to get something done that requires the cooperation or assistance of others. It is much better on such occasions not to be dealing with strangers, to be able to pick up the phone or walk to another office on campus and say, "Hello, Marie. Could I ask your help with something?" knowing that Marie is a thirty-five year old bookstore manager, a mother of two children, and a person with an amiable disposition. A large majority of faculty are by nature introverts (more about this later in Chapter 9). Add to this (a) the lack of leisure time they have at the beginning, with so much to do and new classes to prepare for; and (b) the instinct to feel, as Newprof does, like something of an interloper, and it is understandable that new faculty tend to be slow at widening the circle of acquaintances beyond the department. An extended orientation program for first-year faculty can help with this, but whether your college has such a program or not, this is an initiative you need to take. How should you go about it? What opportunities are there for getting to know people short of wandering the halls and introducing yourself?

First, your first college year will probably begin with one or more social events sponsored by the college administration. While these are not mandatory, they provide occasions for introductions, name tags are conspicuous, and you will meet as many college faculty and staff as you wish. Take advantage of any opening-of-school events announced, circulate as much as possible, and work at remembering names, faces, and functions. Even remembering a small percent puts you on your way.

There is most likely to be an orientation session of some description. There you will meet both key staff members with whom you will be working from time to time, and other first-year faculty as well. Name tags are again a likelihood here. Don't be passive or simply endure the session; study names and faces and put them with functions. If there is not a "Who to See for What" handout distributed, make your own notes as people are introduced.

There is one place for meeting people which a dean always recommends with mixed feelings—the faculty lounge. Your college is likely to have a room somewhere on campus where there is a coffee pot and a place for faculty to sit, sip, and chat. There may also be in the lounge reading materials such as the *Chronicle of Higher Education, Change* magazine, and the like. This is also a common location for a bulletin board where items of general interest to the faculty can be posted. The faculty lounge, you will find, is not frequented by all the faculty, but it is utilized regularly by some. It will be a good place not only to learn veteran faculty's names, but also to have extended conversations with them. The "mixed emotions" mentioned above stem from the certainty, whatever the campus, that the faculty lounge will be a source of gossip, and even the center for the kind of transactional analysis game-playing that can send squalls across a campus from time to time. (More about this in Chapter 9). Adam Newprof, in his third day at the College of Port St. Julian, has discovered the faculty lounge and has picked up some gossip. He likes Carlisle Ravenel, but he is reluctant to accept what Ravenel is reporting about Dean Pennington. There is no organization free from gossip, and that includes the best liberal arts college with the strongest sense of community that you can find in the nation. So you should not be dismayed or frightened by gossip when you hear it. What you want to remind yourself of is this: wait until you have more facts, then draw your own conclusion. But go to the lounge—you will meet people you need to meet, and if it isn't the kind of climate you like, you can become a dropout later.

Finally, there will be a few people beyond your department whose acquaintance you need to make—and who need to make yours—within the first couple of weeks. With these you should take the personal initiative to visit and introduce yourself. You met the dean on the interview, and possibly the president and some other staff members; but you need to add to that list the faculty moderator or chair (if there is one), the registrar, the secretary or assistant to the dean, the director of personnel, the dean of students, the associate/assistant academic dean(s), and (for church-related colleges) the chaplain. These visits are urged, not for purposes of academic courtesy or protocol, but because they will pave the way for communications that will (a) be required frequently, or (b) give valuable insights into dealing with problems that arise with students in your classes. A prior appointment usually isn't needed; just drop by, introduce yourself, and chat briefly, unless you have something specific to discuss. It will be a good investment of time.

The Place

To get the most out of teaching at a college, and to make the most valuable contribution to it, you need to know where you are. That isn't meant geographically, of course, or at least not primarily so. There is an interesting story behind every institution. Take this story, for example:

Shortly after the Civil War, the Caldwell Plantation, a tract of some 500 acres in Gaston County, North Carolina, was purchased by the Reverend

Jeremiah O'Connell, a missionary priest. It was his desire that this tract be accepted by a religious community which would develop on it an institution for the education of youth. At the request of Bishop James Gibbons of Richmond, Virginia, the Benedictine monks of Saint Vincent Archabbey in Latrobe, Pennsylvania, agreed to accept the land and to found a community and school. On 21 April 1876, the Reverend Herman Wolfe, O.S.B., arrived to take possession of the property. The young foundation became an independent abbey on 19 December 1884, with the Right Reverend Leo Haid, O.S.B., being elected the first abbot on 14 July 1885.

The College was chartered as St. Mary's College by the State of North Carolina on 1 April 1886. The College's name was changed to Belmont Abbey College in 1913. Reorganized as a junior college in 1928, it became a senior college in September 1952. In 1972 the College became coeducational for resident students.[2]

To someone on the threshold of a brand new career, the future may seem far more important than the past. There is, in fact, a strong inclination for each of us to feel that the real story of the college began with our coming. That is, of course, illusion. There are people with whom you are working whose memories extend back past vital transition points —like the 1972 move to coeducational status at Belmont Abbey College—and whose view of what has been may be more powerful for them than your own vision of what can be. The power of heritage, its ability to inspire and motivate—or to constrain—is indisputable. The faculty, who have weathered together the ebb and flow of institutional trial and achievement, share a sense of what matters and how things are done that you as a newcomer cannot yet know, but which will nonetheless affect your ability to accomplish your own goals within that culture. The earlier you can learn the history of the college, both distant and recent, the earlier you can begin to be integrated into the community and make your own contributions to it. If there is a written history of the college, make certain to read it within the first couple of months—or even better, before coming to campus, if that is possible. It will not be time wasted.

Other contributions to your sense of place will come from having read the mission statement, institutional goals, the long-range plan, and other college materials. Contributing, too, will be what you have absorbed from conversations during the search and after you moved into the department, as well as whatever you knew about before the general reputation of the college.

A second meaning of "knowing the place" that you should not overlook, though it is a much less lofty concern, is knowing where things are on campus: the bookstore, the snack bar, the cafeteria, the business office, the chaplain's office, auditoriums and theaters, galleries, and athletic facilities. Even if you saw a lot when you were interviewing, only the exceptional person will have a clear recollection of it all. If you are at a small college, you may think

[2] *1989-90 Academic Bulletin*, Belmont Abbey College, Belmont, NC.

that this more mundane connotation of "getting the lay of the land" can't present much of a challenge. But it is always surprising to take note of how many first-year faculty have such limited knowledge of what is where at the end of their first year. A guided tour by a seasoned faculty member as part of an orientation session will help considerably with this, but I would advise the new faculty member simply to get out of the department and spend an hour or two exploring the campus on one's own during the first term. You will have a much better feel for the place as a result, and you will run into a few more people in the process. Familiarity with the physical college, like familiarity with the historical college, will hasten your acceptance and value as a campus citizen.

Learning Your Responsibilities

Any first-year faculty orientation will include a nuts-and-bolts portion intended to acquaint you with a few key responsibilities you will have as faculty member and will need to meet soon after classes begin. This will include such things as what you should do with class rolls, how the grading system of the college operates, and how to handle honor code or academic integrity violations. The remaining delineation of duties will probably take place in the department. Your department chair will make certain you know the class schedule for the campus, and the exact time of your own classes. The chair will also make clear any departmental processes for ordering and purchasing materials, as well as any departmental policies, such as those for handling student challenges to grades or other student complaints. Either the department chair or the dean's office can help make sure you know about college travel policies, and how to get reimbursed for expenses.

Your official contract with the college is the Faculty Handbook. The handbook will cover a large number of items that there isn't time to cover in a formal orientation period. It is the final authority in defining your responsibilities as a faculty member, and you need to be well acquainted with it. Your department chair will help with the interpretation of any section that is not clear.

For Discussion———————————————————

1. As you have attempted to get the lay of the land, what or whom have you found to be especially helpful? What additional things would you suggest be done to assist new faculty in getting oriented to the campus?

2. What initiatives have you taken to get acquainted with (a) faculty outside your department, and (b) staff members?

3. Do you have "the story" of your college at this point?

4. Have you reviewed the Faculty Handbook carefully? If so, did you find it generally easy to read? Did it prompt any questions that need answers?

Becoming a Patriot:
The Liberal Arts Tradition

*The useful is not always good, but the good is always useful. Real
liberal education is, in sum, the most useful of all.*

Earl F. Cheit
The Useful Arts and the Liberal Tradition

This was a great old campus. Lots of camellias and azaleas and
oleanders were clustered under the live oaks, flower beds here
and there, brick walks splotched with shade. On one of the oak-and-
iron benches beside the brick walk that separated the science center
from the library, Adam Newprof was enjoying the setting and the mid-
September weather. It was the first time he had taken an afternoon
break since the term started.

"Hi, Adam!" It was Maggie Morrow, heading toward him down the
walk from the direction of College Street. "You're not in lab?"

Maggie was the other first-year faculty member with Adam at the
College of Port St. Julian this fall. She was in English. Newprof had met
her in the faculty lounge when he returned to get his mail that third day,
after being introduced to the College Street Café by Carlisle Ravenel.
She was friendly and outgoing and had a very relaxed style. She never
seemed as tense about her teaching as Adam tended to be.

"Hi, Maggie. No, no lab on Tuesdays this term. Just getting out for
some fresh air. Come and join me. What have you been doing with the
afternoon?"

She sat beside him, placing a rubber-banded stack of papers between
them on the bench.

"I snuck off to Pete's place to work on these themes. Okay, so I also
had some baklava and a couple of cups of tea while I graded papers. I
confess."

Adam grinned. "No need to be apologetic. Sounds like an ideal way
to do grading. And you missed all the interruptions that would plague
you in the office."

"For a while anyway. Then Pete Makropolos came over to talk. He has a daughter who's going to college next year, his youngest, and he was asking for advice. She wants to be a lawyer."

"He had to ask? Right on the College of Port St. Julian's doorstep, and he had to ask?"

"What he asked, actually, was whether a liberal arts college was a good place for someone to go, if she wants to get into law school. I love talking about the value of a liberal education, so I told him he had come to the right person. We had a good conversation. It was almost a repeat of what I'm doing with my freshmen in class."

Adam was curious. "Your freshmen? What do you do?"

"I'm having them do some readings, then write a paper about the liberal arts tradition. Then we take a period to talk about the history of liberal education, and the implications for college students of today. I told Pete that, being Greek, some of his ancestors may have had a hand in starting it all. Anyway, I think I convinced him that a liberal arts education is what Elena needs."

The Faculty Role as Liberal Arts Advocate

Maggie Morrow sees herself as a champion of the tradition represented by the college where she is teaching. Like Adam Newprof, she is a product of a liberal arts college, places high value on the education she received there, and has a kind of evangelistic fervor about the liberal arts "message." But Maggie has one distinct advantage over Adam. She is grounded in the story of the liberal arts ideal—not merely college catalog prose, but a history with names, themes, and debates in it to prepare her as an advocate. Adam's commitment to liberal education is passionate, but Maggie's is informed as well.

There are no faculty handbooks, to my knowledge—at the College of Port St. Julian or at the college where you have gone to teach—that require either knowledge about or devotion to the liberal arts tradition. There is nonetheless good reason for you to take the time at the beginning of your career to become knowledgeable about the history of liberal education, to become an able articulator of its aims and ideals, and to prepare yourself to answer questions about its value in the contemporary world. There will be questions. Throughout your career, students will ask you to explain why they are required to take this course or that, or why there is a need to take any courses other than those they find naturally appealing, or what is so special about liberal education. Your ability to answer these kinds of questions well can matter considerably to your students' attitudes toward their studies.

For faculty whose own undergraduate experience was in a large university, there may be a bit more homework to do, but it is worth the effort. For those who, with Maggie Morrow and Adam Newprof, have diplomas from liberal arts colleges, the task may consist primarily of sorting out a confusion of impressions and recollections—though the liberal arts colleges are relatively few that can guarantee in their graduates or in their faculty a thorough grounding in the tradition that gave rise to their college. Numerous books and essays are available in every college library to equip you for the weekend reading that can help to remedy any deficits. The best single treatment of the history of the liberal arts ideal that I know about is Bruce Kimball's *Orators and Philosophers: A History of the Idea of Liberal Education.*[1] It is thoroughly researched, replete with references, and full of insight that has influenced the discourse about liberal education during a period of extensive curricular reform. Whatever your preparation, if it is done carefully and with purpose, it will help you feel more like a patriot than a mercenary in the campaign for liberal education.

Origins of the Liberal Arts Ideal

In the Western world we are accustomed to looking to the Greeks for origins of all sorts: the roots of democracy, etymological origins, artistic inspirations, athletic forms, poetic paradigms, and philosophical systems. It is not uncommon for commencement speakers and authors of essays to attribute to the ancient Greeks also the invention of a "liberal arts education." And their contribution to the individual components of that education is indisputable. The evidence points, however, to ancient Rome rather than Greece as the environment that gave rise to a system of education based on the *septem artes liberales* (seven liberal arts), what Kimball refers to as a "normative program" of liberal education. Rome was, after all, a more likely locus for the institution of a uniform system of any kind. The pre-Hellenistic Greek tribes formed city-states, and there were periods when one would be more powerful than the others, but until the time Rome conquered Greece in 197 B.C., there was never a single, united national Greek government. Such circumstances led to strikingly different educational emphases in each city-state. For instance, in Athens, the first democracy in the world, the goal was preparation for citizenship and studies focused on poetry and other literature, writing, arithmetic, music, and physical education. In Sparta, the strongest military center, by contrast, the emphasis was martial and physical, and an "educated" Spartan was likely to be illiterate. Moreover, in none of the city-states was there one single place where a boy (Greek girls were not given an education) could study a standard set of "arts" (the Greek word was *tekhnai*, meaning "techniques"); itinerant masters, among whom there was not even general agreement about the meaning and scope of a specific art, provided the instruction. Even in Athens, the unquestioned cultural leader of the city-states, the preponderance of evidence points to no standard definition of a liberal arts education.

---

[1] Bruce Kimball, *Orators and Philosophers: A History of the Idea of Liberal Education* (New York, NY: Teachers College Press, 1986). Reprinted by permission.

Our debt to the Greeks is nonetheless immense. Rome did not create the normative educational program, which eventually evolved there, from scratch. As with so much else, it appropriated and adapted ideas and traditions found in the Hellenistic civilization. The *septem artes liberales* of the Romans were all individually created and developed by Greek sages. The names of some are among the most recognizable in Western thought: Socrates, Isocrates, Plato, Aristotle, Protagoras, Demosthenes, Euripides, and Pythagoras.

Not all of these voices blended into a harmonious educational chorus. All would concur that education was the province of free citizens with leisure to study; the root word for "school" was in fact the Greek word *skholē*, meaning "leisure." There were, however, differences that went well beyond technical definitions; beyond, too, the general aim of education. The Athenian notion that education should be for citizenship was not the issue. The debate went a level deeper, to the question of the greatest good to be served by learning itself. The two camps that emerged gave rise to two separate traditions, and these have contended throughout the centuries for the "liberal education" banner. Kimball calls these the camps of the orators and philosophers.[2]

The orators were led by the teacher Isocrates (436-388 B.C.).[3] They held that rhetoric was the preeminent art, that the greatest good was served by speaking persuasively, thereby enhancing virtue in the audience. Knowledge of a wide variety was to be pursued, for a full store of knowledge enabled one to speak authoritatively on any subject. But learning as an isolated scholar was insufficient; true learning required a learning community. Philosophy, they contended, should not consist of endless speculation, but should make a difference in society. The orators gave great attention to the epic and hymnic poetry of ancient Greece, the respect for tradition that these texts taught, and the moral lessons that they contained. Homer was not merely "nice reading"; his poetry spoke with authority on virtue and high character. The mathematical arts received only modest attention, and their value was in their contribution to the preparation for rhetoric. The orators saw the central task of education to be not the seeking, but the imparting of truth.

The philosophers, following the lead of Socrates (c. 469-399 B.C.), rejected the dogmatism and absolutism of the orators, insisting instead that the ultimate aim of education should be to prepare the individual citizen to search for truth, wherever it might be found. The greatest good was *philosophia*, love of wisdom, and the search was endless. Virtue, they held, flows from knowing the truth. Eschewing the notion of authority, they taught intellectual freedom.

---

[2] A third camp, the *sophists*, placed priority on arguing persuasively over arguing from truth, and were attacked by both orators and philosophers. The later Roman orators were especially prone to accuse the philosophers of practicing sophistry, argument that was subtly and deliberately misleading.

[3] An orator who suffered, it appears, from both a poor voice and timidity!

The philosophers generally placed far less value on the language arts than did the orators;[4] although his position eventually softened, Plato (427-346 B.C.) saw no place for poets in his *Republic*. He saw, however, tremendous value in the mathematical arts as a means of learning the rigorous analytic thinking that aided one in the search for truth. Plato's student Aristotle (384-322 B.C.) went far beyond speculation and syllogistic reasoning to become the first of the philosophers to engage in scientific investigation. Collectively, the Greek philosophers left an intellectual legacy of enormous magnitude.

The view of the philosophers did not, however, prevail in the shorter term. In 338 B.C. Philip II of Macedonia defeated Greece, and by 328 B.C. his son Alexander the Great had subjugated the Persian Empire. Alexander II greatly admired Greek culture, founded Greek cities throughout his new empire, and thereby spread the Greek influence widely. Alexander was a student of Aristotle, but by the time Alexander died in 323 B.C., a non-Aristotelian "winner" appeared to be emerging in the conflict between the orators and philosophers:

> More and more, the Hellenistic elite looked to the model of Isocrates for their training, as orators such as Demosthenes and Aeschines, rather than philosopher-kings, dominated public affairs.[5]

Alexander gave the world Greek culture and ushered in the Hellenistic Age. Less than two centuries after his death, Greece was a province of Rome and the Hellenistic Age was ended—but not the influence of Greek education. There was in republican Rome, as is typically the case when cultures collide, some resistance to being culturally and educationally altered by the ideas and practices of the subjugated civilization. Such attempts notwithstanding, nearly every aspect of Roman life and enterprise—religion, sculpture, painting, architecture, and literature—was eventually shaped profoundly by the Greeks. Nor could a senatorial ban on both orators and philosophers, shortly after the initial defeat of Greece and Macedonia, do much to delay Athenian ascendancy in education. And that education was dominated by the tradition of the Greek orators.

It was, moreover, a Roman scholar, Cicero (106-43 B.C.), more than his Greek mentor Isocrates, whose name became commonly associated with the origins of the oratorical tradition. His treatise *De oratore* came to be recognized as definitive and it is in his *De inventione* that the phrase *artes liberales* seems to have appeared first. Cicero's contemporary Varro (116-27 B.C.) was an orator whose contributions included the first Roman encyclopedia, *Disciplinae*, and a treatise on the Latin language. A century later, when Rome had became an empire, Quintilian (A.D. 35-97), Spanish by birth but reared in Rome, left a

---

[4] Aristotle nonetheless wrote his *Poetics*, and is considered to be the father of literary criticism.

[5] Kimball, p. 18.

valuable record of Roman oratorical training in *Institutio Oratoria*, a work of a dozen volumes.

A book written as the Roman Empire was expiring and four centuries after Quintilian's death, *De nuptiis Philologiae et Mercurii* (On the Marriage of Philology [learning] and Mercury [eloquence]), set forth a comprehensive codification of the seven arts deemed necessary for the citizen with leisure to study. Scholars have disputed how long prior to the writing of this nine-volume, sometimes pretentious handbook by Martianus Capella (c. A.D. 410) Roman consensus about education had been realized. Cicero, Varro, and other writers were in the first century using the term *artes liberales* (from the Latin *liber*, "free person," thus characteristic of the free citizen), but the number of specified arts differed from author to author. Cicero gave no single, consistent list in his various works. Varro listed nine, including medicine and architecture, and Sextus Empiricus (c. A.D. 200) six. In *De nuptiis* we see what has become universally recognized as *the* list, the *septem artes liberales*: the *trivium* of language arts—rhetoric, logic, and grammar; and the *quadrivium*[6] of mathematical arts— arithmetic, geometry, music, and astronomy.

The Greeks would have found familiar both the individual arts and their association with the education of free citizens. There is a widespread tendency to equate the Greek *enkuklios paideia*[7] (*enkuklios* = general, *paideia* = education) with the Latin *artes liberales*. Kimball argues, however, that neither the orators, philosophers, nor sophists used the two words *together* prior to writings in first-century Rome, so that Cicero's *artes liberales* as a label for an educational regimen for free citizens was almost certainly introduced prior to the coining of *enkuklios paideia*.[8] In whatever period general agreement was reached, it was in the form of *septem artes liberales* that Roman civilization passed along its Hellenistic legacy to the generations that followed.

In addition to the seven liberal arts themselves, Kimball identifies seven characteristics of the *"artes liberales* ideal" that were contained in Rome's legacy to successive generations:

1. The goal of preparing virtuous citizens for leadership.
2. The prescription of certain values and standards for character and conduct.
3. The respect for commitment to these values and standards.
4. The dependence on a body of classical texts as a means of identifying these values and standards.
5. The identification of an elite who gain merit by adopting the values and standards of the texts.

---

[6] The terms *trivium* and *quadrivium* were not actually used in *De nuptiis*; both were coined much later, the former in the Carolingian era, the latter in sixth century Italy.

[7] From which the word "encyclopedia" is derived.

[8] Kimball, p. 22.

6. A dogmatic epistemology.[9]
7. A liberal education as an end in itself.[10]

Inspection of this list reminds us that the Greco-Roman *artes liberales* legacy was in the *oratorical* tradition, with emphasis on virtue, character, and textual authority. Philosophers survived in the Roman Empire, but without status and as groups of nomads not welcome in Rome. Their tradition would rise again, but not for many years.

The Church as Preserver of a Pagan Tradition

Quintilian was a contemporary of St. Paul, whose first-century missionary work did for the Christian religion what Alexander's had done for Greek culture. Quintilian had no reason to suspect that the proponents of the liberal arts tradition would someday owe a debt to this upstart religion. But so it turned out.

By the time of Quintilian's death in A.D. 97, Christianity had spread all over Asia Minor. A century later it had spread all over the Roman Empire, all the way to the northern borders of the empire along the Danube and the Rhine Rivers. Like the philosopher bands, the presence of Christians was not appreciated in imperial circles, nor did denizens of the cities always tolerate their teachings. Their unrelenting persecution by emperors intent on stamping out the new religion is a well-known feature of Roman history. Tradition holds that Paul was beheaded by Nero in about A.D. 67, and it was nearly 250 years before the persecution ceased. In A.D. 286 the empire had been divided into eastern and western regions, each under the rule of a different emperor; in A.D. 306 Constantine the Great became emperor of the West, and later of all the Roman Empire. It was Constantine's conversion to Christianity, and the subsequent establishment of Christianity as the official state religion (A.D. 324) that began the ascendancy of the church as a formal institution of power. An unlikely institution, to be sure, to act as preserver of the educational tradition of the civilization that had tried for three centuries to eradicate it.

Rome was sacked by Alaric the Visigoth in A.D. 410, and again by Vandals from Africa in A.D. 455, and the old (Western) Roman Empire finally ended in A.D. 476, when the German barbarian Odoacer overthrew Emperor Romulus Augustulus.[11] The task was not formidable; the economic, political, and moral decay of Roman civilization eased the path. With Goths, Vandals,

---

[9] A theory of the grounds and limitations of knowledge.

[10] Kimball, pp. 37-38.

[11] Constantine had moved his capital in A.D. 330 to Byzantium, which he renamed Constantinople (now Istanbul). This eastern portion of the old empire survived for a millennium as the Byzantine Empire. Its emperor Justinian in A.D. 529 closed all pagan schools, leaving the Roman church in unchallenged control of education.

Franks, Burgundians, Angles, Saxons, Lombards, and other barbarians swarming over the former empire, the customs of Rome could not survive. These were the "Dark Ages," a time of transition during which barbaric practices gradually supplanted the sophisticated fashion of Rome. It was a time of chaos—art, literature, engineering, and law went into decline. St. Jerome wrote of the period, "The whole world is sinking into ruin." This was clearly not an auspicious era for the practice of *artes liberales* education.

Earlier, St. Augustine (A.D. 354-430), Bishop of Hippo, recognizing the conflict between the Greco-Roman traditions and the ideals of Christianity, wrestled with a resolution. His works *De doctrina christiana* and *De civitate Dei* (City of God) were written in the final days of the Roman Empire, almost as if anticipating their need in the time ahead. Augustine appreciated the *artes liberales*, pagan or not in origin, and saw shared values between classical and Christian teachings. Like the Greeks and Romans, he associated liberal education with leisure time. His *artes liberales* cues were taken mostly from Cicero, and he found the language arts, not mathematics and dialectic, to be of the greatest importance. He was influenced also by a strain of philosophical thought, Stoicism,[12] which made three divisions of *philosophia*: logic, ethics, and physics. His success as a Christian apologist for classical education and erudition had an impact that would influence future Christian thinkers in an important way.

During the Dark Ages, it was in the monasteries that Christian scholarship burgeoned. St. Benedict (c. 480-c. 543) founded the first religious order in Italy, and established there the rule of "work and study." Study at his monastery at Monte Cassino was based on his conviction that education was essential for the preservation of Christianity. Closed away from the chaos outside their cloisters, armies of monks labored at copying volume after volume inherited from antiquity, not merely scripture but classical works as well. It was in Vivarium, a monastery that he founded, that Cassiodorus (A.D. 484-c. 584) wrote his handbook, *Institutiones*. This treatise, like the works of Augustine, attempted an accommodation of classical liberal education to Christianity. *Institutiones* was divided into "divine" and "human" readings, the latter being the *septem artes liberales*[13] which, following Augustinian precedent, were presented according to the teachings of Cicero and the oratorical tradition. The mathematical arts received, of course, little attention, except as they provided underpinnings for scripture. This handbook proved to be of immense import in defining the liberal arts for succeeding generations.

A third and even more popular handbook, *Etymologiae*, was written by Isidore (A.D. 570-636), the Bishop of Seville. As with Cassiodorus, the *septem artes liberales* comprised the core of his treatise, and the language arts were

---

[12] Stoicism held reason to be superior to feeling, and taught that all conditions should be accepted as the result of God's active force; their "God" was, however, the impersonal spirit of the universe, not the personal God of the Judeo-Christian tradition.

[13] Cassiodorus chose to derive *liberalis* from the Latin word for "book," *liber*.

treated far more extensively than the mathematical arts. Of all the arts, grammar (which for him included poetry, prose, fables, and history) was the consummate art. Isidore was apprehensive about the speculative philosophy of Aristotle, leaning toward the Stoic (and Augustinian) partitioning of *philosophia* into logic, ethics, and physics.

Isidore's handbook, like the works of Augustine, Jerome (A.D. 347-420), and Cassiodorus, did not receive universal acceptance among Christian churchmen. There was serious fear in some quarters of the consequences that a compromise with pagan teachings might have for people of the faith. Still, "Christians tended to view classicism as a lesser threat than barbarism."[14]

Despite the barbarians, classical education survived, and institutions of the church were primarily responsible. In addition to the reproduction of important writings, the monks conducted classes in the monasteries; although some liberal arts teaching went on in the form of private tutoring for children of nobles and in some parish schools, it was the monasteries that shouldered most of the responsibility for the *artes liberales*.

By the eighth century, the Anglo-Saxons had assumed leadership in liberal arts education. They had come to this role by way of their own education in Ireland, which had been affected very little by the barbarian conquest that ushered in the Dark Ages. The remote location of Ireland in the old empire had been in its favor, and it had become a center for classical education to which scholars and clerics from all over Europe traveled to study, the Anglo-Saxons among them. The *artes liberales* were, in the eighth century, not the vigorous arts of Greece and Rome, but a version weakened by lingering fear of pagan influence; grammar was there, with hymnic poetry[15] and prosody, but rhetoric was neglected, and only arithmetic remained of the mathematical arts. Still, influenced by the writings of Augustine and the handbooks of Cassiodorus and Isidore, the liberal arts were being promulgated three centuries after Rome was sacked.

Only one barbarian leader, Clovis (A.D. 481-511), of the Franks, had established a durable state. During Clovis's reign in Gaul, Christianity had made inroads in Europe, and the leader of the Franks converted to Roman Catholicism. With that opening, Roman culture began to spread. In A.D. 768 Charlemagne became king of the Franks, and in A.D. 800 was named ruler of the Holy Roman Empire by Pope Leo III. The new emperor established new schools in monasteries and churches, for the poor and wealthy alike. Even before, in A.D. 782 he had recruited an English scholar, Alcuin (A.D. 730-804), to be master of the palace school and to implement educational reform. Alcuin urged that education be based on the *septem artes liberales*, described in his

[14] Kimball, p. 49.

[15] Along with the hymnic poetry was included *historia*, which gave background information and set a context for the respective poems.

Grammatica. His students exported his teachings widely through Europe after his death in the ninth century. In the Holy Roman Empire and in Europe generally, the Carolingian scholars promoted the tradition of the orators, with emphasis on the *trivium*, the label coined by them for the three language arts, grammar, rhetoric, and logic. The *quadrivium* of mathematical arts was taught, as we have seen in other places and times, only as information useful in supporting Biblical and church teachings. Kimball notes that "the seven characteristics of the *artes liberales* ideal may also be identified with this period."[16]

During the ninth century the Carolingian Empire fragmented, and in the tenth century there was a new barbarian onslaught. England and western Europe were invaded by Northmen; France, Germany, and Italy by Hungarians; southern Europe by the Moors. European education waned. Latin language and literature nearly disappeared. But by the late tenth century classical education returned. A thousand years after the birth of Christ the *septem artes liberales* still survived as a system of education for European youth. It survived because of monks, parish schools, and bishops who wrote handbooks. It survived in the oratorical tradition, accommodated to Christianity, with the language arts at the center.

The Philosophers Return

The Roman Catholic Church, as we have seen, preserved the oratorical tradition through the first millennium. The same church proved to be instrumental in the return of the tradition of the philosophers. During the early Middle Ages, the towns of the old Roman Empire had gradually been replaced by a feudal system of self-sufficient baronial castles, with peasant villages and farms adjacent. There was little need for trade, and towns had no purpose without trade. But in 1095 Pope Urban II called for a crusade to rescue the shrines in the Holy Land from the Turks. Shouting, *"Deus vult!"*[17] the First Crusaders marched in the following year, and for two centuries the Crusades continued, totaling seven in all, and eventually going beyond the Holy Land to Egypt and Constantinople. The Crusades ended in the late thirteenth century, a failure when measured against Urban II's original purpose, but a major catalyst in reshaping the world—including eventually education.

Two centuries of crusading meant thousands of Europeans traveling to new lands, seeing splendid cities, encountering new customs, and discovering new arts and crafts. It also meant crusaders returning home with novel products to show others who had not marched. After the eleventh century, there was a revival of commerce, and by the thirteenth century European towns were common again. Interdependence among people grew. Travel led to the discovery, not only of new products, but also new ideas. Intellectual

---

[16] Kimball, p. 54.

[17] God wills it!

activity of all kinds increased. The foundation for modern economic, social, and educational endeavors was laid.[18]

In the medieval towns, the church continued to be a powerful force. Gothic cathedrals, the churches of the bishops, rose as architectural and artistic monuments that still remind us of this age. There was impressive secular architecture as well as the first merchant and then craft guilds grew, using their substantial wealth to build magnificent guild halls in the towns. There were educational guilds too, formed by masters with groups of students. *Universitas* was one of the names commonly adopted by these educational guilds,[19] and it is out of these institutions that the universities of the twelfth and thirteenth centuries grew. They were not independent of the church, but were given great latitude in scholarship. They had a distinctly vocational focus and were intended to train the children of merchants and tradesmen. The former vehicles for liberal education—the parish, cathedral, and collegiate schools—became relegated to providing preparation for study of the liberal arts in the universities. In the latter, there was a faculty of arts that took responsibility for teaching the *artes liberales*, but there was also a "higher" faculty of theology, law, or medicine. After preparatory school, the student attended lectures with masters at the university, participated in logical debates, and demonstrated debating skills to the satisfaction of the masters. At that point the faculty of arts issued the *baccalaurius* title, after which the student was eligible to study to be a master himself.

It would be surprising had the purposes and substance of liberal arts study gone unaffected during the period of great transition that began with the Crusades and produced the universities. Evidence of a shift was very apparent by the eleventh and twelfth centuries, when Scholasticism emerged to dominate the thinking of the Middle Ages. The "Schoolmen," Christian thinkers intent on reconciling the teachings of the church with the philosophies of Plato and Aristotle, turned to the dialectic, beloved by the ancient Greek philosophers and considered logic to be the primary philosophical tool. Many Scholastics, like the philosophers of old, considered the mathematical *quadrivium*[20] the foundation of the liberal arts, and urged that liberal arts education be directed

---

[18] Other factors than the growth of towns contributed, of course, to the collapse of feudalism. Improved methods of warfare made the castles more vulnerable; national languages and literatures tended to broaden ties; a rise of nationalistic feelings transcended loyalty to local lord.

[19] The reader will also recognize other names used for educational guilds: *collegium, communitas, societas.*

[20] So named by the fifth century Roman, Boethius, an earlier advocate of the philosophical tradition, whose translation of two of Aristotle's six treatises on logic helped preserve the thread of that tradition during centuries when the oratorical position dominated education. When the scholastics had rediscovered the remaining four treatises in the twelfth century, Boethius's translations were known as the Old Logic, and these the New Logic.

toward instruction in analytical and critical thinking. The recovery of Aristotle's "lost" works and the influx of writings on mathematics and the natural sciences from non-Western sources further turned attention away from the oratorical tradition. Writings were fitted more and more under some branch of philosophy. Although the *septem artes liberales* were in the 12th century still widely held to summarize liberal education, the preservation of that seven-art structure was taxed by the forced addition of each piece of the expanding new knowledge into so few "boxes." The move toward the philosophical tradition did not take place abruptly, nor was there always perfect clarity and consistency even in the writings of a given scholar.

During the 12th and 13th centuries, a number of scholars attempted to harmonize church teachings with the changed educational canon. In particular, Aristotle's rediscovered writings were a challenge. Aristotle's humanism and rationalism, according to some church leaders, seemed to contradict church positions. Varying attempts were made at accommodating Aristotle within church teachings by writers like Duns Scotus, Peter Lombard, and the greatest of the Schoolmen, St. Thomas Aquinas (c. 1225-1274).[21] Aquinas's approach was Aristotelian; although he rejected some of the Greek philosopher's positions as the products of faulty reasoning, he judged those positions to be, on the whole, consistent with biblical revelation. Aquinas called for reliance on observation, use of logic, and the separation of philosophy from theology. Recognizing how inadequate the seven-art organization of knowledge had become as the vast expansion of learning contributed more and more items to be catalogued under one of seven headings, Aquinas finally concluded: "[T]he seven liberal arts do not sufficiently divide theoretical philosophy."

With the rigid framework of the *septem artes liberales* no longer a restraint, Aquinas and other Schoolmen agreed on an expanded organization for intellectual development, adding to the *trivium* and *quadrivium* of tradition three philosophies: natural philosophy, moral philosophy, and metaphysics. And as Kimball describes:

> Aquinas made logic the heart and soul of the *artes liberales*, which were stripped of direct connection to ethics and oriented purely to intellectual formation.[22]

The impact of Aquinas and the other Scholastics came to be felt in every university in Europe by the 14th century, although the history and emphasis of each affected the timing. The oratorical tradition, with its emphasis on the language arts, held on longer in Italy, for example, where the study of Latin literature and law had long been strong. The patterns of change were also influenced by the interests of the respective graduate faculties, who were assuming greater prominence in the universities as specialized study, which had been

---

[21] Earlier Scholastics were John Scotus Erigena (c.815-c.877), Anselm (1033-1109), and Peter Abelard (1079-1142).

[22] Kimball, p. 67.

criticized by the oratorical tradition, directed attention away from a study of the arts.

With the birth of the Italian Renaissance and the end of the Middle Ages in the fourteenth century, the concept and curriculum of liberal education had been transformed. The rhetoric of the orators had become little more than an appendage to a curriculum that stressed the mathematical arts. Grammar had become primarily a tool in the pursuit of narrow fields of research. Concern for learning virtues had dwindled. Philosophy was classified as natural, moral, or metaphysical, and the old handbooks lost their place. Aristotle, almost lost to the Middle Ages, finally ruled.

Modern Orators: *Studia Humanitatis*

The Renaissance, that time of discovery and intellectual vigor, which began first in 14th century Italy and opened the Modern Age, was also a time of *rediscovery*. There was much that was remarkable about this period: fundamental advancements in science (Copernican revolution, Newton's laws of motion, Boyle's law of gases, discovery of several elements); new forms of art (naturalism in painting and sculpture, Roman arches), literature (the Italian and Shakespearean sonnets), and music (opera, perfection of the violin); explorations of new lands and waters (North America, South America, the Pacific); new approaches to politics (Machiavelli's practical politics, strong central governments). But in the intellectual arena, what was "new" came from antiquity: the rediscovered writings from ancient Greece and Rome.

The movement in Italy is attributed primarily to Petrarch (1304-1374), a poet-scholar who became a kind of "intellectual emperor" of Europe. Early in life he became fascinated with Latin and Greek, and that early interest led him to Cicero and away from the teachings of the Schoolmen. The studies of Petrarch and his disciples was given the label *litterae humaniores* (more humane letters), and from that label came the term "humanist" for those scholars who shared the Petrarchian view that the proper paradigms were not the Scholastics, but the ancients. As this view spread, nobles and churchmen took up the hunt for manuscripts by Greek and Latin authors and rediscovered many works which otherwise would have been forever lost. In contrast to the medieval scholars, the Renaissance humanists tended to hold a rather optimistic view of life and emphasized the continuous improvement of human character. In contrast to the medievalists, their educational program was oratorical.

The program was called *studia humanitatis*, a title taken directly from Cicero, and it was synonymous with the *artes liberales*. In detail, the curriculum consisted of grammar, rhetoric, poetry, history, and frequently included moral philosophy. There was minimal treatment of the *quadrivium*. It could have been taken from Isidore's handbook; the one outstanding point of difference was that Isidore would have connected the arts with the study of theology, while the humanists endorsed learning for its own sake. As with Cicero,

Quintilian, and the other orators, the humanists linked liberal learning with leisure time for study, and with the acquisition of virtue and wisdom.

If the transition from scholasticism to *studia humanitatis*, from the philosophical tradition of the liberal arts back to the oratorical, has seemed easy or swift from the preceding description, that is misleading. There was considerable resistance to a return to the system of the orators. Petrarch's influence was indeed enormous, but it was not immediate or universal in its reach into the universities of Europe. It is not even clear from the literature just when the claim could be made for each of the universities that their curricula were "humanist" in thrust. Not all studies were conducted in the university itself; many were pursued in colleges and schools that came to be built adjacent to the older institutions. Further, although the official listings for the universities might not reflect it at a given point, it is suspected that many of the migrant masters who taught in them brought along and promoted the *studia humanitatis* ideal even before university publications reflected the change. What is unquestioned is that over the approximately four centuries covered by the Renaissance, in the countries of France, England, Germany, and Spain, scholastic education became largely dislodged, and the oratorical tradition advanced by the *litterae humaniores* once more came to dominate.

A Renaissance figure whose stature challenged that of Petrarch was Erasmus of Rotterdam (1469-1536). It was he who was most instrumental in the acceptance of the humanist ideal north of the Italian Alps. His stature as an authority both in the classics and in theology equipped him uniquely to make his own contribution to the movement—and to history; through his influence, *studia humanitatis* became the standard program for the education of Christian citizens, and lead to humanism becoming a factor in the Reformation of the 16th century. In the oratorical mold, Erasmus emphasized rhetoric and the literary aspects of grammar, downplayed the *quadrivium*, and discouraged speculative logic.

The Protestant Reformation was, of course, one of the many history-changing events of the Renaissance. Martin Luther (1483-1546), though opposed vigorously by Erasmus for his role in the Reformation, was, like Erasmus, a champion of a liberal arts education in the oratorical tradition. Most of the Protestant reformers also were followers of Cicero and Quintilian, rejecting speculative philosophy, and endorsing persuasive rhetoric. Like the humanists, they placed great emphasis on moral philosophy. At the Lutheran University of Wittenburg, at Strasbourg, and in the Calvinist schools of Geneva, the humanist liberal arts model reigned supreme, and they in turn were imitated by schools over much of Europe. Further spread of liberal education was accomplished by Roman Catholicism in the mid-sixteenth century when Catholic seminaries were established all over Western Europe, most effected by the Jesuits (of the Society of Jesus).

To the extent that generalization is warranted, the following patterns and sequences of study developed. Formal education began in a grammar school, gymnasium, or college, where the *trivium* was taught to children, called *petits* or "petties." Both rhetoric and grammar encompassed history and poetry, and grammar included a study of Latin and often Greek language. Logic was introduced, but only as a subordinate to rhetoric. In the upper levels of a church college or with the arts faculty at a university, the student studied advanced rhetoric, grammar, and logic. Added to these "trivial" studies were studies in a reduced *quadrivium*, in natural philosophy, in moral philosophy (ethics, politics, economics), and an introduction to metaphysics. Education at a university, but not at a college, led to a master of arts degree.

Across international boundaries, across church lines, despite political and ecclesiastical turmoil, by the end of the seventeenth century there was a widely accepted liberal education based on the humanistic *studia humanitatis*, the Renaissance version of the *artes liberales*. It was strongly influenced by the churches, now Protestant and Catholic, and although it included works of Aristotle, and the residual influence of Scholasticism, it was fundamentally Ciceronian in character.

Education for the Christian Gentlemen

The story of the liberal arts ideal, as related here so far, may have seemed to flow fairly smoothly over the centuries. In part this is because all history gets its storyline by hindsight; in part it owes to so condensed a history as this single chapter being perforce somewhat "smoothed out." But in large measure it is because the story was, in fact, simpler from Cicero to Luther than it was to become soon thereafter. Prior to the sixteenth century, the total number of universities was quite small, fewer than seventy in all of Western Europe. Moreover, college and university education remained a privilege for a very small portion of the male population. As the economic and social blossoming that encouraged the cultural Renaissance in fourteenth century Italy spread to France, Germany, and the British Isles, more and more young men could afford the leisure for study. Old colleges and universities filled up and many new ones sprang up. The Jesuits alone, following fifty years of robust activity, had established nearly 250 colleges by the turn of the seventeenth century. Those of us in 20th century education will not be surprised to learn that these enrollment increases had their impact on the liberal arts curriculum of the Renaissance.

One long-lasting impact came from a growing opinion that young men should be educated for the life of a gentleman. This is a concept not far from the original Greek and Roman view that education was for the *liber*, the free elite. Its proponents held up, however, the image of the medieval knight to suggest what they had in mind. The real knight of the Middle Ages was usually not, of course, a scholar, nor would he want to be mistaken for one. He had been trained, not in the *artes liberales*, but in chivalry, and it was the set of qualities identified with that chivalric standard—courtesy, valor, modesty, honor—that was attractive for young aristocrats. This movement to marry the knightly virtues to humanism began, like the Renaissance itself, in Italy, and by the mid-sixteenth century had spread across the continent and well into England, as demonstrated by the great popularity of Thomas Elyot's *The Boke Named the Gouernour* (1531), which laid out an education designed to form gentlemen. Given the significant influence of the churches on the schools, colleges, and universities, it followed that to the blend of knightly virtues and humanistic education would be added the piety of the educated Christian.

The educational program laid out had an oratorical core: Isocrates, Demosthenes, Cicero, and Quintilian were there, as was Erasmus, who followed the Italian Castiglione in promoting this decidedly utilitarian alteration in the old oratorical program. The point here was not so much education for citizenship as self-refinement, preparation for social and often courtly success. One learned history, politics, economics, geography, law; those things would be needed at court. Arithmetic and astronomy were included, too, along with a bit of logic, natural philosophy, metaphysics, and theology. Gentlemen might study a non-classical language, most likely French or Italian, in addition to their Greek and Latin grammar. Keen oratorical skills were highly encouraged. They would, however, avoid assiduously any specialization. They would study broadly, but not too deeply, and their aim was to acquire wisdom rather than the ability to search for truth.

In seventeenth and early eighteenth century colonial America, new colleges came into being—Harvard (1636), William and Mary (1693), and Yale (1701). Founded respectively by the Congregationalist, Anglican, and Congregational-Presbyterian churches to prepare men for the ministry and leadership, they followed the English model of liberal education for the Christian gentleman. Because their primary purpose was to prepare boys for admission into the colleges, the colonial grammar schools had curricula appropriately classical in nature. The *artes liberales* had come to America.

Redefinition: Impact of the New Philosophy

The "gentrification" of liberal education was a curricular modification of a quite different and less drastic sort than that resulting from certain extra-curricular intellectual movements that were also taking place while the colleges and universities were educating Christian gentlemen. We have noted already that the Renaissance was a remarkable period, a time of intense intellectual activity and discovery. It was out of the search for new knowledge about the heavens that a new philosophy sprouted and grew. Copernicus (1473-1543), the Polish mathematician whose work *Concerning the Revolutions of the Celestial Spheres* recast the solar system, was followed by Galileo (1564-1642), who designed the first telescope and confirmed the heliocentric model of the Pole. Galileo's German correspondent, Kepler (1571-1630), produced three mathematical laws that described the movement of planets in their solar orbits, removing any reasonable doubt about the Copernican theory, and later providing a basis for Newton's (1642-1727) law of universal gravitation. In Elizabethan England, Francis Bacon (1561-1626) set aside religion as an unsuitable object for the intellect and instead concentrated on scientific pursuits. Bacon's inductive method became, in fact, the principal means by which the empirical discoveries of the scientists became laws. His younger contemporary, Thomas Hobbes (1588-1679), also made a sharp break with the past and his Oxford education, describing a mathematical, materialistic world of motion. Descartes (1596-1650), the French mathematician-philosopher, taking his cues from the astronomers, also proposed that the whole of nature must be capable of mechanical and mathematical explanation. This kind of work was not a look back at the golden age of antiquity,[23] the preoccupation of the Renaissance universities; it was the beginnings of modern science, the New Philosophy.

The churches opposed this radical revolution, and their colleges and universities did not welcome as masters its practitioners and preachers. Most of the scientific investigation of the seventeenth century was conducted privately, without an institutional base of operation, or with the support of one of the scientific societies established to advance science and publish the findings of the scientists—the Royal Society of London (1622), the Academie des Sciences in France (1666), the Societas Regia Scientarium in Germany (1666), and others. The spread continued into the eighteenth century Enlightenment and into America, where Benjamin Franklin's American Philosophical Society (1743) catalyzed investigations by a network of amateur scientists.

Not only were the New Philosophers operating outside the universities, they were also actively disputing the established curriculum, proposing to replace it with one of their own which Kimball calls the "liberal-free ideal." Never contained in a single treatise nor advanced whole by a single philosopher, it owes something to Locke (1632-1704), to Hobbes, to Descartes, to Hume (1711-1776), to Rousseau (1712-1778), to Kant (1724-1804), and to other scientists, philosophers, and freethinkers of the sixteenth century and the Enlightenment. Kimball attributes to the liberal-free ideal seven emphases:[24]

1. individual freedom (Locke, Rousseau)
2. intellect and rationality (Descartes, Newton, Diderot)
3. critical skepticism (Descartes, Locke, Hume)
4. tolerance (Locke)[25]

---

[23] The New Philosophers were not universally opposed to study of the ancients, but they generally found it to be inadequate as a total program of education.

[24] Kimball, p. 119 ff.

[25] Heretofore tolerance was considered to be a weakness, not a virtue. But with the fundamental skepticism of the new science of the eighteenth century came a corollary view that no position can be absolute, and so all views must be given weight.

5. egalitarianism (Hobbes, Locke, Rousseau)
6. primacy of individual will over responsibilities of citizenship (Locke, Rousseau)
7. freedom of intellect as an end in itself (Kant).

To call this approach to learning "liberal" was to redefine the word.[26] The traditional educational meaning had associated "liberal" with the qualities of a "free" gentleman, i.e., one with leisure time; the alternative meaning suggested a lack of moral restraint characteristic of a libertine. By the time of the Enlightenment the secondary meaning of "liberal" had shifted to denote freedom from restraint in all areas, including "unreasonable" restraints that might come from ecclesiastical or cultural traditions. It is this new emphasis on individual, universal freedom, as opposed to freedom for citizenship, that leads to the label "liberal-free" for this new intellectual strand.

The New Philosophers, departing from the classical scholarly tradition of centuries, wrote in their own modern languages—English, French, or German—no longer feeling bound to the long-time "official" language of scholarship, Latin. They emphasized empiricism (reliance on observations and experiment) and the teaching of the findings of science. They were critical, too, of the use of classical works and approaches in teaching, eventually developing a new, simplified rhetoric and striking at the heart of the oratorical ideal. Their skepticism, their anti-authoritarianism, and their science were long resisted by the churches and universities. There were hints here and there over the seventeenth century that the New Philosophy was making inroads into the formal institutions, but it was late in the eighteenth century before any unquestioned gains could be pointed to in the curricula of the schools, colleges, and universities. Even then, and in both Europe and America, the writings of Descartes and Locke, and the study of modern science were little more than educational afterthoughts in the colleges. Until the American Revolution transformed the intellectual environment, the Enlightenment remained essentially extramural.

"Freedom" became the battle cry of the Revolutionary leadership. This was the freedom, not of classical education, but of Locke and Rousseau, freedom from the old authorities. And freedom was linked prominently with other emphases of the New Philosophy. Simultaneously, the revolutionary spirit of the times nullified appeals to authority and tradition, weakening the hold of *studia humanitatis* in the colleges and universities. As the nineteenth century got underway, Americans grew more ambitious for their new nation, and they saw modern science as a means of national progress. Study at German universities encouraged a zest for free inquiry in young American academicians.

---

[26] Not all modern scholars agree that the scientists, *philosophes*, and freethinkers differed significantly from the humanists in their definitions of liberal education. See Kimball's references, p. 115.

The liberal-free proponents called for replacing the classics in the university curricula with modern language and science. Defenders of the classics, one observes, began to shift their arguments. Studying the classical letters, they pointed out, teaches the principles of liberty and trains the intellect—both liberal-free emphases. These shifts, along with the move in English and German universities toward studying the Greek and Latin classics *critically*, thus advancing specialized research, resulted in a very visible accommodation by the *artes liberales* to the liberal-free ideal.

Recognition of this accommodation did not signify a wholesale replacement of the old classical curricula in the colleges and universities with a new, liberal-free curriculum. Far from it. The modern languages were taught, yes; but they took a decidedly back seat to Greek and Latin. The sciences could be learned, yes; but they did not include experimentation, and in the grading systems they were weighted lightly. Prior to the Civil War, while the philosophers had made definite gains, the orators still controlled the curriculum.

After the emancipation of the slaves and the fighting of the Civil War, "free" was a very popular word again. If introduction of the liberal-free ideal had not blurred enough the common understanding of what "liberal" education meant, the new connections of "liberal" with "liberating" certainly added to the confusion. President Alfred Upham of Miami University, for example, suggests the definition:

> The liberal arts, we say, are the liberalizing arts, the studies that liberate the mind and send it questing on strange and alluring adventures.[27]

Included in all this liberation language was the view that there should be a certain equality of subjects, a drastic change of view that led to increased choice by students as the twentieth century approached, and ultimately to the elective system introduced at Harvard in 1867.

The elective system was in harmony with the expansion of university research which was imported from Germany in the late nineteenth century. The universities, in contrast to the four-year Christian colleges of the time, invested heavily in specialized research, and the numbers of disciplinary departments greatly multiplied. But the momentum was too great for the colleges; by the new century some of them had relaxed their staunch defense of the old purist version of the *artes liberales*, and had begun emphasizing modern languages, the sciences, and specialized studies. In America the stage was set for a century of increasing pluralism in education labeled "liberal."[28]

---

[27] A. H. Upham, "The Liberal Arts," *Association of American Colleges Bulletin 16*, (1930): 332.

[28] I have not discussed here the situation in late nineteenth century England. While the effects of the intellectual forces of the time were less pronounced there than in America, the trend was the same: toward the German and away from the classical model.

The Present State of the Arts

As we near the end of the twentieth century and look about us, we recognize among American institutions of higher learning abundant pluralism. There are the megaversities and the small colleges, the community colleges and the conservatories, the secular and the sectarian colleges, the open-door and selective institutions, the pre-professional and liberal arts colleges. Even within the last of these categories, the liberal arts colleges, the range of diversity among institutions is enormous. It is not a matter, either, of a handful of differing but distinct qualifiers—of just having one set that is "oratorical," another that is "philosophical," and another that is "liberal-free." The variations are too numerous and too non-systematic for easy cataloging.

During the decades since the century turned, much has been debated about what liberal education "ought" to be. Consensus—at least *lasting* consensus—has been hard to come by on any particular issue, much less on the larger question of normative programs. Add to this the complication of having had several generations now in which not even educational leaders and most of the modern "masters," the faculty themselves, have been grounded in a knowledge of the enduring arguments. The statements of purpose can seldom be counted on to help sort things out; nor can formally stated curricular goals of the colleges. These reflect the understandings of their authors, and in them one will generally find phrases that mix the traditions rather hopelessly. Taken on the whole, the century belongs, however, to the philosophers. In the liberal arts colleges, as in the universities, devotion to the department of the discipline runs generally stronger than devotion to the larger cause of liberal education. But in the small colleges the oratorical tradition can still be distinguished, particularly in humanities departments. Joseph Featherstone describes the situation:

> Today there are nods in the direction of the orators, but most of our great research universities are a modernized version of the program of the philosophers. Outside the religious colleges and a few liberal arts institutions, the free Socratic mind is the dominant ideal—even as a rationale for reading the classics, curiously enough. The orators have been losing out for some time: both great texts and the creation of a learning community have taken a long time.[29]

Among the arguments that are worth pausing to examine briefly is "liberal" *versus* "useful" arts, and the place of the latter in a liberal arts education. Nowhere has the argument against the inclusion of the utilitarian been made more eloquently than when it was made by Cardinal John Henry Newman (1801-1890) in his 1853 "Discourse IV":

> [T]hat alone is liberal knowledge which stands on its own pretensions, which is independent of sequel, expects no complement, refuses to be *informed* (as it is

---

[29] Joseph Featherstone, "A Note on Liberal Learning," *Colloquy*, (Fall 1988).

called) by any end, or absorbed into any art, in order duly to present itself to our contemplation. The most ordinary pursuits have this specific character, if they are self-sufficient and complete; the highest lose it, when they minister to something beyond them....And so of the learned professions altogether, considered merely as professions; although one of them be the most popularly beneficial, and another the most politically important, and the third the most intimately divine of all human pursuits, yet the very greatness of their end, the health of the body, or of the commonwealth, or of the soul, diminishes, not increases, their claim to the appellation in question, and that still more if they are cut down to the strict exigencies of that end.[30]

Newman insisted, with Cicero, that knowledge is a worthy end in itself, and that learning with some "useful" end cannot *ipso facto* be "liberal." His essentially oratorical position can be heard on liberal arts colleges campuses today over a hundred years later, when a newly-proposed course, for instance, is judged to be aimed more at developing skills than at nourishing the intellect. A contrary position was articulated by Alfred North Whitehead (1861-1947), when commenting on the legitimacy of a school of a very "useful" subject, business, at Harvard:

> But the primary reason for [the] existence [of universities] is not to be found either in the mere knowledge conveyed to the students or in the mere opportunities for research afforded to the members of the faculty....The justification for a university is that it preserves the connection between knowledge and the zest of life, by uniting the young and the old in the imaginative consideration of learning.[31]

For the veterans who poured into American colleges and universities after World War II, the matter was not debatable. They, along with the materialistic students of the 1980s, sought higher education for reasons that tended very much toward the pragmatic. These populations, along with others entering the colleges and universities as access to baccalaureate programs has been expanded, have brought in practical goals of their own which stand outside any recognized liberal arts traditions, adding to the tensions on liberal arts campuses and creating pressures to compromise ideals.

One of the compromises of the 1960s and early 1970s was the creation of general education curricula of wide assortment and minimal structure. It was a time of permissiveness, of unprecedented accommodation to individual wishes. Student selection of courses was at a zenith, and "general education" consisted of "distribution requirements," a kind of Chinese-menu approach to encouraging breadth in learning. *Enkuklios paideia* was forgotten; students

---

[30] Cardinal John Henry Newman, "Discourse IV: Liberal Knowledge Its Own End," *Scope and Nature of University Education* (London: J.M. Dent, 1915), p.99.

[31] Alfred North Whitehead, *The Aims of Education* (New York, NY: Macmillan, 1929), pp. 138-139.

were chasing diplomas, and faculty were teaching their specialties to students who had chosen to be there. The disciplinary curricula of the colleges had much in common, but their general education curricula had become very institution-specific and not obviously connected with any identifiable historical strand of education. For two decades liberal learning realized, at best, some lowest common denominator, but it was an elusive denominator, hard to articulate and too feeble to provide inspiration.

On the campuses as the 1970s progressed, one occasionally began to hear grousing about the condition of general education. There was a growing uneasiness about the choices students were making in the educational cafeteria, a certain recognition that something important was being lost, and a growing worry about the future of a society in which, with nothing more than preference as a guide, the naive constructed their own education. In 1978 Harvard moved toward more structure with its new core curriculum, and across the country college faculty began thinking about curricular reform.

In the following decade the reform began in earnest. Study groups and task forces were formed by the National Institute of Education, the National Endowment for the Humanities, and the Association of American Colleges, and the resulting reports issued proved portentous and extremely influential in the colleges and the universities. The NIE study group observed:

> As we write, signs of interest in undergraduate education are beginning to reappear. College faculty are once again beginning to ask what every educated person should know and therefore what their students should learn. They are talking with one another across disciplinary boundaries about their mutual interests, and are experimenting with new courses and programs.[32]

With even more feeling, William Bennett asserted, with definite oratorical accent, in the NEH report:

> Although more than 50 percent of America's high school graduates continue their education at American colleges and universities, few of them can be said to receive there an adequate education in the culture and civilization of which they are members. Most of our college graduates remain shortchanged in the humanities—history, literature, philosophy, and the ideals and practices of the past that have shaped the society they enter. The fault lies principally with those of us whose business it is to educate these students. We have blamed others, but the responsibility is ours. Not by our words but by our actions, by our indifference, and by our intellectual diffidence we have brought about this condition.[33]

---

[32] Study Group on the Conditions of Excellence in American Higher Education, *Involvement in Learning: Realizing the Potential of American Higher Education* (Washington, DC: National Institute of Education, 1984), pp. 1-2.

[33] William J. Bennett, *To Reclaim a Legacy: A Report on the Humanities in Higher Education* (Washington, DC: National Endowment for the Humanities, 1984), p. 1.

And from the AAC report, from the chapter entitled "The Decline and Devaluation of the Undergraduate Degree":

> The educational failures of the United States are emerging as a major concern of the 1980s. The abundance of reports diagnosing and prescribing for our schools and colleges, the urgency with which they are argued, the evidence that they summon, and the analyses that they offer are persuasive evidence that there is a profound crisis.[34]

The reports went on to recommend sweeping changes in existing undergraduate curricula, and the colleges responded with action. Many of the new general education curricula being planned and implemented in the late 1980s and early 1990s restore coherence through explicit goals and enabling structure. Both oratorical and philosophical traditions are interwoven. Faculty are attending to the need of future generations to know about what has gone before (oratorical); to the need for competence in oral and written communication (oratorical); to the need for "values" to guide decision-making and human relations (oratorical); to the need for clear, critical, and analytical thinking (philosophical). The result is not exactly a new normative program or a fresh definition of the *artes liberales*, but it is an encouraging new chapter in liberal education.

The yearning for community, even among highly autonomous and individualistic academicians in late twentieth century America, is perennial. One hears the call for community in the speeches of college presidents and keynoters at meetings of educational associations; in college planning documents that picture a stronger future; in campus task force reports addressing student retention and faculty morale. Community comes easily when there is a sharing of purpose and direction, values and aspirations. But for a long stretch now the dominant emphases have been individualism, skepticism, and tolerance. And for two decades supply-demand imbalances have produced compromises in the search for college-faculty fit. Add to these two factors the commitment of most colleges of the 1990s to the worthy goal of increasing faculty racial and ethnic diversity, and the picture begins to emerge: the mix of educational histories, allegiances, passions, and antipathies is apt to be a scramble indeed, even on the campuses of small liberal arts colleges. The assortment of those who would commune is, as a consequence, often formidable, and true community is correspondingly difficult to forge. How then do we forge it? I find the new curriculum reform a hopeful sign and a promising pointer. Perhaps it is in consensus—not unanimity on detail, but broad and substantial agreement—about what we want our curricula to achieve in the education of our liberal arts college graduates that we can find common ground.

---

[34] Project on Redefining the Meaning and Purpose of Baccalaureate Degrees, *Integrity in the Curriculum: A Report to the Academic Community* (Washington, DC: Association of American Colleges, 1985), p. 1.

Becoming a Patriot

You may sense some need, having reviewed the history in this chapter, to choose between the orators and philosophers. Featherstone points instead to a need to recognize the honest state of the tradition:

> [A] liberal education is the confrontation of philosophy and oratory: In each generation, Socrates must challenge Isocrates' texts in the name of reason and a mind freed from the past. Isocrates must argue perennially against Socrates that the dialectic needs to be grounded in commitments to community and tradition. Isocrates alone ends in the fetishism of texts at the expense of the living human spirit and the living human community. The Socratic dialectic alone yields a naked questioning without commitment to any human community or tradition. Socrates lacks human commitments; Isocrates lacks the jugular instinct for the truth.[35]

Featherstone is arguing that becoming a liberal arts patriot does not call for taking sides. "Oratorical" or "philosophical," "liberal" or "useful"—these are not imperative choices, but historical arguing points that can and have been taken repeatedly to excess. We need to know the arguments and beware of the excesses.

As a new citizen of a liberal arts campus, whatever the mix of other faculty by educational experience, academic specialty, and ethnic background, you will find your greatest satisfaction in "fighting for a cause" that has meaning and value for you. Real meaning will come from knowledge of and thoughtful reflection about the history of the venerable tradition that has produced your college. And the cause will have growing value for you as you settle in your own mind the distinctive ends of liberal education. You will know that you have escaped the status of "mercenary" and claimed the status of "patriot" when you can answer with confidence and zeal the questions from students (and often parents) about the nature and merit of a liberal arts education.

There are many wrong notions out there about what a liberal arts education of today is and isn't. Students and parents choose liberal arts colleges for all kinds of reasons, some of them not very profound and some of them very mistaken. As a defender of the tradition, it is good to be alert to these, and ready to offer corrections. Here are corrections to some of the common misconceptions that you will encounter:

+ A liberal arts education is *not* just any broad collection of "general" studies.
+ A liberal arts education is *not* one that emphasizes the fine arts.
+ A liberal arts education is *not* a particular variety of education for those uncertain about an area of specialization.

---

[35] Featherstone, Ref. 29.

✦ A liberal arts eduction *is* a good preparation for graduate study in the sciences and humanities, and for the study of medicine and the law.

On the positive side, you will, as I have suggested, have frequent opportunity to speak about the worth of a liberal arts education for someone preparing for life in the modern world. It will usually not suffice (let us face it) to answer queries about worth with assertions about the value of knowledge for its own sake. Someone trying to decide between a relatively modest tuition at a large state university and a more costly private liberal arts college will quite rightly want to know just what commends the latter over the former. You should, of course, have ready what might be called "environmental" responses, those that stress the personal attention and small classes that are hallmarks of education in a small liberal arts setting. There are, however, other answers that can be persuasive, answers that go beyond course requirements and address educational outcomes—the ideal "product" of liberal learning:

1. A liberal arts college graduate has broad knowledge. Study of a broad, but purposefully selected core body of knowledge equips the graduate to:
   • learn from history, science, and literature
   • set personal experience in context
   • make enlightened, informed decisions
   • converse intelligently with a wide variety of people
   • understand and frame arguments of diverse types
   • understand the functioning of political, social, and economic institutions
   • escape provincialism.

2. A liberal arts college graduate thinks effectively. Practice in logical, analytical, and creative thought disciplines the graduate for:
   • identifying flawed arguments
   • solving problems
   • coming to sound conclusions
   • recognizing and proposing options.

3. A liberal arts college graduate can communicate effectively. Discipline in thinking, coupled with practice in writing and speaking, prepares the graduate to:
   • communicate information, ideas, analyses, and arguments clearly
   • persuade others
   • work collaboratively
   • provide leadership.

4. A liberal arts college graduate can make discriminating judgments. Formal attention to enduring principles, and to systems of values and their application to specific situations readies the graduate to:

- make ethical judgments
- better appreciate art, music, theater, and literature
- live a richer, fuller, more contributive life.

5. A liberal arts college graduate can see connections. Guidance in getting beyond disciplinary and political boundaries conditions the graduate to:
   - integrate experience
   - anticipate outcomes in complex situations
   - acknowledge and value interdependency
   - work productively with people from other cultures.

6. A liberal arts college graduate is quantitatively conversant. Introduction to and practice in using mathematical approaches equips the graduate to:
   - employ quantitative methods in solving practical problems
   - assess arguments that include quantitative and statistical information
   - use quantitative and statistical information appropriately in decision-making.

7. A liberal arts college graduate is committed to learning. Inculcation in the techniques and pleasures of learning, including specialized learning in the major, enables the graduate to:
   - pursue graduate and professional education
   - remain open to new experiences, insights, and points of view
   - ferret out new information
   - enjoy learning over a lifetime.

This is not an exhaustive list, but I hope it is enough to make the point: A liberal arts education is, I would argue, the most truly "useful" of all, for its product is an educated person capable of reasoned reflection and effectual response. The ideal product of a liberal arts education is a graduate prepared for leadership, for vocation, for good citizenship, and for a satisfying and productive life. That prospect is what we have to sell, and it is a worthy product.

For Discussion————————————————

1. To what extent did you feel able to trace the history of the liberal arts ideal prior to joining the faculty of your college?

2. Do you feel yourself instinctively drawn to one of the curricular "camps," oratorical or philosophical, more than the other? If so, what is the basis of your preference?

3. Consider the following statement of curricular goals adopted by the College of Port St. Julian faculty. Label each goal (or phrase within it), to the extent that is possible, as "oratorical" or "philosophical" (or liberal-free). Is the College closer to one tradition than the other? Try the same exercise with the curricular goals or statement of purpose of your college.

A graduate of the College of Port St. Julian should possess:
1. a sound, broad intellectual foundation, including the ability to think logically, analytically, and creatively and to make judgments and evaluations as a result of that process; the ability to be flexible, to assume new tasks, and to adapt to changing realities; the ability to function effectively, both independently and in groups.
2. an understanding of our world and the ability to communicate that understanding, including effective mathematical, computer technology, and communication skills; knowledge of scientific and social-scientific thought, methodology, and contributions; sound historical perspective, appreciation for diverse cultures, and an aesthetic appreciation and understanding.
3. an integrated, mature perspective, including an understanding of the interrelationships among various disciplines; a set of moral and ethical values and a commitment to lifelong learning; awareness of the importance of mental and physical well-being.
4. a comprehensive background in a specific discipline, including the ability to recount and explain the basic facts and postulates of the discipline and to use them in the solution of problems; proficiency in the use of techniques and tools of the discipline to seek out and assimilate knowledge not a part of the classroom experience.

4. When considering new courses being proposed for addition to the curriculum, how should the faculty of a liberal arts college draw the line between "useful" and "liberal"? Or, if you would argue that they need not draw such a line, how should a decision be made about whether a proposed course "belongs" in a liberal arts college curriculum?

5. Isocrates and his students valued the writings of Homer for the "virtues" they imparted. In his book *New Life for the College Curriculum*, Jerry Gaff makes this observation: "[H]igher education has, for the most part, abandoned values education. It gave up trying to shape the morals of students through the curriculum earlier this century..."[36] How would you relate the "virtues" education of Isocrates' and the "values" education included in so many of the new general education curricula of the 1980s? Gaff reports that 57% of the colleges

---

[36] Jerry G. Gaff, *New Life for the College Curriculum* (San Francisco, CA: Jossey-Bass, 1991), p. 190.

he has surveyed include education in "ethics and values."[37] Speculate on reasons for the disappearance of this educational component
in the 1960s and 1970s and its reappearance in the 1980s.

6. In the 1990s the colleges are turning their attention to "multiculturalism," making a serious effort to recognize the great variety of cultures represented in modern America, and to accommodate the
histories, interests, and concerns that the students coming from these
cultures bring to the academy. In what ways do you see "liberal education" addressing the issue of multiculturalism? In what ways
would you expect multiculturalism to shape liberal education?

---

[37] Gaff, p. 73.

6

Good Teaching

While learning has many ends, teaching has only one: to enable or cause learning.

K. Patricia Cross
"In Search of Zippers"
AAHE Bulletin, (June 1988)

*H*e felt great! Pete Makropolos's strong, hot coffee tasted better than ever this morning, and Adam Newprof waved for a refill.

"So, Professor," Pete said as he poured, "how's it going? You like the College? It's okay? They treating you right?"

Adam made an O with forefinger and thumb. "They're treating me just fine, Pete. Sure are."

Carlisle Ravenel and Maggie Morrow were sitting on the other side of the booth, facing Newprof. "Hey, don't forget *us*, Pete," Maggie said. "Carlisle and I are getting low."

"Sorry, sorry. Here you go, professors."

When Makropolos had gone back behind the counter across the café, Maggie said to Adam: "I hope your eight-o'clock went better than mine. My class was deader than Shakespeare."

"As a matter of fact," Adam told her, "*my* eight-o'clock was superb! Best class I've had in the month I've been here, if you want the truth."

"Is that a change?" Ravenel teased. "When we hired a Phi Beta Kappa chemist, we expected him to be superb all the time. Is this something new?"

Adam grinned and took a sip of Pete's coffee. He remembered that first class a month ago. *Not* a pleasant memory. Right in the middle of his freshman lecture on scientific measurement, with some students squirming, quite a few looking conspicuously bored, and a couple actually dozing off, a thought had hit him: Maybe I'm not really cut out for teaching. He had wrestled with that thought for the rest of the day, and it had not entirely left him until this morning. Back in the apartment that first night he had put in extra hours preparing for the organic chemistry class the next day, reading and re-reading not only the text, but several other references he had pulled off his office bookshelf. Organic had gone better, but even there he could tell that he just didn't have a high percentage of the students with him. Something was wrong. He had spent nearly four weeks trying first one thing, then another, but what he had done this morning had produced a kind of breakthrough. This morning he saw *eyes* light up!

"So tell us," Maggie prodded. "What made it so superb?"

"Well, because the students were awake for the first time. I had more questions from them today than all semester up until now. Don't tell anybody, but I think they might be starting to *like* chemistry."

"Never happens in *my* classes," Carlisle said. "What produced this dramatic turnaround?"

"You know Marty Fresch, either of you?"

"Marty? Yes," Maggie answered, "he's in my rhetoric and composition class on Tuesday and Thursday afternoons. Bright boy."

"Well, it was actually Marty who gave me the idea. He came to my office after class last Friday, and he said, 'Dr. Newprof, I'm just not getting the hang of chemistry.' Not too encouraging, right? So I asked him what the problem was, and he told me he kept looking for the ways that what we were talking about applied to the real world. That's what he said: 'the real world.' He said he had thought chemistry would be about pollution, and medical cures, and explosives, and things like that, and we never came close to those kinds of topics in class."

"Did you ask him if he wanted to teach the class?" Carlisle asked.

"No, wait. What he was saying was that he needed a reason to learn the chemistry I'm teaching, that he needed to be motivated. The students were falling asleep because I wasn't motivating them to pay attention."

Carlisle shook his head. "Unh unh. No. Motivation is not my job. I give them a good biology course, and that's my contribution. They have to supply their own motivation. If nothing else, they should be motivated by wanting to pass the course."

"Well," Adam replied, "I guess that was my assumption going in. But if they aren't tuning in, not learning, what good's the exercise? I mean, what's the good of my burning the midnight oil putting lectures together, and talking and writing on the board for three hours a week, if in the end three-fourths of the students aren't learning chemistry?"

Carlisle looked into his coffee and shook his head again, and Maggie said: "So what did you do?"

Adam smiled. "I walked into that class at eight o'clock this morning with a big brown paper bag, and I set it on the desk, and I said, 'Class, what is chemistry?' Well, they just looked at each other, naturally. And

I said, 'Marty, what is chemistry?' And he said, 'Well...it's the name of this course.'"

"Smart-mouthed kid," Carlisle Ravenel muttered.

"So the class laughed, and I said, 'I'm going to tell you what chemistry is, ladies and gentlemen.' And with that I put my hand down into the bag—they can't see anything in it—and I pulled out an oak leaf, and I said, 'Let me tell you why green leaves turn red.' So I explained in very simple terms about the green of chlorophyll yielding to the red of anthocyanins, and I said, 'Ladies and gentlemen, that's chemistry. Now let's see what else is in this bag."

He explained how he pulled out a polyester tie, then a vial of an antibiotic, then a bottle of blue ink, then a firecracker. And with each object he talked briefly about the chemistry involved, and the role of chemists in producing so many of the products that had impact in their everyday lives.

"I paused for questions—and there really were some. And at the end I told them, 'What I just did with the bag was actually sneaky. I could have put anything in the bag, because everything is chemistry. If you want to understand the world you live in every day, you have to know something about chemistry. They were actually *listening*, Carlisle. They listened because they had a *motive* for listening—and it wasn't grades. Two of them even came up after class and said how much they enjoyed it."

"Maybe so," Carlisle grumped, "but I bet two more asked if they had to know it for the test."

Maggie Morrow laughed.

The Central Mission

Of all good starts, the most important to the conscientious faculty member is a good start in teaching. Teaching is, at least in a liberal arts college, far and away the dominant interest of the majority faculty, and that is as it should be. The HERI study cited back in Chapter 2 documents this commitment,[1] as does the Carnegie Foundation for the Advancement of Teaching survey of 1989,[2] with both studies reporting that 84% of the liberal arts college faculty see teaching as their chief interest. The Carnegie Foundation report contrasts this with research university professors, only 38% of whom select teaching as a

---

[1] Alexander W. Astin, William S. Korn, and Eric L. Dey, *The American College Teacher, National Norms for the 1989-90 HERI Faculty Survey* (Los Angeles, CA: Higher Education Research Institute, 1991).

[2] Ernest L. Boyer, *The Condition of the Professoriate: Attitudes and Trends, 1989* (Princeton, NJ: The Carnegie Foundation for the Advancement of Teaching, 1989).

preferred activity. The rise of the research university in the late nineteenth century (see chapter 5) resulted in a bifurcation of American higher education, but in the liberal arts colleges teaching remains the central mission.

Perhaps we have said that wrong. Is teaching really the central mission? Consider the quote from Pat Cross at the beginning of this chapter. And this assertion by Paul L. Dressel and Dora Marcus:

> The only purpose of instruction is to enable students to learn, and the individual who engages in teaching without stimulating others to learn cannot be considered an effective member of the teaching profession.[3]

Is not the true reason for the existence of liberal arts colleges, rather than teaching *per se*, actually student learning? The distinction may seem subtle, and the person just entering the profession may find this to be so much quibbling, but I think there is a point to be made. If you start off your career believing that teaching is, in and of itself, the reason that the college was chartered, the buildings were built, and the faculty are hired, you may well mistake your responsibilities, and so enjoy less success than you should. To the extent that there is no learning, there is no teaching. Teaching is never an end in itself, unless teachers take it to be so. And when they do, the true purpose, the hoped-for end result, of teaching gets missed.

It is a good idea, as you begin the profession of teaching, and if you are committed to this central mission of the college, to reflect before plunging into the task of teaching on the following kinds of preparatory questions:

✦ What are my motives for choosing teaching as a profession?
✦ What is my preparation for teaching?
✦ What conditions are known to encourage student learning?
✦ What are found to be the characteristics of an effective teacher?

If teaching is a sacred mission, it must warrant our most thoughtful preparation for doing it. What is the typical formal preparation of a new college professor for a life of teaching? That answer is abundantly clear: For very nearly every Adam and Eve Newprof starting out, there has been no training at all, none, prior to that first day in the classroom. If one were going in for surgery, it would be small comfort to know that one's surgeon had been to the top medical school in the country, had learned the human body literally inside and out, had observed scores of master surgeons at work, and had finished at the top of the class—if that surgeon had not both studied and practiced the art of surgery. That is very close to what the student faces who enters a college class in America. In his often caustic book, *The Professor Game*, Richard Mandell notes:

---

[3] Paul L. Dressel and Dora Marcus, *On Teaching and Learning in College* (San Francisco, CA: Jossey-Bass , 1982), p. *xiii*.

A working assumption throughout academic life that is almost never stated is that anyone with a Ph.D. can teach well enough for any college students he might be required to teach.[4]

And of course he is correct. The graduate of a baccalaureate college, who aspires to a career of college teaching prepares—how? He or she spends four to eight years doing graduate study, but all of it focused on an academic discipline and research in a very small corner of that discipline. Educational philosophy and pedagogy are never mentioned, much less studied in this period. The graduate schools assume that they are manufacturing experts, and so they are—but experts in Renaissance History, Herpetology, and nineteenth Century British Literature, and Analytical Chemistry; certainly not in what works best in the teaching of undergraduates in a liberal arts college. And so, carrying with them the enduring assumption that the Ph.D. guarantees readiness to teach, they teach.

Maryellen Weimer includes this assumption in a list of three that she is convinced not only interfere with a good start in teaching, but also hinder faculty from making improvements in their teaching as they gain experience:

> Faculty make a number of flawed assumptions about teaching and learning. Unfortunately, these seemingly obvious truisms seriously inhibit both individual and institutional efforts to do something about instructional quality....If you know it you can teach it....Good teachers are born....Faculty teach content.[5]

She goes on to discuss the error inherent in each of these assumptions. We will get back to the second two later in this chapter, but you can see the tacit supposition: college teachers don't need training in how to teach, they only need to know their subjects thoroughly. If things aren't going too well in the classroom, well, they probably just need to increase their knowledge of the material they're teaching; and, if that doesn't work, it's probably because some teachers are born with more natural talent than others, and there's not much to be done about that.

Adam Newprof comes to the College of Port St. Julian not only eager to teach, but believing he is ready. After all, he has spent twenty years in classrooms as a student, and his father was a teacher. No passive observer, he began to note by his junior year in high school what "good" teachers and "bad" teachers did, and by his senior year in college he had some rather firm notions about things teachers *should* do and other things they should *never* do. By the time he had decided on his future career, he had synthesized a kind of mental model of himself as Teacher. This kind of preparation for teaching, a perfectly standard one in my experience, is an *imitation-and-avoidance* process,

---

[4] Richard D. Mandell, *The Professor Game* (Garden City, NY: Doubleday, 1977), p.156.

[5] Maryellen Weimer, *Improving College Teaching: Strategies for Developing Instructional Effectiveness* (San Francisco, CA: Jossey-Bass, 1990), p.3 ff.

wherein the incipient teacher imitates the practices of "good" teachers he or she has known, and avoids those of the "bad" teachers. Valuable techniques can be learned this way; it is as responsible an approach as is ordinarily available to those whose graduate study was not in education itself. I hope you will agree, however, that it represents a more haphazard and dubious strategy than preparation for the college's central mission deserves.

The motives that bring most of us into the teaching profession will be something of a mixture. We should be honest about that, too, at the outset. Included in the mix are likely to be:

+ *the Evangelist dream:* a desire to advance the ideals of liberal learning
+ *the Maestro dream:* a wish to be appreciated as a disciplinary expert
+ *the Mentor dream:* a desire to contribute to the intellectual and personal development of students
+ *the Thespian dream:* a yearning to enrapture audiences with impeccable performances
+ *the Godship dream:* the longing to create one's own world and to rule over it.

I hasten to underscore that these are all, to my mind, perfectly good dreams to have. They all represent natural human yearnings of the sort that have propelled history and produced grand achievements in every arena and every age. Between the motives and the outcomes there lies, however, the matter of full readiness for the work.

The above critique is offered, not to plant some seed of guilt or doubt in the mind of those beginning a new career with zeal and high purpose, but rather with the intent to encourage a beginning on the soundest base possible—what is true. You, as a new professor on the job, must begin where you are, and where you are has been largely determined by the approach taken by higher education to supplying teachers for the education of college and university students. Your zeal and disciplinary proficiency are vital, but they are not all that you will need. It will be your challenge, recognizing where you are strong and where you are weak in preparing for teaching, and accepting your own mix of personal motives, to assure the highest quality student learning possible during your years on the watch. You have no reason to feel guilty, but you have abundant reason to think actively about how to acquire teaching expertise equal to your disciplinary expertise. That kind of reflection at the start can produce great rewards both for you and your students early on in your teaching career.

One final caveat remains in this discussion of the central mission of the liberal arts college. Just as it is easy to confuse the difference between "teaching" and "student learning" when talking about mission, so one risks forgetting that "teaching" has an implied object. The central mission is to teach—but what? The obvious answer is that one teaches whatever the assignment calls for—calculus, Shakespeare, macroeconomics, physical chemistry, the New

Testament. In other words, the answer depends on the discipline of one's expertise. But that is a more limited answer than is merited. For *accomplishing the mission of the college requires more than summing up the syllabi of its courses.* Every faculty member in a college needs to have the fullest possible knowledge of and fealty to, not only one's own discipline and courses, but also the general education goals and curriculum of the college. It is all too commonly accepted that a student's experience is more patchwork than holistic, more a checklist than an integration. Absorbed in the teaching of the major, one risks losing and transmitting to one's students the overarching aims of the total curriculum that they are required to negotiate. In the tension between the major and general education, the latter, in recent decades, has usually lost, with faculty no less than with students. For the best possible start in teaching at a new college, you will add considerably to your value if you are prepared to explain the general education curriculum to students, and to make explicit connections across all the disciplines as you teach your own. Indeed, the understanding of students that there are values, ideals, and principles that simultaneously transcend and permeate the curriculum will depend squarely on the self-conscious effort of dedicated teachers to teach such notions along with sociology, statistics, western civilization, and physics.

The Students

They come to us in all varieties—affluent and pampered, poor and deprived, intellectually ravenous, sick of school, clear in their purposes, unsure why they're here, self-reliant, hopelessly dependent, brilliant, dense, male, female, young, middle-aged, Jewish, Wasp, Black, Hispanic, Asian. They are the mirror of America. They remind us of ourselves at the same age, yet they are strangers. They are confused by some of the simplest concepts, yet they have flashes of insight that amaze us. They can be maddeningly selfish, yet they will voluntarily give up a vacation to help with a Habitat project. They give us inspiration to get up in the morning, yet they leave us weary at the end of the day. We love them and we hate them. They are our reason for being here, the object of the enterprise.

If we accept that the central mission is accomplished only when students learn, it follows immediately that the presumptions we make about the nature of these creatures, these "students," and what causes them to learn will be crucial to our success in accomplishing the mission. In addition, once we discover what conditions are conducive to student learning, we must then decide how far our own responsibility extends in seeing that these conditions are realized.

Sitting in the College Street Café, Professor Ravenel has drawn a line regarding responsibility. "Motivation is not my job," he says. "I give them a good biology course, and that's my contribution." What if the conditions conducive to student learning turn out to include a teacher who is good at providing motivation? What if the amount and quality of learning depend significantly on that factor? Has Ravenel chosen to draw the line here because he is indifferent to students and how much they learn? Not at all. Although the importance of motivation (perhaps particularly to a biologist) is self-evident, whether it is rats being trained or students being taught, Ravenel is expressing a view that is extremely common among college teachers. It is a corollary to the "faculty teach content" assumption that Weimer points out (see above). If one enters teaching accepting that disciplinary expertise is the sole criterion for teaching, then the presumption that motivating is not the business of a teacher is a rather natural one. Weimer says:

> The problem is that sometimes their allegiance to the content is much stronger than their loyalty to students. This explains why some faculty members end up teaching *content* but not necessarily *students*.[6]

Paul Morrill and Emil Speer note the perennial difficulty that this business of "motivation" gives college professors:

> Motivation has always been a troublesome aspect of teaching. College teachers must become aware of the necessity of the examination of motivation of "thinking" when thinking is conceived as an aspect of knowledge-seeking behavior.[7]

Psychologists have, in fact, discovered a great deal about how learning occurs and what conditions contribute to student learning. Morrill and Speer outline the commonly offered conditions as important in the learning process:

+ Motivation: the student must want something.
+ Stimulus: the student must notice something.
+ Response: the student must do something.
+ Reinforcement: the student must get something.

The fact is that Carlisle Ravenel and—let us face it—thousands of other faculty members have a kind of immunity to what research shows about teaching and learning. It is a fascinating phenomenon, albeit a dismaying one. Presented with what research has discovered in these areas, the college teacher is apt to react, not merely with indifference, but with scorn. Yet there it is. Really caring about student learning calls for serious attention to each of these four conditions—*all* four: motivation, stimulus, response, and reinforcement.

Let's look first at motivation. Perhaps never before in history have teachers who are striving at finding ways to motivate students had such a hard time settling on methods for doing so. Much of the college and university enrollment growth that has taken place in this century is the result of expanded access, a manifestation of our dedication as a society to the ideal of universal

---

[6] Weimer, p. 7.

[7] Paul Hampton Morrill and Emil R. Speer, *The Academic Profession: Teaching in Higher Education* (New York, NY: Human Sciences Press, 1982), p. 45.

education. The idea that education is for the aristocratic few who have leisure time was long ago abandoned, and we see a college education instead as requisite to any member of the American society who aspires to a significant share in its prosperity. Recognizing this shift of college education from an aristocratic to a democratic instrument, it follows that the characteristics—including the motives—of the clients of higher education have shifted over the century. And indeed they have. Those seeking a college education with a view to acquiring knowledge and qualities appropriate for "a gentleman or lady" had a strikingly different motivation for enrolling in college than does a young person whose dominant interest is getting a well-paying job. Motives are influenced, too, by the generally lower academic readiness of those whom expanded access have added to the campuses; many are first-generation college students; many were not in a college preparatory track in high school; and many simply have lower aptitudes than those entering when higher education was the abode of society's elite. Add to this the changing nature of the college population that has resulted from the large influx of adult students, whose motives are inevitably affected by the point in their lives at which they are getting a formal college education, and one sees abundant reason for the large shifts in the perceived purposes of college.

Alexander Astin, through the Cooperative Institutional Research Program (CIRP)[8] has been surveying college freshmen for many years, and the accumulated data show trends that are well worth the consideration of any new (or seasoned) faculty member. There are two items that have been tracked over time which are seen as indicators of this shift in motivation for attending college. They are (1) "Develop a meaningful philosophy of life" and (2) "Be very well off financially." In 1970 a good majority of freshman (about 75%) placed high priority on developing a philosophy of life in college, and a minority (about 39%) were primarily motivated by a desire to make more money. By 1987 the two motivators had switched places, with the "philosophy of life" item moving to 39%, and the "money" item moving to 76% (see Graph 6.1). Little wonder that one has been hearing faculty say for decades, "Students just aren't the same as they used to be."[9]

The point of this illustration is not that faculty must cater to the crass motives that some students bring with them to college, but rather that our failure to take the existence of these motives into account has implications for our success in bringing about student learning. As a new faculty member, you need not demonstrate to the student for whom a large personal income is a major goal how your course, or even college itself, promises to further that

---

[8] The results of these surveys are published annually by the Higher Education Research Institute, UCLA Graduate School of Education. The project staff for the 1990 survey were Alexander W. Astin, William S. Korn, Ellyne R. Berz, and Robin Bailey.

[9] Since 1987 the trend has been reversed, although the financial item in 1990 still came out (74%), well ahead of the philosophy of life item (43%).

Graph 6.1
Trends in Freshman Life Goals

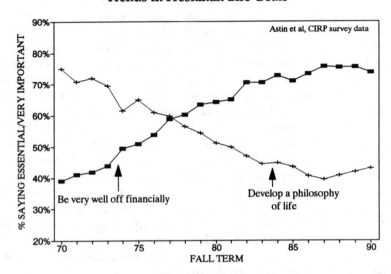

objective. But you ignore at great jeopardy the pragmatic view that students—and their parents—take of the purpose of college. A very helpful way of seeing what has happened, and the challenge it represents for faculty, is to look at the very great differences in basic personality type of (1) students now and students three decades ago; and (2) the typical student and the typical faculty member. While a study of cognitive developmental theories might give a deeper understanding of the sources of learning-style variations in college classrooms, a great deal of insight into the resulting challenges of these variations for the teacher can be derived from a consideration of fundamental differences in what the psychologist Carl Gustav Jung termed "function types." The Myers-Briggs Type Indicator (MBTI),[10] based on Jungian theory, was devised in the 1950s as an instrument for assessing psychological types. Following the MBTI approach, we recognize four primary preference polarities, as shown in Table 6.1.

It is easy to see that a student's preferences will influence tremendously how he or she learns most easily. Consider these examples:

(1) **E *vs* I:** A student whose natural interests are externally directed (E-type) will learn best in a setting where there is action and conversation; whereas the internally oriented student (I-type) will prefer a setting that is quiet and less active. Furthermore, while the E is stimulated by group discussions, the I tends to be very uncomfortable and resistant when forced into this approach to learning.

[10] Isabel Briggs Myers, *The Myers-Briggs Type Indicator* (Palo Alto, CA: Consulting Psychologists Press, 1962).

(2) **S** *vs* **N**: A student who by nature takes in information primarily through the five senses (S-type) will grasp abstract ideas best when they are approached through the doorway of the senses, i.e., through concrete experience. Someone whose information is acquired primarily through intuition (N-type) will, by contrast, prefer to deal directly with the abstract ideas. S students are very good at memorizing; N students dislike memorizing, and much prefer theoretical subjects. S students like the repeated use of familiar, defined processes; N students are curious about new concepts and possibilities. S students will be absorbed in the moment; N students are constantly looking toward the future, and in a classroom will be racing ahead mentally.

(3) **T** *vs* **F**: A student who is inclined to make decisions (judgments) based on objective, impersonal considerations (T-type) will be motivated to learn by logical explanations; he or she is stimulated by the prospect of learning *why* things happen (cause and effect). Someone

Table 6.1
The Four Myers-Briggs Type Indicator Preference Polarities[11]

Preference	Polarity and Occurrence in the General Population	
Natural Interests	**Extroversion** **E** *external orientation* 75%	**Introversion** **I** *internal orientation* 25%
Ways of Perceiving	**Sensing** **S** *primary reliance on the senses* 75%	**Intuition** **N** *primary reliance on insight* 25%
Ways of Judging	**Thinking** **T** *objective, impersonal judgment* 50%	**Feeling** **F** *subjective, value-based judgment* 50%
Attitude toward the Outer World	**Judging** **J** *preference for order, process, planning* 50%	**Perceiving** **P** *preference for flexibility, adaptability* 50%

[11] The terms used here are those that Jung proposed. They are sometimes confusing, particularly his use of "judging" and "perceiving" as alternative attitudes toward the outer world, since two of the *preferences* are themselves labeled "perceiving" and "judging."

inclined to make decisions based on more subjective, value-based considerations (F-type) will, on the other hand, be motivated by seeing the human perspective on a subject; to this student, why something happens is less important than its relevance to human situations. The T student wants to be respected for his or her competence, the F craves personal appreciation and encouragement.

(4) J *vs* P: A student whose preference is for order, process, and planning (J-type) responds well to a structured learning environment with clearly-stated goals; whereas a student whose preference is for flexibility and adaptability (P-type) sees learning as open-ended, and feels constrained by too much structure. The J-type is very task oriented, and pays serious attention to deadlines; the P-type tends to see deadlines as "guidelines," and will often be late getting to class and turning in assignments.

There are sixteen different ways in which the four letters—E or I, S or N, T or F, J or P—may be combined. Each four-letter combination identifies a distinct personality type, and what emerges in combination gives a personality picture that goes well beyond simply "adding up" the four preferences. The interested reader is encouraged to consult a reference that gives more detailed discussion of the underlying theory and of the sixteen types.[12] We will include here simply a summary table. Table 6.2 gives thumbnail personality descriptions that focus on learning-related characteristics. The table, even though its use has limits, can prove extremely valuable to the teacher determined to reach as many students as possible. There is, it should be noted, an actual scoring involved in the determination of MBTI type, and there are matters of varying degree in the four preferences. A "borderline P," for example will not test the teacher's assignment deadlines, for instance, nearly so much as a "raving P." Further, there are effects from prior training that can shift one along a preferences scale, although Jung believed that one's basic type was inborn, and that the only possible change was a scale-shift change (e.g., a T-type who over the years comes to take human factors more into account when making decisions).

The sixteen personality types will not be equally represented in your classrooms. In the typical medium-selective liberal arts college the type most fre-

---

[12] There are several references that can help in addition to Myers' 1962 book. Some examples : (1) Gordon Lawrence, *People Types & Tiger Stripes: A Practical Guide to Learning Styles*, 2nd. Ed. (Gainesville, FL: Center for Applications of Psychological Type, 1979). (2) Isabel Briggs Myers with Peter B. Myers, *Gifts Differing* (Palo Alto, CA: Consulting Psychologists Press, 1980). (3) David Keirsey and Marilyn Bates, *Please Understand Me* (Del Mar, CA: Prometheus Nemesis Book Company, 1984). Another reference that focuses on applications in higher education, with chapters by a number of contributing authors who have experience in using MBTI is: (4) Judith A. Provost and Scott Anchors, *Applications of the Myers-Briggs Type Indicator in Higher Education* (Palo Alto, CA: Consulting Psychologists Press, 1987).

quently encountered in the freshman class will be the ENFP, which will account for maybe 20% of the students. The type least frequently encountered will vary and is harder to predict; the INTJ or INFJ are good candidates, but the ISTJ and ENTJ are also possibilities in a given year. Whatever the type least frequently found, there are likely to be no more than a tenth as many of these students as of the ENFP type. The specific programs that attract students to your college will, of course, make a difference in the distribution of types there. A popular program in business may, for example, result in a larger population of ESTJ students. And a program in nursing may attract more ESFJ personalities. At a technically-oriented university such as MIT, a far larger portion of the class will be INTJ and INTP types, the types attracted to the physical and life sciences and to computer studies. If your college has a male/female ratio that differs significantly from 1.00, the ratio of T-types to F-types will reflect the imbalance; F-types are about twice as prevalent among women as are T-types, whereas T-types slightly outnumber F-types among men. This is the only polarity where there is a significant gender difference. The MBTI profile for a typical freshman class is shown in Graph 6.2.

Graph 6.2
MBTI Freshman Profile

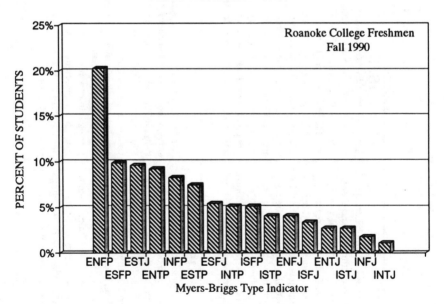

Table 6.2
Student Personality Types[13]

ISTJ	ISFJ	INFJ	INTJ
Are serious and quiet. Earn success by concentration and thoroughness. Are practical, orderly, matter-of-fact, logical, realistic, and dependable. See to it that everything is well organized. Take responsibility. Make up their own minds as to what should be accomplished. Tend to have a need for materials and directions, and for teachers to be precise and accurate.	Are quiet, friendly, responsible, and conscientious. Work devotedly to meet their obligations and serve their friends and school. Are thorough, painstaking, and accurate. May need time to master technical subjects, as their interests are usually not technical. Are patient with detail and routine. Are loyal, considerate, and concerned with how other people feel.	Succeed by perseverance, originality, and desire to do whatever is needed or wanted. Put their best efforts into their work. Are quietly forceful, conscientious, and concerned for others. Are respected for their firm principles. Look for small groups of people who understand and appreciate them. Write and communicate well because of a desire to express their ideas clearly.	Usually have original minds and great drive for their own ideas and purposes. Have a fine power to organize a task and carry it through with or without help in areas that appeal to them. Are skeptical, critical, independent, determined, and often stubborn. Tend to be serious and to set high academic standards. Prefer challenging teachers. Don't readily follow fads.

ISTP	ISFP	INFP	INTP
Are cool onlookers—quiet, reserved, and observing. Analyze life with detached curiosity and unexpected flashes of original humor. Usually interested in cause and effect and in how and why mechanical things work. May enjoy physical, risk-taking games. Lead by setting an example. Would rather show their feelings through actions than words.	Are retiring, quietly friendly, sensitive, kind, and modest about their abilities. Shun disagreements and do not force their opinions or values on others. Usually do not care to lead but are often loyal followers. Are often relaxed about getting things done. Learn best from direct experiences and find it hard to learn in rigid and highly structured classrooms.	Are full of enthusiasms and loyalties, but seldom talk of these until they know you well. Care about learning, ideas, language, and independent projects of their own. Tend to undertake too much, then somehow get it done. Are friendly, but often too absorbed in what they are doing to be sociable. Are reluctant to ask others for help and would rather do things for themselves.	Are quiet, reserved, and brilliant in exams, especially in theoretical or scientific subjects. Are logical and impersonal and may be somewhat shy. Are usually interested mainly in ideas, with little liking for parties or small talk. Tend to have sharply defined interests. Need to choose careers where some strong interest can be used.

ESTP	ESFP	ENFP	ENTP
Are matter-of-fact. Do not worry or hurry. Enjoy whatever comes along. Are likely to be involved with sports or after-school activities. Are good at math and science when they see a practical use for them. Dislike long explanations. Are best with real things that can be worked, handled, taken apart, and put together. Prefer teachers who are entertaining and make learning active and fun.	Are outgoing, easygoing, accepting, and friendly. Make things more fun for others by their enjoyment. Like sports and making things. Like learning when it is fun and active. Find remembering facts easier than mastering theories. Are best in situations that need sound common sense and practical ability with people as well as with things.	Are warmly enthusiastic, ingenious, and imaginative. Are able to do almost anything that interests them. Are quick with a solution for any difficulty. Are interested in people and skillful in handling them and their problems. Often rely on their ability to improvise instead of preparing in advance. Dislike uninspired routine and attention to detail.	Are quick, ingenious, and good at many things. Are clever and outspoken and can be stimulating company. May argue for fun on either side of a question. Are resourceful in solving new and challenging problems, but may neglect routine assignments. Tend to be independent, analytical, and impersonal in their relations with people.

ESTJ	ESFJ	ENFJ	ENTJ
Are practical, realistic, and matter-of-fact. Want ideas, plans, and decisions to be based on solid facts. Are not interested in subjects they see no use for, but can apply themselves when necessary. Like to organize and run activities. May value traditional activities such as team sports, band, and class offices.	Are warm-hearted, talkative, popular, conscientious, born cooperators, and active committee members. Need harmony and may be good at creating it. Are sensitive to criticism. Think best when talking with people. Work best with encouragement and praise. Are mainly interested in things that directly and visibly affect people's lives.	Are responsive and responsible. Generally feel real concern for what others think or want, and try to handle things with due regard for other people's feelings. Value harmony and inspire cooperation. Like to get matters settled and organized. Are sociable, popular, and active in school affairs, but put in enough time on their studies to do good work.	Are intellectually curious, insightful, able in studies, and leaders in activities. Are usually good at anything that requires reasoning and informed talk, such as debates and public speaking. Are usually well-informed and enjoy adding to their fund of knowledge. May sometimes be more positive and confident than their experience in an area warrants.

Leading into this discussion of MBTI theory, I underscored the pragmatic view that today's students tend to take of college, and I referred to the change that has taken place over the past thirty years. This change is not, needless to say, a consequence of change in genetics that has resulted in a redistribution of personality types in the general population, nor is it simply the effect of a society that has become radically materialistic (though materialism doubtless has had its influence). The shift is instead largely the consequence of the greatly-increased access to higher education, mentioned earlier in this chapter, that has marked this century. While MBTI theorists emphasize that there are no "good" nor "bad" types, only differences in preference, a quick scanning of the sixteen personality types in Table 6.2 is sure to produce in any teacher certain feelings of preference of one's own. When considering potential scholars, phrases like "put their best efforts into their work" and "care about learning, ideas, language" inevitably produce a very different reaction from phrases such as "often rely on their ability to improvise instead of preparing their work in advance" or "are often relaxed about getting things done." The personality types that you would probably label as unlikely scholars were present in far lower concentration in the first half of the twentieth century than now as the century is ending. Extroverts (E) accounted for only about 56% of liberal arts college students in the 1960s;[14] now they comprise about 75% of an incoming freshman class,[15] the same percentage as is found in the general population. Sensing types (S), grounded in the present, realistic and practical, were not nearly so abundant in colleges in the 1960s, representing only about 34% of the population; in 1990 nearly half of a liberal arts college freshman class may be S-types.

E and S characteristics present special challenges for the typical liberal arts faculty member, who is likely to be an IN-type.[16] The increase of E and S students in colleges has led to articles and presentations on "the new student," as both faculty and student life personnel adjust to a generation of students which, more than any before it, prefers having fun to studying, values physical over intellectual activity, and demands to see relevance between what is being taught and their own interests and aims.

But again, this is not a call to despair but rather one to start the teaching task with an understanding of the facts as they are, and to plan for success out of that understanding. We all know the proclivity one has for raising one's voice when talking to a person who doesn't speak English very well. Sometimes faculty try the equivalent with students who seem not to comprehend,

[14] See Myers (1962).

[15] Data from Roanoke College freshman classes, 1986-1990.

[16] Read the description of the INTJ, the most common faculty type, in Table 6.2 to get an idea of how disparate faculty and students can be in type.

losing patience and escalating demands rather than learning to speak their language in the interest of good communication—and thus, ultimately, of student learning. Language that motivates an IN personality (the typical faculty member) will fail to motivate an ES personality (a commonly-encountered student). When you wish to communicate with an E student about a concern, it is always far more effective, for instance, to talk rather than write to the student. And if you want to communicate with an S student, try to use concrete examples and facts rather than talking in generalities.

The ideal student is (we are prone to be convinced) as we were at nineteen—quiet, studious, punctual, and well-read. The real student of today is far more likely to be *un*like us: gregarious (over half spend eleven or more hours per week socializing), not studious at all (over half spend fewer than five hours a week studying), a stranger to reading (only 12% read anything beyond course requirements),[17] often tardy (about two-thirds are P-types, who pay little attention to deadlines). But the real student is the one who is there to be taught. And a good start with teaching means learning the motivating language required to reach that student.

We will look further at the other three conditions for learning—stimulus, response, and reinforcement—in the following section on teaching styles.

Teaching Styles

The term "teaching style" would probably suggest to Adam Newprof something like "lecturing with verve and panache." The phrase might even smack of too much showmanship at the expense of substance. It really has never occurred to Newprof that there might be more than one fundamental approach to teaching. Some did it better than others, but "teaching" for him means "lecturing." Doesn't "improving teaching" mean "finding ways to lecture more effectively"? Adam's experience, the footing for his imitation-and-avoidance strategy for learning how to teach, tells him that, while there were various degrees of teaching capability, there is only one "style."

A few first-year professors will have had a teacher now and then who strayed from the lecture path, perhaps one who spent most class periods leading discussions in which students were strongly encouraged and perhaps even required to participate. A very few may even have been in a class that divided into smaller discussion groups and then reconvened as a whole class for reports. But these professors will be in the minority. Research has shown that college teachers are lecturing a large majority of the time (80%).[18] Let me

---

[17] Alexander W. Astin, William S. Korn, Ellyne R. Berz, and Robin Bailey, *The American Freshman National Norms for 1990* (Los Angeles, CA: Higher Education Research Institute, 1990).

[18] Howard R. Pollio, "What Students Think About and Do During College Lectures," *Teaching-Learning Issues* 52, 1-18 (1984).

confess that, while I mixed in demonstrations and used visual aids frequently, I fell within this 80% norm in every one of the seventeen years that I taught. And let me say quickly that I found the lecture method to work well most of the time. Indeed, there is no orthodoxy as to teaching style. Students will respond to and learn from various styles and from teachers with a multiplicity of personality types.

In your "Godship" role, you will be doing more than practicing a teaching style, you will be creating in your classroom a total environment for learning. That environment will not be a function merely of whether you lecture, lead discussions, or sit with your class in a circle under a tree; contributing as well will be your own self-image, your view of the place of students, the emotional feel of the classroom, the kinds of assignments that are given, the standards that are set, and the degree to which the authority of the professor is asserted. Dressel and Marcus have identified four prototypes of teacher orientations, based on N.T. Hardy's doctoral dissertation at Michigan State, and have delineated their components in what I find to be a useful tabular fashion, an abbreviated version of which appears in Table 6.3.[19] I urge that you take a close look at this analysis of teaching styles, and that you use it as you decide the best environment for the students to learn what you hope to teach them. It's your choice!

The four prototypes of teaching orientations given above are, not surprisingly, not the only way to look at one's approach to teaching. The literature contains many other suggested ways of looking at styles of and attitudes toward teaching. More valuable certainly than labels is the introspection and reflection you do as you examine such suggested prototypes.

Another, less structured, way of coming at the question of teaching style is simply to consider what the research, if it has been done, has shown to be the shared characteristics of effective teachers. The research has, of course, been done—repeatedly, with all kinds of groups. Investigators have used studies with students, alumni, faculty members, and administrators to identify what qualities these groups with some basis for judging associate with "good teaching." Well over a score of reports have now appeared in the literature, and while the exact wording may vary slightly from study to study, the picture is sharply defined by now. In a summary, Wotruba and Wright extracted from these studies the qualities most frequently cited as being identified with effective teaching:[20]

---

[19] Dressel and Marcus, pp. 10-11. In addition to the five components shown in the abbreviated Table 6.3, the authors include seven more: the classroom setting, assignments, objectives and evaluation, adaptation to or in student groups, originality or creativity, individualization, source of standards, and objectivity. A study of the entire table is strongly recommended.

[20] T. R. Wotruba and P. L. Wright, "How to Develop a Teacher-Rating Instrument: A Research Approach," *Journal of Higher Education, 6* (1975); 653-663; cited in John A. Centra, *Determining Faculty Effectiveness* (San Francisco, CA: Jossey-Bass, 1979), pp. 18-19.

+ Knowledge of subject
+ Good organization
+ Communication skills, clear interpretations of abstract ideas
+ Enthusiasm for subject
+ Interesting lecturer, good speaker
+ Encouragement of students to think for themselves
+ Willingness to experiment, flexibility
+ Favorable attitudes toward students
+ Fairness in examinations and grading.

Knowing the characteristics of good teachers should give the new faculty member an immense advantage. Teaching is supremely important, but it really is not some kind of mysterious, priestly activity into which only those gifted by the gods can enter successfully. Prototypes aside, this list is not a bad place to start as you decide on how you will teach.

Given what we now know about the most notable qualities of successful teachers, and what we know about the nature of today's students, we begin to see how the stimulation condition, mentioned earlier, turns out to be consequential for student learning—and thus for effective teaching. Let us suppose that you are Adam Newprof, and you have in the classroom (to pick up the description again) one of the "new" students, say Marty Fresch, who has been successfully motivated to learn about, say, acid-base reactions in chemistry. You want him to understand the process of "neutralization" of acid by base. Your next task, according to the model for the learning process presented above, is to stimulate Marty. You launch into a high-blown, abstract verbal description of what happens when one begins to mix an acid and a base. Before you can say "hydrogen ion" twice, Marty's eyes are beginning to glaze over.

But suppose instead of a verbal description alone, you give Marty a small beaker of hydrochloric acid and a dropping bottle of sodium hydroxide (a base). You have him add a small drop of dye to the acid, and nothing happens. Then you have him add, drop by drop, the base to the acid. Marty begins to notice that where the drop is hitting the dye is changing to pink, then the color disappears and the solution in the beaker remains clear, like water. He adds more drops of base. All at once—wham!—the whole solution in the beaker turns red. Clear one instant, red as blood the next. Marty notices. He is stimulated, and he has demonstrated a response. He has experienced an acid-base neutralization; he is now prepared to understand what was involved chemically.

Now this kind of demonstration and student involvement will enhance learning for *any* of the personality types, but for an ES student like Marty Fresch it will prove particularly effective as a stimulus. The "new" student sees things in very concrete terms. Abstract descriptions, which the student with intense concentration may follow, do not provide the kind of stimulus

Table 6.3
Four Teaching Orientations

Components	Teaching Orientations			
	Discipline-Centered	Instructor-Centered	Student-Centered (Cognitive)	Student-Centered (Affective)
Course content	*Disciplinary concepts, principles, theories & methods*	*Based on teacher's preferences & perceptions*	*Materials interesting to students & producing cognitive outcomes*	*Content secondary, used to help student's maturation*
Method of instruction	*Lectures & standard text covering body of knowledge*	*Lecture or teacher-dominated discussion highlighting teacher's personality*	*Discussion, with special lectures to focus on important issues*	*Emphasis on student involvement as a means of personal & social development*
Student-faculty interactions	*Familiarity and intimacy with students discouraged*	*Discussions with students focused on clarifying lecture points*	*Interactions planned to be intellectually stimulating to students*	*Interactions in groups, with instructor acting as moderator*
Professorial self-image	*Identifies with the discipline rather than with teaching role*	*Has strong ego and radiates self-confidence*	*Developer of student's ability to analyze, reason, etc.*	*Counselor and resource person*
Students	*Viewed as would-be majors and graduate school candidates*	*Viewed as an audience or a source of acolytes*	*Regarded as individuals who must become self-reliant in using knowledge*	*Viewed as individuals who must achieve self-insight and accept full responsibility for behavior and goals*

Dressel and Marcus, pp. 10–11.

that an S student needs. Something concrete to focus on and do draws the attention you are seeking.

The mid-1980s saw, as we noted in Chapter 5, several national reports on baccalaureate education in America. These differed in their details, but all leveled keen criticism at what was happening in undergraduate education in American colleges and universities alike and offered extensive recommendations for improvement. One of these, published by the National Institute of Education, was entitled *Involvement in Learning,* a title chosen to stress one of the three "critical conditions of excellence" identified by the eminent study group that produced the document. That condition—student involvement—they saw as "the most important for purposes of improving undergraduate education." (The other two were high expectations and assessment and feedback.) The authors of the report went beyond the classroom itself in their use of the word involvement, but it is certainly applicable there as well. They state this fundamental principle:

> The amount of student learning and personal development associated with any educational program is directly proportional to the quality and quantity of student involvement in that program.[21]

That sentence is worth reading several times. The matter of getting students involved in their learning may be even more critical than is selecting a "teaching style"—although the two may well become related. In a technical sense, learning cannot take place at all except when the student becomes involved, or at least engaged on some level. But "involvement" called for in the NIE report and advocated in this chapter goes well past the limited engagement that one observes in too many teaching/learning situations. Approaching any classroom door on any campus on any day, one can predict the scene ahead of time: professor up front talking, students sitting and (maybe) taking notes. Now, the point is not that the professor shouldn't be talking and the students shouldn't be taking notes. The point is that taking notes represents the only involvement, other than cramming for exams, that many students will practice in the course. Their forty hours or so of classroom time will be spent transcribing—usually poorly!—what the professor is saying and writing on the board. Motivation—stimulus—response—reinforcement: the gears must be turning if effective learning is to take place. There are too seldom any intellectual gears turning in college classrooms. It is too often a passive business.

"Instructors should give greater attention to the passive or reticent student," *Involvement in Learning* says. They go on to note that not every apparently passive student is uninvolved. "But passivity is an important warning

---

[21] Study Group on the Conditions of Excellence in American Higher Education, National Institute of Education, *Involvement in Learning: Realizing the Potential of American Higher Education* (Washington, DC: U.S. Government Printing Office, 1984), p. 19.

sign that may reflect a lack of involvement that impedes the learning process and leads to unnecessary attrition." (p.23). The second of the recommendations made in *Involvement in Learning* reads: "Faculty should make greater use of active modes of teaching and require that students take greater responsibility for their learning." (p.27). There are many ways of doing this, of course, and they vary with the discipline and sub-discipline. The authors go on to suggest a "mix of teaching styles" and suggest these specific means of providing "active modes of teaching and learning":

- ✦ Student-faculty research projects and field classes
- ✦ Internships and other experiential learning (carefully monitored)
- ✦ Breaking large classes into small discussion groups
- ✦ Required in-class presentations and debates
- ✦ Simulations
- ✦ Practitioners as visiting teachers
- ✦ Individual learning projects and supervised independent study.

A good start in teaching will, then, need to include strategies for getting students involved in their learning. No matter how superb you are at lecturing, student learning will be advanced far more effectively by the use of mixed teaching styles that require them to become involved—really involved—in their own learning. The returns will be great.

I conclude this section on teaching styles with an admonition so elementary that I almost left it out. But an old friend who has been teaching for twenty years reminded me of its overriding importance. Here it is: Think about the student; forget about yourself.

That is not easy advice to take, particularly for the person not yet reassured by success as a teacher. But it is perhaps the most useful advice—if you take it—that this chapter can offer. The conscientious new faculty member can all too easily become so preoccupied with how well he or she is doing before the classroom audience that empathy—intellectual identification—with the student becomes impossible. And that empathy is crucial to the planning of and successful implementation of learning strategies. Imagine yourself as a student again. Now imagine yourself (this gets harder!) as a *typical* student. You are uninitiated to the subject; you are thinking about diploma and job more than joys of learning; you are hoping to find the path of least resistance through this course; you are even majoring in something else. If this student were you, what would be necessary to engage you in ways that produce the desired learning? As an empathetic teacher, you should choose your words, your visual aids, your demonstrations, your out-of-class homework and projects with that typical student sharply in your mental focus. Even when you're standing before the classroom—maybe particularly then—you should not be saying to yourself: "*I wonder if I'm really cut out to be a teacher?...Did I get that point across?...Are those students snickering at what I just said?...*" Just imagine that you are out there sitting in one of those desks, uninitiated and trying to make sense of what that professor is saying.

Think about the student; forget about yourself. It works.

Testing and Grading

It lurks in the corners of the classroom, even during your most brilliant and inspirational lectures. It infects the learning environment. It sullies half the conversations between students and teachers. It comes with the territory: Testing and grading.

When we dreamed about ourselves as Teacher, this was not part of the dream (well, maybe just a *smidgen* in the Godship dream!). In what must have been my first year of college teaching, I happened to read a book called *The Profane Comedy*.[22] It was about teaching and learning in America, and the author, lamenting the effect of testing and grading on the relationship between student and teacher, proposed that colleges simply stop doing it. It was his thesis that, if we made the condition for obtaining a college diploma not the passing of so many courses with such-and-such a grade-point average but rather faithful attendance of the required courses, we would have no less learning going on—and we would save both the student-faculty relationship and a lot of time. I doubted then, as I doubt now, that he was correct, and I certainly am not prepared to try the experiment. Still, it set me thinking about how testing and grading do affect mightily how student and teacher see their relationship.

The philosophy of testing and grading that I adhered to throughout my teaching career was shaped by reading that book, as were my conversations with students. I set down these assumptions:

1. The teacher and student are collaborators in the student's learning; *they are not enemies.*
2. Tests are primarily tools for encouraging and guiding learning; *they are not arbitrarily constructed hurdles.*
3. Test grades are only symbols reflecting the grader's best judgment about the degree of mastery being demonstrated by the test-taker on a limited portion of a discipline; *they are not precision measurements.*
4. Final grades are expressions of the mastery demonstrated over the course of a term, judged from all of the data available to the grade-giver; *they are not the final balance in an academic banking system nor the product of an arithmetic sausage grinder.*
5. Conversations between student and teacher about tests should be collaborative in tone, and should focus on what the student has and has

---

[22] Kenneth E. Eble, *The Profane Comedy* (New York, NY: Macmillan, 1962).

not demonstrated by way of mastery; *they should never be debates about the fairness of the grade.*[23]

I began every course with a discussion about the role of tests and grading and explained with an example on the board how I arrived at final course grades. I told them that I gave only letter grades, not numerical ones, and why. I also distributed a brief written version of my testing-grading philosophy and approach—along with a list of "taboo" questions. This last item included: How much does this count? Do we have to know this? Where do I stand? In other words, I tried to head off the kinds of counterproductive questions that tend to dominate conversations between teachers and students. It was my aim to direct our time together toward the common goal of student learning, to resist allowing what should ideally be seen as a side product (grades) to displace the central purpose (learning).

New faculty may, as many of my colleagues did then, see all this as just an eccentricity, but I offer the story to invite you to set aside all biases about how you will do testing and grading that you may have accumulated in an imitation-and-avoidance phase of preparing to teach. Think afresh about how you will test, how you will use grades, and what underlying philosophy will guide you in deciding your own approach. That decision will have consequences for the learning environment you create in your classes. If we return to the four teaching orientations of Dressel and Marcus outlined in Table 6.3, we may now add one more component, "objectives and evaluation," as depicted in Table 6.4. As you can see, there are very definitely options for the new teacher, even as to the fundamental role that testing and grade-giving will play and how they will be approached. You are in a wonderful position to influence students' thinking, not only about your course, but about the very purposes of education, from which they are so often distracted by the language we use in talking to them about their studies. The old friend I mentioned above has always refused even to call tests "tests," but instead types across the top of the page: "Opportunity to Succeed #2"!

As you think about how you will start your practices of testing and grading, some thought as to the frequency of testing is in order. As a new teacher, you will be exceedingly occupied in the beginning simply being prepared for class every day. There will be a strong temptation, unless you have already published a list of test dates to your classes, to delay testing longer than it is good to do. One of the purposes to be served by testing is to supply the reinforcement (feedback) step of the learning process discussed earlier in this chapter. Frequent feedback can give the student both incentive and direction. A delay in

---

[23] This is not to say that the teacher should not be prepared to reconsider whether some error might have been made in assessing the level of mastery. That reconsideration should, I propose, take place without the student looking over the teacher's shoulder in an attitude of mistrust.

Table 6.4
Objectives and Evaluation in the Four Teaching Orientations

Components	Teaching Orientations	
	Discipline-Centered	**Instructor-Centered**
Objectives & Evaluation	*Students judged and graded by comparison with mastery standards*	*Students judged and graded on ability to imitate professorial approaches, perspectives, and formulations*
Components	**Student-Centered (Cognitive)**	**Student-Centered (Affective)**
Objectives & Evaluation	*Students judged and graded on tasks that require new resources and strategies*	*Students evaluated (perhaps by themselves and their peers) on participation and self-expression*

After Dressel and Marcus (1982).

feedback can not only impede learning, it can also allow it to get onto a spurious track. A second function of testing (especially with freshman classes early in the fall semester) is to give evidence to students that this course *is* about learning by calling on them to demonstrate that they are doing it. Too long a delay after the term begins, or testing done only infrequently, can convey the wrong message about the seriousness of the course. A third benefit of frequent testing is that it encourages students to stay actively engaged with the course, rather than concentrating their "learning" into a few spurts of mad cramming, a technique that is notoriously worthless if mastery is a goal. Even when many of the tests are simply short quizzes that take but a few minutes of class time, their worth may be well out of proportion to the time they take. To these I would add a fourth value for testing: It provides important feedback and guidance to the *teacher*. Carol Copperud, in her very practical handbook, says:

> Tests are one method for giving students an opportunity to show you what they know or what they can do—hopefully, as a result of your instruction.[24]

We may lose sight from time to time of the fact that test results tell not only the students, but also the teacher, something about what has been learned—and by implication, what has been taught. All of us who have taught very

---

[24] Carol Copperud, *The Test Design Handbook* (Englewood Cliffs, NJ: Educational Technology Publications, 1979), p. 3.

much have had the experience of believing that we have done a perfectly fine job of teaching a concept or skill, only to discover from a disastrous test that we missed the students entirely. It is particularly beneficial, if the topic concerned is foundational in nature, to learn at the earliest time possible if students have or have not mastered it; tests can give us that vital information in a timely fashion.

A good start with testing will also mean appreciating that it is a measure of limited precision. While we may report grades to students to two decimal places or more, we never truly know precisely and absolutely the level of mastery that a student has acquired. There are too many factors that affect that final grade, and each factor may contribute to error in the grade assigned. Copperud (p. 5) notes these three factors affecting test reliability:

+ the question itself
+ test administration
+ scoring.

A human being designs the question. The test is administered by a human being in circumstances that may vary in their conduciveness to clear thinking and concentration. The completed test is scored by a human being. At each point, if we hope to establish a measure of the student's degree of mastery of the objectives we have in mind, we lose exactness in that measure.

So what does one do? Does this mean that grades are something close to wild guesses about the level of mastery? Let us hope not. The degree of test validity (how well it measures what we mean to measure) will depend perhaps most on how clearly one communicates learning objectives to the student. This is another point at which college professors—excluding those whose discipline is education, but not including many others—may begin to roll their eyes. Phrases like "learning objectives" do not trip lightly off the tongue of most college faculty members; why, I cannot exactly say, but so it is. Yet the fact is that unless the student knows what you want him or her to learn, *expressed in very clear and understandable terms*, you guarantee both unreliability in your tests and frustration as you grade. A learning objective will give an unambiguous answer to the student's question: What should I be able to *do*? For example, "To understand acid-base chemistry" is *not* a well-stated objective. "To be able to write a balanced chemical equation for the reaction between any acid and base" is. In the first case, the student is left quite uncertain as to what the word "understand" implies for him or her. In the second, the required demonstration of mastery is clear. My counsel to the starting teacher here is to try mightily to overcome any prejudice against drafting and publishing learning objectives; they can make a vast difference in how reliably you test what you want to test. And they can contribute very directly and significantly to student learning.

Assuming you have resolved the matter of learning objectives, there remains the chore of actually constructing the test itself. A basic decision now will be that of choosing between objective and subjective test items, or "questions." You will get plenty of pronounced opinions from experienced faculty about which is better. Table 6.5 sums up the typical arguments on either side of the issue.

Table 6.5
Objective and Subjective Testing

Type of Testing	Typical Assignments and Items	Advantages	Disadvantages
Objective	• Multiple-choice • True-false • Matching	• More questions • Greater reliability • Easier to grade	• Harder to construct • Less organization & integration required • Less freedom for student expression • Allows guessing
Subjective	• Essays • Short-answers • Completion	• Easier to construct • More organization & integration required • More freedom for student expression	• Fewer questions • Less reliability • Harder to grade • Allows bluffing

After Dressel and Marcus (1982).

Neither pro-objective nor pro-subjective faculty can claim compelling research that establishes the overall superiority of one type of testing over the other. While the reliability (consistency of scores when readministered) of objective tests is greater, owing to the greater number of questions that can be asked, only subjective tests call on students to write, a skill that most colleges hope to encourage in students. Proponents of subjective tests often disparage objective tests as shallow in their probing of student knowledge and abilities; how true that turns out to be will depend, of course, very much on the skill and scruples of the test designer. As Robert Ebel points out:

> ...Most good objective test items require the examiner to develop, by creative, original thought, the *basis* for choice among the alternatives. Good objective test items do not permit correct response on the basis of simple recognition, sheer rote memory, or meaningless verbal association....The quality of an objective test is determined largely by the skill of the test constructor. The quality of an essay test is determined largely by the skill of the reader of student answers....In

item writing, perhaps unlike creative writing, the more nearly a sentence means exactly the same thing to every person who reads it..., the more claim it has to respect as an example of literary craftsmanship.[25]

While in Ebel's opinion "it is probably true...that the typical essay test falls farther short of its potential as a measure of educational achievement, than does the typical objective test" (p.130), he underscores as well that both objective and subjective tests can be used to measure almost any important type of classroom learning, and to encourage students to "study for understanding, organization, and application."

I would urge striking a healthy balance in the matter of testing. Extremes are usually a mistake here as they are in other affairs. One should recognize the advantages and disadvantages of both objective and subjective testing, and put together a mix of question types on each test. Including some multiple-choice and matching items can allow you to sample a much wider spectrum of material, and including essay questions will permit students some freedom in demonstrating what they have learned while giving them experience in writing. And lest we forget the impact on the instructor, "balance" will provide some relief to the pro-subjective teacher when tests are being graded, and some to the pro-objective teacher when tests are being constructed.

There have been a great number of books and papers written over the years on the topic of testing and grading (or "evaluation"), and we cannot possibly do justice to the subject here. I will conclude this section with some references that are strongly recommended,[26] and a list of guidelines for testing that I would commend to the new college teacher:

◆ Provide the students with the clearest possible learning objectives.
◆ Design test items that are:
  • clearly related to learning objectives
  • plainly stated
  • practical and relevant, as often as possible
  • not dependent on one another.
◆ Keep test lengths reasonable.
◆ Use a good mix of objective and subjective items.
◆ Keep the testing environment as free from distractions as possible.
◆ Return tests *promptly*, with corrections indicated.

---

[25] Robert L. Ebel, *Essentials of Educational Measurement* (Needham Heights, MA: Allyn & Bacon, 1986), pp. 124, 130, 131.

[26] Some examples: Carol Copperud, *The Test Design Handbook*. (See reference 24); Patrick W. Miller and Harley E. Erickson, *Teacher-Written Student Tests: A Guide for Planning, Creating, Administering, and Assessing* (Washington, DC: National Education Association, 1985); Howard B. Lyman, *Test Scores and What They Mean* (Englewood Cliffs, NJ: Prentice-Hall, 1986); Robert L. Ebel, *Essentials of Educational Measurement*. (See reference 25).

✦ In discussing tests and grades, avoid language that (1) suggests that teacher and student are on opposite "sides," or (2) shifts attention away from learning and onto grades.

Student Evaluations of Teaching

It is better to know nothing than to know what is not so.
Anonymous

I start this section with this quote because there can scarcely have been a larger store of common knowledge—all of it wrong—about any subject discussed perennially on college campuses than there is about student evaluations of teaching. This is not for lack of research, for the research is abundant. It is also not for lack of publicizing by secondary sources,[27] for several have pointed out the persistent "myths" about the reliability of student evaluation data. The new faculty member has an opportunity here, even though it may not be easy to challenge the common wisdom, to start with fact rather than fiction.

In the 1940s and 1950s, few colleges and universities were using student ratings of instruction; by the 1990s, a large majority do. They are used for two purposes, one called summative (used for detecting *whether* there is a problem, and for making decisions about salary, tenure, promotion, retention), the other formative (used for determining *what* the problem might be, and for directing the improvement of one's teaching). A great deal of the debate has been muddied by a failure to get these two uses separated, and arguments made with validity about one are erroneous for the other. It is also very likely that when you, as a new faculty member, ask to see a student evaluation form, you will be unable to discern which items on the form are seen as "summative" and which as "formative." At some institutions the form does separate the two quite well, and the statistical ratings of instruction go to department chair and dean only for the summative items; the instructor alone sees the results for the formative items. True summative items will always be *global* in their nature, for example, "Rate the instructor" or "Rate the course." Formative items will be worded descriptively, for example, "The instructor is well organized" or "The instructor is available to answer questions," and students will be asked to express their level of agreement with these statements.

One reason that many are inclined to be skeptical about the use of student evaluations for deciding promotion and tenure is the confusion between (1) statistical and anecdotal data, and (2) student opinion of instruction and the "true" quality of instruction. Sitting in a faculty lounge, you may well hear this kind of conversation:

---

[27] For example: Lawrence Aleamoni, "Evaluation Myths," *Academic Leader*, October 1985.

Bob: "It's crazy to use those student ratings to judge my teaching."

Mary: "Why?"

Bob: "Well, because there are students in there who just don't like me. Joe Malice in my American History course told my student assistant he was going to get me when student evaluations came around."

Mary (shaking her head): "Oh my goodness! That's what scares me about student ratings. How can they measure how good you are as a teacher, when so much bias creeps into them?"

Bob: "That's what I say. I think we should just use the written comments. Joe would be too lazy to write anything anyway, and the comments help me *much* more than those numbers do."

Here are corrections to the misperceptions revealed by that brief interchange:

Correction #1: Student ratings are, when used appropriately, taken to reflect only how positively students responded to your teaching, *not* to "measure" your actual teaching effectiveness. Student perception surely suggests *something* about effectiveness, but it is only one piece of information to be considered.

Correction #2: One of the values of using *average* ratings for a whole class is that the only number that gets used is that average, not what rating Joe Malice or any other single student assigned. The average rating represents, then, a *class consensus* about your teaching. Unless the class is very small, Joe's bias will matter little to the average.

Correction #3: Written comments by students can indeed be very helpful for *formative* purposes. They are, however, notoriously poor for *summative* purposes, where *statistical* data are far more reliable. The consensus inferred from reading written comments turned in will be distorted by (a) the fact that not everyone takes time to write; (b) the opinion of, say, a very angry person who writes well, can have a disproportionate influence; (c) written comments are hard to analyze and generalize from.

Much of the fallacious conventional wisdom comes simply from drawing statistical conclusions (generalizations) from anecdotal experience (experience with an individual student whose opinion is suspect). We will not take time to discuss the many points at which one's intuition turns out to mislead in this area of student evaluation data, but it is well worth while, as you seek to get off to a good start in teaching, to contemplate what decades of research have established. I add this summary of **corrections to common fallacies** to others that have appeared; the following are *true* statements:

✦ Students rate higher those instructors from whom they learn more.
✦ Students give higher ratings in courses in which they must work harder.
✦ Student ratings are *not* appreciably affected by:
  • gender of instructor or students
  • age of instructor or students
  • grades
  • personality of instructor or students
  • class level (freshman, etc.)
  • class size
  • time class meets.
✦ Student ratings provide reliable data for judging teaching effectiveness.[28]

Teaching is at the heart of the mission of every liberal arts college. Surveys show that about 80% of liberal arts colleges in 1988 said that they always used systematic student ratings in evaluating teaching performance of their faculty, up from 68% in 1983.[29] It should be reassuring to know that these kind of data, used properly, can help assess how well that mission is getting carried out.

Student evaluations are, it would appear, now a firmly entrenched part of the academic scene. They can be of tremendous help to the new faculty member who wants to be the best possible teacher. I have, over the years, seen a great deal of denial on the part of faculty whose student ratings are consistently low; their attempts to "kill the messenger" (student ratings) have inevitably led to their failure to use vital feedback to make improvements that are needed. Student ratings "measure" nothing more than how positive the learning experience, taken overall, has proved for a class. Low student ratings are a symptom that something is amiss, as the students see it. The appropriate response on the part of the teacher is to try in all earnestness to examine the situation objectively, and to see whether anything needs fixing. A conscientious professor will not lower academic standards or forego substance for entertainment, but will aim to make the learning experience as positive as possible. After all, the most basic psychology teaches the reinforcing value of positive experiences—and the avoidance of negative experiences. Given the choice, it simply makes good sense that learning is advanced by a positive environment.

If your campus uses a typical student evaluation form, it has a five-point rating scale. If it has a five-point scale, the campus mean for the "rate the instructor" question (or its equivalent) will be 4.00 ± 0.1—trust me on this! There is no sharp line separating ratings of the "good" from ratings of the "bad." Still, as a rule of thumb, if you find your ratings falling *consistently* more

---

[28] A good summary paper on this topic, and one which contains many useful primary references is: William E. Cashin, "Student Ratings of Teaching: A Summary of the Research," *IDEA Paper No. 20*, (Center for Faculty Evaluation & Development, Kansas State University, 1988).

[29] Peter Seldin, "How Colleges Evaluate Professors, 1988 vs. 1983," *AAHE Bulletin 41*, 3 (1989).

than, say, 0.15 point below the campus mean, you have reason to look for ways to make improvements. Remember, I said *consistently*; you should not get the blues when ratings fall below the mean in one course in one term. You need to look for patterns. An inspection of the set of formative items may give you a clue as to where there is a problem.

Consider the following example of Dr. Adam Newprof's ratings in all his courses for his first fall term. His average was 3.80 on "Rate the instructor," where the college mean was 4.00. There are eight formative items on the form. He puts on a graph (Graph 6.3) his own ratings and those from campus means. On both of the first two items—which are the summative items—"Rate the course" (Crs) and "Rate the instructor" (Instr), he has fallen below the campus mean. He looks next at the eight formative items to the right, beginning with "The instructor improved my knowledge of the subject" (ImpKn) through "The instructor was willing to provide assistance" (Asstc). He is below the mean on four of the eight (ImpKn, Comm, Stim, Grdg), and above on the other four (Org, PosF, Open, Asstc). Obviously, the students were not negatively influenced by those items rated more positively than the campus mean; they found him to be better organized (Org), to display a more positive feeling toward his subject (PosF), to be more open to student questions (Open), and slightly more willing to provide assistance (Asstc). He looks back at the four items where he was rated below the mean. Only on two of those, improving knowledge (ImpKn) and communication (Comm) was the deviation from the mean significant enough to suggest that the students saw his instruction as weaker than that from other instructors on campus. So, he has to reflect on what he might be able to do to work on these two areas. It is worth noting that, while most colleges now use student evaluations and administer them near the end of the term, it can be exceptionally valuable—and can affect positively the final, "formal," end-of-term ratings—for the teacher to have students in a course to do informal midterm evaluations. This is not surprising, since it gives the teacher an opportunity to discover, *at a time when the students can profit from any midcourse adjustments,* how things are going in the students' view. The effect on end-of-term ratings, particularly when the instructor discusses the results with someone else, can be dramatic.[30]

How Much Time Should Teaching Take?

This is your first term of full-time teaching. You have four courses assigned to you. How much time should you be spending on the various aspects of teaching?

When we first took a look at teaching load, back in Chapter 2, we saw what was typical for baccalaureate colleges: 47% of baccalaureate faculty spend 9-12

[30] P. A. Cohen, "Effectiveness of Student-Rating Feedback for Improving College Instruction: A Meta-Analysis of Findings," *Research in Higher Education 13,* (1980) 321.

Graph 6.3
Student Ratings of Dr. Adam Newprof

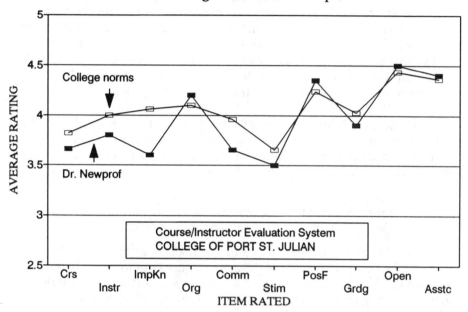

Graph 6.4
Daily Time on Teaching

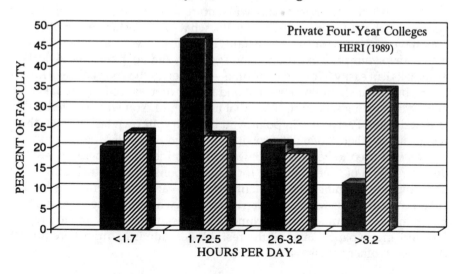

hours per week in the classroom, and 53% spend more than twelve additional hours in preparation for teaching. Those are the figures for *all* faculty, first-year and veterans. Plainly, faculty just preparing courses for the first time, designing tests for the first time, and dealing with student problems for the first time, will find themselves spending far more than twelve hours per week on teaching-related tasks. Some colleges, though not very many, will take into account this disproportionate time investment required for those just beginning their teaching and will lower their in-class obligations during the first year.

It may be more helpful to look at the teaching load data from Chapter 2 on a *per-day* rather than a per-week basis. Graph 6.4 presents teaching load data in these terms, and further simplifies the picture by using fewer ranges. Let's now make some suppositions about you as a new faculty member:

Worst-case Suppositions:
- Your scheduled teaching time is near the mode of 1.7-2.5 hours/day.
- The time required for preparation is high, > 3.2 hours/day.

Let's pin things down further, assuming that "near the mode" actually becomes 2.6 hours/day, and "high" actually turns out to be 5.4 hours/day. This would allow you to be in class 2.6 hours in a given day and spending 5.4 hours preparing for the next day's lectures, grading, and all the rest—a total of 8.0 hours/day. That's a full day by non-academic workplace standards. You will, of course, work more than 8 hours on some days, work less on others (maybe), and do some work outside the five-day week assumed here.

How much time you personally will require will, of course, depend on how you approach your work (see Chapter 10), what prior teaching experience you may have had as a graduate assistant, how closely your assigned courses match up to your prior experience and specialty, and your personal style. Perfectionists can easily allow *all* their time—not merely the "normal" workweek hours, but what should be personal and family time as well—to be taken up getting everything set *just* right for that next lecture. You will need to be alert to that danger. Past a certain point, you become your own task master; there will be no one there saying, "Stop! It's time to go play golf."

You will need to be careful not to let the instinct to "be there for my students" rob you of time you need for other responsibilities—including other dimensions of teaching. One's "Mentor dream" can be powerful. It is hard to cut off conversations with appreciative students who are sitting in your office. But in the end, too much time "schmoozing" means too little time to prepare for class, grade papers, and all the rest. Moderation is in order here no less than it is on other occasions.

Summing Up

The calling to teach—and most beginning faculty in liberal arts colleges do see teaching as a "calling"—is powerful. The vision of teaching well will keep the blood rushing and the midnight oil burning for the committed new faculty member like no other aspect of the faculty profession. And in a profession that pays modestly by the measures of the world, the rewards that come from generating an epiphanic glow on a student's face, or mentoring a neophyte on to demonstrated mastery, are beyond measure. The good start in teaching is indeed the most vital of all.

It is in some respects also the hardest of good starts to make, and that needs very much to be recognized. We come to it, those of us who choose teaching, without formal preparation for the task—but more critically, without *knowing* that we are underprepared, without recognizing that we are mistaking a thorough grounding in the discipline for preparation. Content and process are *both* imperative to good teaching. It is essential to acknowledge that, and to act on it. The challenge, once accepted, is not daunting. The well-grounded disciplinarian will not find reaching pedagogical proficiency overwhelming. I have tried in this chapter to point toward approaches that can afford proficiency, to illumine pathways that I wish someone had lit for me at the outset.

If you are intent on a good start as teacher, you will give thoughtful attention to the objects of that teaching—the students. You will begin your work by recognizing what they are, as opposed to what you wish them to be. You will think of them as *becoming* something more than they were, and welcome your opportunity to help them get there. You will search for insights into what motivates them and recognize their differences from one another—and from you. You will settle on your teaching style with their predilections and receptivity factored realistically into the formula. And you will take seriously their responses to your teaching. You will not react irrationally to the results of student evaluations, but you will be intent on extracting from them helpful clues about what is working and what is getting in the way of learning.

You will look, too, beyond student evaluations to tell you how effectively you are teaching and to guide your teaching improvement over time. One promising new approach is the use of a teaching portfolio. This practice calls for faculty to help select individualized criteria for appraising their teaching, then to document success in meeting these criteria by a wide variety of means. Employment of teaching portfolios may well prove to be a remedy for the enduring concerns that one hears expressed about evidence for effective teaching when faculty personnel committees meet or when department chairs evaluate faculty. Whatever their long-term acceptance for these more formal purposes, they can be most valuable to the individual professor seeking to gain strength as a teacher and confidence about the outcomes of his or her teaching. Peter Seldin's book *The Teaching Portfolio* [31] offers a concise, straightforward

[31] Peter Seldin, *The Teaching Portfolio: A Practical Guide to Improved Performance and Promotion/Tenure Decisions* (Bolton, MA: Anker Publishing Company), 1991.

guide, as well as a number of examples, to assist the new (or experienced) faculty member who is interested in trying this approach.

As you set out, perhaps most important of all is to be clear about the mission you are undertaking as teacher. The mission is *student learning*. Teaching is not an end, but a means. To go further, you and your students will profit from the time taken to reflect just *what* learning you are striving to cause or enable. Your college will be far stronger and those who teach in it more fulfilled if its faculty articulate with evangelistic fervor its ambitions for the broad, enriching study that characterizes the serious liberal arts institution. Those of your students who will profit most are those who see in you not only an authority in statistics or French literature or botany, but also a masterful weaver of cross-disciplinary connections.

For Discussion

1. When did you first begin thinking about becoming a teacher? What was the primary motive for your decision to teach professionally in a college?

2. What do you expect to be your greatest source of satisfaction and reward in a teaching career?

3. Considering that the INTJ personality is the most common MBTI type among college teachers, what teaching difficulties might be anticipated with students whose preference is "E"? "S"? "F"? "P"? What approaches might the teacher employ in working with students of each type?

4. Considering the variety of personality types, and therefore learning preferences, in your classroom, just how far do you believe a college teacher should go in accommodating these preferences?

5. Which of the four teaching orientations described in Table 6.3 do you feel you encountered most often in college? in graduate school? Which do you find most appealing as you decide on an approach for yourself?

6. What are some ways that you can think of to:
   (a) encourage student-teacher conversations to focus on learning rather than on grading?
   (b) use grading to encourage mastery rather than point-counting?
   (c) encourage students to see the student-teacher relationship as collaborative rather than adversarial?

7. What is your reaction to the suggestion in Chapter 6 that:
   (a) a college teacher might take some responsibility for motivating his or her students?

(b) a college teacher might take some responsibility for finding ways to involve students in the learning process?

(c) grading might be a very imprecise process?

(d) student evaluations of teaching might give valid information about teaching effectiveness?

(e) it is possible to invest too much time in your role as teacher?

8. Are you familiar with the services and programs available at your college in support of teaching? Do you know whom to contact to get additional information?

9. Examine the graphical representation (below) of the average student ratings for Dr. Maggie Morrow of the College of Port St. Julian in a recent term. What would you say the students see as Dr. Morrow's principal strengths? To what would you advise her to give more attention? On the whole, how positively are students responding to her teaching relative to that of other College of Port St. Julian professors?

[Key: **Crs** = Rate the course. **Instr** = Rate the instructor. **ImpKn** = The instructor improved my knowledge of the subject. **Org** = The instructor was well prepared and organized. **Comm** = The instructor communicated effectively. **Stim** = The instructor stimulated my intellectual curiosity and interest. **PosF** = The instructor conveyed a positive feeling about the material. **Grdg** = The instructor's grading procedure was impartial. **Open** = The instructor was open to questions. **Asstc** = The instructor was wiling to provide assistance.]

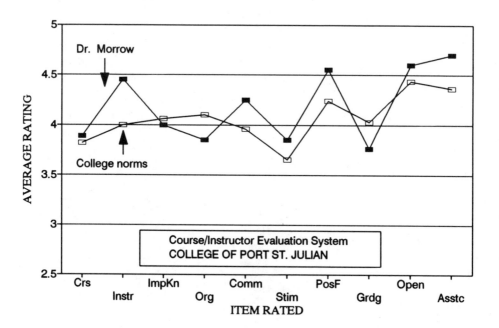

7

What About Scholarship?

The enemy of good teaching is not research, but rather the spirit that says that this is the only worthy or legitimate task for faculty members....The finest teachers are often the best researchers. Imparting to students some of the sense of the wonders, complexities, ambiguities, and uncertainties that accompany the experience of learning and growing can and often should be intimately connected with the dissemination of new knowledge.

Integrity in the College Classroom
Association of American Colleges

ivulets wormed down the long panes of the antique windows. A front had stalled along the coast, and the summer rain that had started in Port St. Julian last night was still coming down. The resurrection ferns that yesterday had been shrivelled and brown were unfurled and green today along the top surfaces of the arthritic live oak limbs outside the laboratory window. After two years at the College of Port St. Julian, Adam Newprof still marveled at that miracle.

But at the moment he wasn't thinking about the rain or the ferns. He was engrossed in the chromatograms that Marty Fresch had spread out on the top of the lab desk. Marty was pointing at one of the tracings, agitated.

"It's crazy!" Marty said. "You can see the ketone. There." He stabbed at one of the peaks that rose up from the baseline traced on the chromatography paper. "But—no product peak. How can that be?"

Newprof stroked his chin and studied the chromatogram. Then he pulled another graph over and studied it. "None here either," he mused. "Strange. Tell me again what you did."

"Okay, I took the ketone and dissolved it in hexane. Then I injected the butyllithium—the new stuff that just came in, brand new bottle—and bubbled in the gas. Stirred it and heated it—under nitrogen, of course—for two hours, took off samples at fifteen-minute intervals, quenched them, and dried them over calcium chloride. That was yesterday. Then today I came in and cranked up the gas chromatograph and ran the samples." He waited for Newprof to comment.

"Sounds right. I wonder...."

"Hey, Einstein!" a voice interrupted. Carlisle Ravenel. "Grab your umbrella and let's beat the crowd to Pete's place."

"Marty, let me think about this over lunch. At the moment, I don't have an answer. But you think about it, too. Go over everything you did again. I'll be back in the lab probably by one."

The rain was steady, but not hard. It pattered on their umbrellas as they crossed the soggy campus and crossed over to the College Street Cafe. People were already in three of the booths, but their favorite up front by the window was still open. They stood the dripping umbrellas in a corner by the doorway and slid into the booth. Pete was there inside a minute. They both ordered "The St. Julian Special," the Greek's famous hamburger that had just a bit of mutton ground up with the beef, grilled in olive oil, and served with a slick slice of purple onion.

"You have Marty pushing back frontiers this summer?" Carlisle asked Adam. "He seemed pretty excited about something."

"Yeah." Adam chuckled. "He's a great kid. I never dreamed he would get as much done this summer as he has. Seems to be a natural."

"*I* never dreamed you would snag him as a chemistry major," Ravenel said. "How'd that happen?"

"I'm not sure. We just seemed to hit it off during his freshman year. He hadn't had high school chemistry and had to work at it pretty hard in the fall, but by the spring term—I don't know—he had sort of caught fire, and he turned out to be the top student in the class that term. After that he signed up for organic and analytical, and last spring he asked me about majoring."

"You let rising juniors do research with you? I don't take anybody but seniors. If I take anyone at all."

"We mostly take rising seniors, too, for summer projects. But Marty was *so* intent on doing a project with me that I couldn't turn him down. And it was a good decision. I let him pick up where Angela Park left off when she graduated last spring, and he's already accomplished enough in a month to do an Academy of Science presentation, or pretty close to it."

"I heard Angela's presentation last year. She did a *terrific* job. Better than some of the professors from the university."

"Yeah, that gave me a real payoff. Do you know, when she first tried to rehearse her presentation, she was *frozen*. I mean, she couldn't say a *word*. But once I got her started, she picked up confidence like a freight train picking up steam. We rehearsed about five times, and she was ready. I was really pleased to see her win the Outstanding Undergraduate Paper award."

Pete showed up with the St. Julian Specials. The onions smelled marvelous. Newprof took a bite and chewed with relish.

"Well," Ravenel said, "I teach biology, not research. And I don't know how you find time for it all. This fall will start my fifth year at the college, and I just can't get cranked up. I came out of Duke feeling really on top of my field and thinking I'd keep up with the herpetology literature, but..." He shrugged, and chomped down on the S.J. Special, as he, Adam, and Maggie Morrow called them.

Newprof sipped iced tea. "I'm not doing anything big-time. But I guess teaching students to search somewhere besides a textbook is one of my motivations. I think that's our responsibility."

"Whatever keeps the dean happy," Ravenel said wryly.

Newprof found himself thinking about Marty Fresch's mystery. There *should* be a product peak on those chromatograms. Why was it missing? The ketone peak was shrinking as it should. So why—? Ah! He had an idea. He was anxious to get back and check with Marty on it.

The Role of Scholarship in a Liberal Arts College

The title of this chapter is a question: *What about scholarship?* It is, in a way, a strange question to have come up on a college campus, the approximate equivalent of asking, "What about physical fitness?" in a gymnasium. Is not scholarship the *sine qua non* of the academy? Is it not the ideal we are committed to instilling in the hearts and minds of the new high school graduates who come onto our campuses every fall? Yet it is a question asked by hundreds of faculty members entering the teaching ranks each fall—and one asked by whole colleges as well. It is a question that will be very real to you as a new faculty member; you will need to answer it, and act on your answer. No matter the degree of formal emphasis your first college puts on research and scholarship, you will discover in some future year that your own career as an academic, your sense of continuing mastery of your discipline, your recognition by peers, and your professional options have been affected by your decisions now—at the start. How should you answer?

Perhaps we should begin to find an answer by going back for a second look at how the liberal arts colleges and the research universities became separated, a process that we noted in the section on "The Central Mission" in Chapter 6, then see where that has brought American higher education with respect to this question of research and scholarship. The original, ancient notion of *artes liberales*, Aristotle's investigations notwithstanding, surely did not carry with it a requirement for research. It was, as we have seen in Chapter 5, an orator's curriculum and was aimed, not toward the creation of new knowledge, but toward preserving and passing on a body of knowledge accepted as fixed. The transformation of American higher education began after the Civil War and proceeded rapidly after 1900, when knowledge, particularly in the sciences, began to burgeon rapidly. In the speeches and writings of the college and university presidents, one hears the commencement of debates raging still in the halls—and faculty lounges—of academia. Charles Eliot, who became president of Harvard in 1869, remarked, for example:

> ...[A] university which is not a place of research will not long continue to be a good place of teaching.[1]

And Johns Hopkins' president, Daniel Coit Gilman, looking at the same connection from the other direction, observed:

> The scholar does but half his duty who simply acquires knowledge. He must share his possessions with others. This is done, in the first place, by the instruction of pupils...The process of acquiring seems to be promoted by that of imparting.[2]

To some *artes liberales* purists, it was as if a germ had crept into education. Nineteenth century American professors, after experience with German universities, were coming back singing the praises of *Lehrfreiheit* and *Lernfreiheit*— freedom to teach and freedom to learn whatever one wishes—and the specialized study going on there. The appeal of the German model took hold firmly. By the early 1900s not only the activities, teaching methods, and responsibilities of their faculty, but the very organizational structures of the American universities had changed permanently.

With the prominent rise of research as a focus of higher education, and with a recognition that the smaller liberal arts colleges were unable to afford the libraries, much less the scientific equipment, needed to carry on research, some educators expected the eventual demise of the small college—and some even called into question the need for attention to liberal education.[3] But the liberal arts colleges had other ideas. Their leaders, although often at odds with one another about the proper definition of the liberal arts, nevertheless agreed that their colleges represented the intellectual and philosophical bulwarks against the anathema of utilitarian and preprofessional education, the keeper of the *artes liberales* tradition. They failed to die.

But they did not survive unaffected. As Kimball describes it:

> It was natural...that in the American liberal arts college the oratorical tradition of civic and polite learning militated against the specialized research of the uni-

---

[1] Charles W. Eliot, *Educational Reform: Essays and Addresses* (New York, NY: Century Co., 1898), p. 231.

[2] Daniel C. Gilman, *University Problems in the United States* (New York, NY: Century Co., 1898), pp. 57-58.

[3] See for example: (1) William R. Harper, *The Prospects of the Small College* (Chicago, IL: University of Chicago Press, 1900); and (2) Daniel C. Gilman, "Is it Worth While to Uphold Any Longer the Idea of Liberal Education?", *Educational Review* 3 (1892).

versity...But [their] commitments alone...in the ideal of the Christian gentleman could [not] long withstand the pressures of urbanization and industrial-
ization, the decline of evangelism, the advance of Darwinism, and the general
success of the university model. By 1900, even the small Christian colleges
began to devote themselves to the transmission of specialized learning.[4]

That does not mean that the liberal arts colleges embraced research in their
mission statements. There remained the conviction in many quarters that any
subject that was "useful" did not belong in the curriculum, and neither did
the research of the German university. The only valid mission for any liberal
arts college was to transmit knowledge to others.

The polemics have not waned as the decades of the new century have
passed. Further evolution has, however, taken place, and as we approach
another new century, the research climate spectrum looks roughly like the
scheme shown in Table 7.1. Distinctions in reality can never be drawn as
sharply as they are shown there, of course; there are institutions that are a
challenge to classify, where there may even be contradiction between what is
supported by rhetoric and what tenure and promotion policies require, for
instance. The research colleges represent the most public compromise with
tradition. These are very selective four-year colleges with considerable stature,
where the aim is to combine the conduct of first-rate research with the curriculum of the liberal arts college. Both liberal arts and comprehensive colleges
can, in theory, fall anywhere to the left of the research universities; i.e., may
consider themselves "research colleges" or any one of the three "teaching college" types.

One should not, let me underscore, imagine that the device represented by
Table 7.1 is meant to suggest that there are *equal numbers* of the five different
institutional types. Indeed, I suspect that if the counts were done and the table
were redrawn showing a proportionality to climates experienced by *numbers*
of students and faculties, it would appear to collapse, for all practical purposes, into *three* columns, except that the middle column should be far smaller
and the right-hand column still much larger.

TEACHING	TEACHING with RESEARCH	RESEARCH with TEACHING

[4] Bruce A. Kimball, *Orators & Philosophers* (New York, NY: Teachers College Press, 1986), p. 165.

There are more small colleges than large universities in America, but the enrollment of a liberal arts college averages about 1/20 that of a research university and has far fewer faculty. In other words, in terms of climates for learning and teaching, the student and faculty member are faced with essentially *two* likely climates, the teaching-only or the research-dominated climate. The teaching-with-research colleges are still small in number, although all indications are that the number is growing. It is hard to know just how far the trend will spread, but for faculty members who want a small-college environment with support for the active scholarship that they came to enjoy in graduate school, the prospects are, at present, improving.

Robert Pirsig, a former college professor, wrote in *Zen and the Art of Motorcycle Maintenance*, about the typical climate as described on the far-left of Table 7.1:

> The school is what could euphemistically be called a "teaching college." At a teaching college you teach and you teach and you teach with no time for research, no time for contemplation, no time for participation in outside affairs. You just teach and teach until your mind grows dull and your creativity vanishes and you become an automaton saying the same dull things over and over to endless waves of innocent students who cannot understand why you are dull, lose respect and fan this disrespect out into the community. The reason you teach and you teach and you teach is that this is a very clever way of run-

Table 7.1
Climates for Research

TEACHING COLLEGES			RESEARCH COLLEGES	RESEARCH UNIVERSITIES
Tolerant	**Welcoming**	**Supporting**		
• Allow research	• Welcome research	• Encourage research	• Expect research	• Emphasize research
• Do not encourage by rhetoric	• Welcome by rhetoric	• Encourage by rhetoric	• Encourage strongly by rhetoric	• Demand by rhetoric
• Do not encourage with funds & time	• Do not encourage with funds & time	• Encourage with funds and time	• Encourage with funds and time • Encourage external grants	• Encourage with funds and time • Demand external grants
• Not considered for tenure & promotion	• Not important for tenure & promotion	• Influential for tenure & promotion	• Important for tenure & promotion	• Demand for tenure & promotion

ning a college on the cheap while giving the false appearance of genuine education.[5]

There is cynicism, to be sure, in Pirsig's description. But there is no disputing its essential accuracy as a depiction of many small colleges in America. There is an American tendency toward extremes. Much of the debate about the place of research and scholarship in the liberal arts college you will hear couched in conflictual terms, with research set *against* teaching. One sees articles or headings in books with titles like "Teaching *vs* Research," for example. Or you will hear in the faculty lounge someone drinking coffee and declaring, "I came here to *teach*. I can't possibly teach and do research too." As a new faculty member trying to get one's bearings in this rhetorical weather, you need to recognize that, however heartfelt the convictions of the debater using that kind of language, there is a pronounced red-herring quality to such arguments. It is true that there are only twenty-four hours in a day, and that one cannot use any one of them twice, but the claim that research only uses up time that would otherwise be spent improving teaching can rarely, if ever, be substantiated. Examples of good research can be found on campuses sprinkled from one end of the spectrum to the other. Faculty, like anyone else, usually find time to do the things they want to do most. Arguments against research on grounds that it is in mortal combat with teaching will, on close scrutiny, turn out to be arguments by faculty members whose priorities are quite simply somewhere else other than on active scholarship.

You will often hear arguments for research emphasis in a college on the grounds that "it makes you a better teacher," something referred to as the "spillover effect." Research has, not surprisingly, been done on this question of spillover. In one study, for instance, when colleagues were asked to rate both research and teaching effectiveness, the two correlated positively.[6] Yet the picture is not clear: Some studies have supported this thesis; others have not. For example, a study by Centra found a moderate positive correlation between research productivity and student ratings of instruction only for teachers of social science; for others the correlation was very nearly zero. Even this study has bearing, however, on the contention that time on research detracts from teaching. Centra notes: "The lack of consistent negative correlations between research productivity and teacher ratings in this and other studies indicates that performance as a scholar or researcher does not significantly detract from performance as a teacher."[7]

[5] Robert M. Pirsig, *Zen and the Art of Motorcycle Maintenance* (New York, NY: William Morrow, 1974), p. 147.

[6] P. Wood, "Student and Peer Ratings of College Teaching and Peer Ratings of Research and Service." Paper presented at the annual meeting of the American Educational Research Association, Toronto, March 1978; cited in Ref. 7.

[7] John A. Centra, "Research Productivity and Teaching Effectiveness," *Research in Higher Education* 18, (1983) 379-389.

   This assurance is reinforced by what faculty on liberal arts college campuses say themselves. In the Carnegie Foundation for the Advancement of Teaching survey of 1989, about two-thirds (68%) report that they are currently engaged in a scholarly work that they expect to lead to publication, an exhibit, or a music recital. A significant number (44%) also reported receiving some institutional support for their scholarly work. And while 39% said that it was difficult for a person to achieve tenure there without publishing, only 21% felt that pressure to publish reduced the quality of teaching. These various factors relating to research emphasis on liberal arts college campuses are summarized in Graph 7.1.[8]

   The very best liberal arts colleges (in my view) have, as we wind up the century, kept teaching connected to research, have defined scholarship broadly, and have avoided the two extreme climates. In colleges where trustees and administrators have cared most deeply about the climate in which teaching and learning take place, where they have determined to keep faculty alive and lively over a full career, and to keep students learning in an environment that is intellectually stimulating, "running a college on the cheap" has never been entertained as an option. At these colleges, the choice is not at all teaching *or* research, for the two are not seen as enemies. Far from it. On these campuses,

Graph 7.1
Research on Liberal Arts Campuses

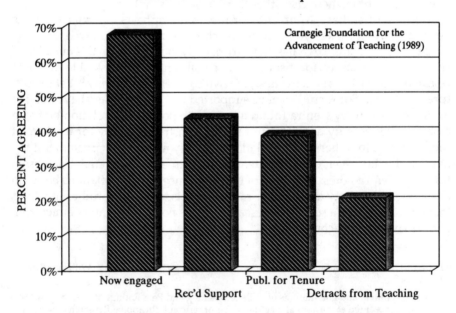

[8] Ernest L. Boyer, *The Condition of the Professoriate: Attitudes and Trends, 1989* (Princeton, NJ: The Carnegie Foundation for the Advancement of Teaching, 1989), pp. 47ff.

the connection between scholarly inquiry—call it "research" or whatever—and the preparation of students for a life of intellectual satisfaction and deftness—call it "teaching"—is self-evident to faculty and administration alike. They have observed the football hero who graduates in top physical form, but who returns years later as a coach with the fitness turned to flab—and they see the academic analogy. Intellectual activity, people on these campuses recognize, is a necessary means of keeping intellectually fit enough to be always at one's best as a teacher.

So—how should you, as a new faculty member deciding on priorities, answer the question: *What about scholarship?* I would contend that the best course is to choose scholarship. Active and visible commitment to scholarship, while it offers no guarantee that you will *automatically* be better as a teacher, will *interfere* with teaching *only* if you permit that—and it can surely *enhance* your effectiveness as teacher, if you enter into the profession of teaching self-consciously *planning* to connect teaching with scholarship. Your first college may very well be a "tolerating" institution, where there are neither overt pressures nor subtle enticements to enter a life of research and professional vigor. And that may seem the most inviting of environments for your career. But down the road—and not very far down the road at that—the faculty member who has stayed current in the discipline, has been productive as a scholar, and has built a *vitae* that reveals a continuing record of scholarly vitality, will have a professional currency and a set of options that are slipping quickly away from the faculty member who chose at the start to shelve his or her dissertation, pick up a textbook, and eschew active inquiry and creativity forever.

We all have known students who neglected serious study in a course from the start. The first week there was no problem and no panic; the second week there was a little quiz where things didn't go so well, but, well, the *big* test was up ahead; the third week the big test came, and there was so much more material to master than expected, and the test was a bomb; and...until a hole has been dug that is too big to climb out of. That is a very apt metaphor for the first-year faculty member faced with the question of scholarship. The start is important. The seeds of the finish are in the start. You have the choice. Choose scholarship.

Payoffs from Scholarship

Back in Pete Makropolos's College Street Café, Professor Carlisle Ravenel has suggested one kind of impetus for a new faculty member to get started with a program of scholarship. "Whatever keeps the dean happy," he just said. There are better reasons, as I suggest above.

A dean's hopes or expectations for faculty may or may not get translated into reality. To the extent that they do get taken seriously, it should never be, of course, just because they are the dean's hopes or expectations. Each faculty member—junior and senior—must decide to what extent scholarship promises a "payoff," and whether that payoff is worthy of motivation for a dedicated teacher. There are three generally recognized areas of benefits for investments of teachers in active, personal scholarship. Some types of returns have been pointed out above. These and others are included in the following summary.

✦ Payoffs for the student
  • Students working directly with faculty members as co-learners receive a perspective on learning otherwise unavailable to them.
  • Students who do research and independent study with faculty learn to function more independently.
  • Students who see a faculty mentor actively engaged in a discipline are more likely to see the discipline as an area for continuing study rather than just a subject to be "passed."
  • Students are more likely to be stimulated by faculty who bring information, anecdotes, and illustrations into the classroom from their own investigation and study of the discipline.
  • Students who present or publish papers co-authored with faculty gain a special confidence in themselves as scholars and strengthen their opportunities for graduate study and employment.

✦ Payoffs for the faculty member
  • Faculty usually enjoy learning more about their discipline and getting answers to questions in the discipline.
  • Faculty who feel they are staying current maintain their confidence as professionals over years of teaching.
  • Faculty who have records of professional accomplishment are more mobile in their careers.

✦ Payoffs for the college
  • The college whose graduates leave with a high degree of intellectual independence and a special appreciation for intellectual inquiry and creativity enhance the reputation of their alma mater.
  • The college whose reputation is enhanced by the visible scholarship of its faculty and graduates attracts more of the high-caliber students and faculty.
  • The college whose reputation is enhanced by the professional accomplishments of its faculty and graduates attracts more financial support from benefactors who want to be associated with success and to advance worthwhile enterprises.

Evidence of Scholarship

As with teaching, you will hear faculty worrying aloud in faculty lounges on liberal arts college campuses that when the time comes to have their scholarship judged, "the system" will fail. This is not different from the worry of students that they might study and master the material to be covered by an exam, but that the exam might be too flawed to discover their mastery. If one *is* devoted to scholarship and one *does* scholarly things, the challenge to a college is, indeed, to recognize that scholarship. What can you, the new faculty member, expect?

Peter Seldin has surveyed liberal arts college deans at five-year intervals to determine what their campuses consider to be "major" factors in evaluating overall performance of faculty. Of the thirteen items included in the survey, five relate to one's professional activity: research, publication, public service, consultation, and activity in professional societies. The results are informative. Looking at what emphasis has been given to research, publications, and activity in professional societies, three common types of evidence, we see that each of these is considered more important now than it was ten years ago. Graph 7.2 shows the trends, which suggest confirmation of the continuing shift of expectations toward increased scholarship in liberal arts colleges. It is also worthwhile noting that, as Seldin points out, "scholarly research/publication" is "always used in evaluating *teaching* performance" by no less than 29% of the colleges [*emphasis added*].[9]

Graph 7.2
Major Scholarship Factors in Faculty Evaluation

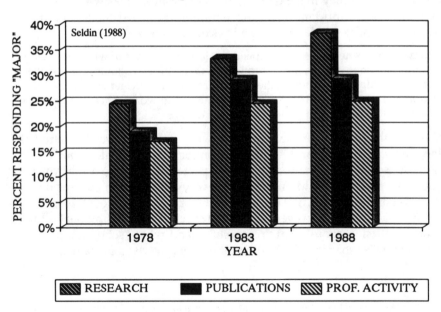

---

[9] Peter Seldin, "How Colleges Evaluate Faculty," *AAHE Bulletin 41*, (1989).

The language in this chapter has been slightly slippery, let me acknowledge, until now. "Research" and "scholarship" have been used fairly interchangeably. I suspect that faculty worry over expectations for and evidence of scholarship because the small word "research" conjures up an image of the whole research university environment that so many of us selected *against*. In most liberal arts colleges, there have been sincere efforts to respond to the calls for a redefinition of scholarship such as that found in *Involvement in Learning*:

> We believe that keeping current in one's field is vital to good teaching and that any attempt to denigrate the importance of scholarship will be harmful to the quality of undergraduate instruction. We favor a learned professoriate, and we believe that love of subject matter is essential to effective teaching. *A broader definition of scholarship*, we believe, will encourage faculty members and institutions to be more realistic in their expectations...[Emphasis added.][10]

Ernest Boyer, in his book, *Scholarship Reconsidered: Priorities of the Professoriate*, elaborates such a proposed broadened definition, one that includes—along with "the scholarship of discovery"—"the scholarship of integration," "the scholarship of application," and "the scholarship of teaching."[11] This call by so prominent an educator will surely be wrongly used in some quarters as permission to abandon the pursuit of research, and simply to relabel whatever kind of teaching they may be doing as "scholarship." This would be an outcome that I am confident Boyer did not intend; his insistence on universal practice of faculty scholarship is made clear elsewhere:

> Scholarship is not an esoteric appendage; it is at the heart of what the profession is all about. All faculty, throughout their careers, should, themselves, remain students. As scholars, they must continue to learn and be seriously and continuously engaged in the expanding intellectual world. This is essential to the vitality and vigor of the undergraduate college.[12]

Whatever the risk that "reconsideration" will result in an overdrawn redefinition, I am convinced that this kind of attention to and debate about what we mean by "scholarship" is needed, and I expect much good to come from it, for it strikes a resonant chord on campuses everywhere—even in some quarters on university campuses, and certainly at the liberal arts colleges. It strikes me that we in academia , however, lean far too much toward definitional solutions to this confusion about what "research" is and what "scholarship" is, and whether one is broader than the other. We worry overly, too, about *lists* of evi-

[10] National Institute of Education, *Involvement in Learning: Realizing the Potential of American Higher Education* (Washington, DC: U.S. Government Printing Office, 1984), p. 50.

[11] Ernest L. Boyer, *Scholarship Reconsidered: Priorities of the Professoriate* (Princeton, NJ: Princeton University Press, 1990), 23-24.

[12] Ernest L. Boyer, *College: The Undergraduate Experience in America* (New York, NY: Harper and Row, 1987), p. 131.

dential items. As a new faculty member, particularly if you are in a "research college," you may well have asked already about "how many publications are required for tenure" at your new college. While one's intent in asking such questions will be both innocent and practical, let me encourage you to look at the matter of evidence in a different, and I hope a more reassuring way.

If one is devoted to scholarship and one does scholarly things, I suggest that the evidence will take care of itself. Think of it this way: if scholarship were a crime, could you be convicted? The evidence will not consist of lists, but of patterns. It will not come from mindless "number crunching," but from honest and sensitive study of the record. At a liberal arts college, the specific patterns will be varied and individual, but they will all be recognizable. In most liberal arts colleges, one would expect to see these patterns heavily colored by the central mission of teaching. I would expect all of the following to be found in the patterns of some teacher-scholars, but no one pattern would contain them all.

+ Investigation and inquiry
  - student research and independent study direction
  - individual research projects in the laboratory or library
  - collaborative research projects with peers elsewhere
  - research into effective pedagogical approaches
  - classroom research
  - works in progress

+ Writing
  - papers for on-campus discussion
  - monographs, books, essays and papers for publication
  - texts, study guides, manuals
  - poetry
  - fiction
  - reviews
  - progress reports on research projects

+ Presentations
  - at local, regional and national symposia
  - at on-campus symposia

+ Creations
  - works of art
  - musical compositions
  - computer software

+ Editing and refereeing
  - editing professional journals
  - refereeing manuscripts
  - reviewing grant proposals

✦ Professional recognition
  • professional awards
  • invited reviews
  • invited papers
  • election to office in professional societies

✦ Grants
  • internal awards in support of projects
  • external awards in support of projects

✦ Professional society activities
  • travel to professional meetings
  • participation in programs (panelist, session chair)
  • service as officer

✦ Collaboration
  • college-school collaborations in academic disciplines
  • consulting

Although the above has the look of a list, one should not use it that way. It is meant to enumerate all the reasonable ways that occur to me to give clues to others that one is a practicing scholar. Those reviewing the evidence will need to examine it for compelling patterns. A dash of this and drop of that are not apt to be seen as a compelling pattern. And there are no equivalencies that say, "Four professional meetings equals one published paper." But if someone sees that Adam Newprof has directed a student in a butyllithium project, given a butyllithium paper at the Southeastern Regional American Chemical Society meeting, attended the national meeting of the American Chemical Society, received a Faculty Research Grant for an investigation of butyllithium reactions with alkyl halides, and given an invited seminar at Furman University— the pattern emerges without strain.

To give some idea of the portion of four-year college faculty who actually have published, inspect Graphs 7.3 and 7.4. While more attention is being given to research and scholarship, if writing and publication were used as the only measure of "scholarship," a great many would be in trouble; over half have written nothing professionally in the past two years (Graph 7.3), and in their overall career to date, over 30% have never published an article, about 60% have never published a book, and nearly 75% have never published chapters in a book or monograph (Graph 7.4).

These graphs are intended, not to convey the message that publication doesn't matter, but rather to show the actual extent of involvement of liberal arts faculty in this kind of scholarly activity. Every college is individual, obviously, and the level of scholarly activity, particularly the frequency and quality of publications, is set locally in light of local traditions and goals. You will need to make abundantly certain that you have a sense of the expectations at

Graph 7.3
Number of Faculty Writings

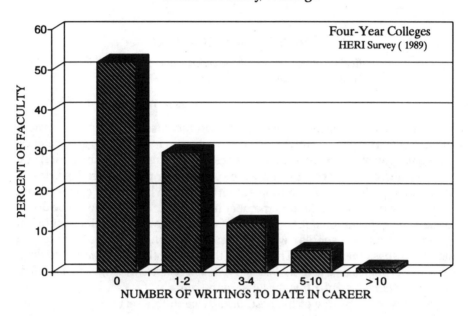

Graph 7.4
Faculty Publishing

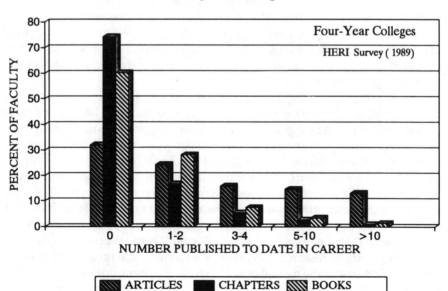

your college. And remember: Whether everyone else is doing it or not, it is one excellent way to keep sharp as a scholar and to keep your own options more open.

Getting Started As a Scholar

Alice: Would you please tell me which way I ought to go?
Cheshire Cat: That depends on where you want to get to.
Lewis Carroll
Alice in Wonderland

There has been a steady trend toward an increased attention to demonstrated scholarship for faculty, we have noted, even in the liberal arts colleges. Yet a great gap still separates these colleges from the research universities, and the spectrum of standards is quite wide even among the small colleges themselves. In a guide like this, nothing authoritative can be said, of course, about what a specific first-year faculty member in a specific college should be doing to meet the expectations of that college. So I am approaching this section on getting started as a scholar with an assumption that you are not seeking merely to "pass the course." This will be the assumption: *You want to establish a program of professional activity that will keep you competent, confident, and stimulating as a teacher-scholar throughout an entire career.*

If you want to be one of the best, the advice in this section will serve you well. If your college at this point in its history places minimal interest on active scholarship, and you are positive you will never want to leave, you can do less. Even then, it is well to consider, as Spenser said, that "all is mutabilitie." Colleges do change. A new president, a new dean, a new chairman of the board, and new directions get set, new expectations held up. So I am assuming from here on that (a) you have indeed chosen scholarship as a way of life; (b) you are planning a career in a liberal arts college setting; and (c) you want to get off to the best possible start.

The first thing you should accept is that only the very exceptional first-year faculty member can land running. The first year, if you have had no prior full-time experience, will be more full than you can imagine. If you have negotiated a reduced teaching load in your "neophyte" year, that will help some, but even with that you will feel very pushed. Part of that feeling will come simply from being in a new environment and from being uncertain much of the time about what is the wisest way to spend your next hour. Many of those hours you will spend preparing brand new courses. You will be able to handle it, even when the papers start coming in for grading, but you owe it to yourself to begin with realistic expectations for yourself. There will be strong temptation to forget about research and other professional activity altogether in the first year. Remember the metaphor of the student starting out in a course; your first year is the first week of the course. Psychologist Roger Baldwin says to the first-year faculty member:

The new teacher must avoid becoming so consumed by instructional responsibilities that professional development and research are neglected.[13]

Good advice. But I would urge that your professional activity goals that year focus simply on planning and preparing, getting ready for the second year. Unless you have something left over from graduate studies that is practically ready for presentation or publication, that will be enough. Let teaching take its rightful place at the head of your priorities, and just expect that it will dominate your days (and nights!) in year one. I make more specific suggestions about that first year in Table 7.2. The primary goal for the first year: *Get a plan in place for a* program *of scholarship.*

After that first year, you should be ready to move purposefully forward, picking up your pace. There will still be some new course preparations, very probably, but you will have a year of experience under your belt, and less energy and time will be demanded for keeping your teaching strong. It will be important to make certain that your professional development plan is moving forward. Goal for the second year: *Get work underway.*

The third year should put you in still firmer territory, both with your teaching and your scholarship. You should have a routine established for yourself, at least approximately, and should be feeling a sense of accomplishment. By now you should be able see some product from your plans, perhaps a presentation somewhere, or, if you have used your two summers especially well, you may even have a modest paper ready for submission. The point is to have begun establishing an indisputable pattern of scholarship. Goal for the third year: *Realize a product.*

After the third year, you will be 3/5 or 3/6 or 3/7 (or in a few places, 3/10) of the way towards your college's tenure decision. You should lay out a plan each year for the year following, and should assess progress at the end of one year before planning for the next. Assess progress *explicitly*; I would suggest in the form of a brief, written progress report that compares the year's outcomes with both your own stated goals and the institutional standards for tenure. Each year should be adding to the scholarly record. By that I am not proposing that you feel pressure to publish every year, but as a rule of thumb *you should be publishing or presenting papers about every other year at a minimum.* (Remember, this is not advice for "passing," but for doing well. In a few colleges this would be minimal "C" work, but in most liberal arts colleges, where teaching loads are twelve hours or more per week, this will, as part of a larger pattern of professional activity, establish you as a solid scholar.)

---

[13] Roger G. Baldwin, "Faculty Career Stages and Implications for Professional Development," in Jack H. Schuster, Daniel W. Wheeler, and Associates, *Enhancing Faculty Careers* (San Francisco, CA: Jossey-Bass, 1990), p. 32.

In addition to this suggested plan for movement into full-fledged status as a scholar, these continuing emphases are offered:

+ Use student and colleague collaborators as often as possible.
+ Keep your "niche" defined narrowly enough to focus your study/investigation.
+ Start modestly and work up; don't wait for a master work.

In a liberal arts college especially, collaboration with students is the most obvious way to connect research with teaching. Efficient and effective progress with scholarly inquiry, either in the library or the laboratory, is to kill as many

Table 7.2
Suggested Timetable for Establishing a Program of Professional Activity

Year	Major Goal	Suggested Objectives
Year 1	Map out a professional plan	• Decide on a "niche" for research (scholarly investigation/study). • Write out a plan for beginning a program of research. • Investigate support, released-time, schedule. • Investigate opportunities for peer collaboration. • Arrange for student collaboration next year. • Go to a professional meeting. • Scan the literature, mark for summer reading.
Year 2	Get the plan underway	• Keep current with the literature. • Direct a student in a project connected with your research. • Begin a regular schedule of library/laboratory study/investigation. • Apply for a grant in support of your research. • Prepare for presentation/publication next year. • Arrange for student collaboration next year. • Go to a professional meeting. • Write during the summer. • Evaluate your progress; write a plan for next year.
Year 3	Realize a product	• Keep current with the literature. • Direct a student in a project connected with your research. • Keep a regular schedule of library/laboratory study/investigation. • Present/submit manuscript for publication. • Go to a professional meeting. • Write/study during the summer. • Evaluate your progress; write a plan for next year.

birds as one can with a single stone. Properly planned and directed, a student research or independent study project will contribute to your own work while contributing with no less value to the student's educational experience. Adam Newprof has discovered that; Carlisle Ravenel has not. Working directly with a faculty member provides opportunity, too, for mentoring that cannot be equaled in the classroom. You will also be much better able to give expert and enthusiastic direction to the student whose research is in your "niche." People in the sciences usually manage to make better use of student collaboration than do faculty from the humanities and social sciences, although there are exceptions. There is no inherent reason that a student cannot, for example, contribute to the library work of someone in, say, Elizabethan history, and the Elizabethan historian involved in collaboration with that student can truly be *collaborating*, i.e., learning *with* the student as the faculty member reviews bibliographic references unearthed and reports written.

Collaboration with peers, either in your own department or outside it, is also a fine way to make more substantial progress with research when time is limited. Some faculty in liberal arts colleges have established profitable, long-term working arrangements with colleagues in corresponding departments of nearby (or sometimes distant) universities. Working solo is a more natural mode for the typical faculty member, but the benefits of collaboration make it worth consideration.

Keeping a narrowly defined niche staked out for your research also makes eminent sense. The use of the word program is meant to imply that one has defined that niche, is keeping up with the literature for that manageable area, and is aligning the rest of the professional development plan with it: student projects, grant support, collaborations, and products. It is too common to see faculty at tenure time whose professional efforts have been so scattered, that no pattern is detectable in them other than disarray and even dilettantism.

You should not hesitate, if your department chair does not think of it first, to ask for a class schedule in the second year (and every year!) that puts together as large a block of unbroken time as can be managed. Grouping classes on, say, Monday, Wednesday, and Friday can leave several hours uninterrupted by classes on Tuesday or Thursday during which you can work on your study and research with greatest advantage.

The summers can also provide an ideal time for the scholar in a liberal arts college. You know the old story: someone is asked what three things he likes best about teaching, and he answers, "June, July and August." For many of us who chose teaching there was unquestionably a strong attraction to a work that pinned us down for only nine months of the year. We liked the prospect of reading, reflecting and writing during three pleasant, low-pressure months. It *can* be that way. Summers can be the time that you get caught up on the literature, write a few chapters on a book, pull together the work of the last two years for a paper, and ponder where your research should go next. Whether it turns out to be that way will depend squarely on the kind of start you get in your use of summers. Summer teaching, the allure of an added summer salary, will tempt you exceedingly. But, if you can avoid "getting hooked" on that extra income, the summers can be an extraordinarily productive and rejuvenating time. If your college offers stipends for summer researchers, you should apply for one at the earliest possible point, and as often thereafter as policies will allow. This will help to relieve your guilt over not "working" (i.e., teaching), and assist financially while you do the work of a scholar. There are also often opportunities, particularly in the sciences, to get funding through a university to do collaborative work on the university campus.

The pace recommended in Table 7.2 will need to be speeded up if your college has established greater expectations. And the objectives in the table will obviously need to be modified somewhat for faculty in the arts. The yearly major goals are the same. Of course, there are also opportunities for artists to present and publish as well as to create artistic works. Indeed, the table is intended only as a means of giving direction as one sets out; modifications will surely be needed to fit anyone's specific circumstances, artist or biologist, historian or economist.

How Much Time Should Scholarship Take?

We saw earlier that the studies support the contention that spending time on research does not have a detrimental effect on teaching,[14] all conventional wisdom to the contrary. But it *does* take time. How much should you plan to devote to scholarship activities? From the discussion and timetable (Table 7.2) above, it is clear that what is being recommended is a phase-in of scholarship activities as the time required to prepare for teaching diminishes. In the first year, the important thing to assure is that your plans for research don't become moribund just when they should be aborning.

In the HERI survey of 1989 (see Graph 7.5), faculty of private, four-year colleges reported their investments of time in research and writing. The mode in that study was 1-4 hours per week, with 38% falling in that range. Another 38% invest more than four hours per week, and 24% give no time to scholarship at all. If we assume that you are in the first year of your timetable (Table 7.2), devoting most of your first-year energies to teaching, but with serious plans for scholarship, an estimate of five hours a week—an hour a day—is reasonable. To the extent that you can shift some of that time expenditure into the summer, you will be able to reduce the weekly expenditure. In subsequent years, more time will be needed if you stay on track.

Summing Up

A good start as a scholar is, in every way except the psychological, rather easy. You have learned thoroughly in graduate school the literature and tech-

---

[14] See Centra reference 7 above.

niques of your discipline. You know the large unanswered questions and many of the principal scholars in the field who are pursuing the answers. You have produced at least one scholarly work, your dissertation, that has passed muster with established experts in the field. The odds are good that you still feel the exhilaration of productive intellectual inquiry. The odds are equally good that you feel more trepidation about getting started as a scholar than about any other aspect of your new career. It can help a great deal to get beyond vague anxiety, to reflect on what is producing it, and to act on what you discover.

The first instinct is nearly always to attribute a halting start as a scholar to lack of time. Let me suggest that time, while not irrelevant, is also not the number one hindrance. The academic woods are full of very busy teacher-scholars who schedule time for work in the library and the laboratory, and who integrate into their workday periods for writing and creativity (more about this in Chapter 10). The new faculty member who waits until there is "extra" time for scholarship can expect never to get started at all. If time is not the barrier, what is? It is this: At the very beginning of the faculty career one finds in the way of scholarship a unique psychological mountain, what a chemist like

Graph 7.5
Time on Research and Writing

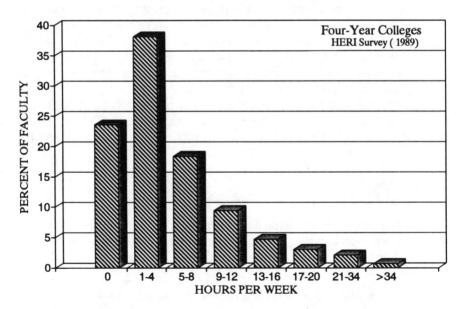

Adam Newprof would call an "energy barrier." It is unique among the triumvirate of professional responsibilities—teaching, scholarship, and service—in its demand that the beginning faculty member act absolutely alone. In teaching there is a teaching assignment (you know what your duty is) and a class schedule (you know when you are supposed to do it). In service you get elected or invited to do something specific, the meeting times are set, and an agenda is announced. But in scholarship, it's your initiative. *You* decide what needs to be done and when to do it. In graduate school, where your time was dominated by research, it was never *yours* in the same way. A research director set directions; you had deadlines to meet; grades were given. Now, as you start a career, it is time to fly solo. You are not scheduled by your department chair to retreat to the library between three and five in the afternoon. No mentor is there to pick the intellectual problem to be addressed. If there is anything like a scholarship deadline, it is probably down the road at some remote evaluation time, and even then it might not be clear exactly what is expected. Lacking a specific assignment and time to complete it, the tendency is to spend the time instead on the tasks that show up on your calendar. After a semester or a year, what was by default postponed has grown in impression to enlarged proportions. Better to get over the hump before it becomes truly daunting.

Once you have scaled this psychological slope, chosen your own direction, and staked out your own intellectual terrain, the travel of the scholar is no harder than the travel of the teacher and citizen. In fact, unless you insist on separating them, the scholar and teacher will be traveling arm-in-arm. You will not be taking off your teaching hat in order to do research, but will be thinking as teacher-scholar and looking always for ways to link the two. You will see scholarship as empowering you for teaching, and teaching as a way of making scholarship come alive for students.

We have looked at specific, effective ways of getting off to a good start as a scholar in this chapter. But in the final analysis, you are still flying solo. I encourage you to have the confidence to take off expecting favorable winds.

For Discussion

1. Recalling the history of the liberal arts ideal (Chapter 5), discuss the conversation between Adam Newprof and Carlisle Ravenel in the College Street Café in terms of the perennial orator-philosopher debate.

2. In which of the "climates for research" (Table 7.1) did you do your own undergraduate work? Which of the climates from Table 7.1 do you believe comes closest to describing the college where you are beginning your career as a faculty member?

3. Suggest ways in which you might go about connecting your scholarship with your teaching so that the two are not seen as being in competition. Do you feel that making that kind of connection is easier in some disciplines than others?

4. In *Scholarship Reconsidered*, Ernest Boyer says: "What we urgently need today is a more inclusive view of what it means to be a scholar—a recognition that knowledge is acquired through research, through synthesis, through practice, and through teaching. We acknowledge that these four categories—the scholarship of discovery, of integration, of application, and of teaching—divide intellectual functions that are tied inseparably to each other. Still, there is value, we believe, in analyzing the various kinds of academic work, while also acknowledging that they dynamically interact, forming an interdependent whole."[15]

   What are some specific activities that exemplify each of these four categories of scholarship? Would all be accepted as scholarship on your campus?

5. In this chapter, a broad definition of "scholarship" has been proposed, and numerous types of evidence of scholarship suggested. Comment on the validity of each of the following, in your own judgment, as evidence of scholarliness:
   (a) developing and marketing an instructional video tape to be used by church choir directors
   (b) publishing a volume of poetry
   (c) publishing a short story in a college literary magazine
   (d) publishing a six-page paper in a refereed sociological journal
   (e) intradepartmental circulation of a progress report on continuing research in biochemistry
   (f) producing an exhibit of early Renaissance paintings
   (g) composing a sonata
   (h) reviewing new fiction for a local newspaper
   (i) chairing a panel on euthanasia at a regional professional meeting
   (j) preparing to teach a new course in your specialty
   (k) preparing to teach an interdisciplinary course in a new general education curriculum.

6. What adjustments, if any, will you need to make in the timetable suggested in Table 7.2 to meet the expectations for scholarship at your college?

7. What programs of support for scholarship are available in your college? To whom would you go to get additional information about support for scholarship and professional activities?

---

[15] Boyer, pp. 24-25.

Citizenship and Service

Lord Lilac thought it rather rotten
That Shakespeare should be quite forgotten,
And therefore got on a Committee
With several chaps out of the City.
　　　　　Gilbert Keith Chesterton
　　　　　The Shakespeare Memorial

he gas chromatograph was an elegant apparatus that provoked mixed sentiments in Adam Newprof. On the one hand its power to give the chemist a view of what was happening in a chemical reaction was almost magical. On the other hand, there were days when it illustrated perfectly what Doc Paradigm used to call "the perversity of the inanimate." Today was one of those days.

"Hand me that screwdriver, please, Marty," Newprof said.

Marty Fresch leaned across from the opposite side of the lab table and handed his mentor a small Phillips-head screwdriver. The professor touched it gingerly to a capacitor visible but out of reach beneath a circuit board. The faintest metallic tinkle confirmed what he had feared.

"Rats!" he muttered.

"What is it?" Marty asked.

"There's a bad solder joint to the capacitor. Poor quality control at the factory. Electronics are a lot simpler these days. Most of the wires have disappeared from instruments, but even with transistors and printed circuit boards, there can be problems."

"Can't you call someone in to repair it?"

Newprof snorted. "Don't I wish? The nearest service person is in Atlanta and would cost us a hundred dollars an hour portal to portal." He straightened up. "No, I'm the designated instrument repair person for the department. If something is absolutely beyond my ability to deal with—and if we absolutely have to have the instrument before a new budget year—then we call Atlanta."

"This time...?"

"This time it's simple and I'm it. Took me long enough to find the problem, but it's only maybe a half-hour job to get it repaired. In fact, you can help me with it." He looked up at the wall clock. "Heck—I've got a Curriculum Committee meeting in six minutes. Want to see if you can yank the circuit board while I'm gone?"

"Sure. What do I have to do?"

"Come around here and I'll show you."

As Fresch was rounding the end of the lab bench, a voice called out from the door into the hall. "Dr. Newprof. *There* you are! I was by your office twice this morning and couldn't find you."

Newprof looked over his shoulder. It was Gertrude Posey, one of his advisees who wanted more than anything in the world to be a veterinarian, and who was a class-A worrier. Yesterday he had helped her work out her pre-registration schedule for the spring.

"Hi, Gert. What can I do for you?"

"Well, you know my schedule? You signed me up for Dr. Ravenel for biology, and now I'm hearing that he's real hard, and I need good grades to get into vet school. So could I get into another section?"

Newprof opened his mouth to answer, but was interrupted by a call from Charles Noble, the department chair, who slipped past Gert in the doorway.

"Adam, can I see you for just a minute? Excuse me, Miss Posey. I just need him for a minute."

Newprof asked Marty Fresch and Gert Posey to wait in the lab, while he left for the hallway.

"Yes, Charles?"

"Sorry to interrupt, Adam, but President Fitzgeorge dropped by to ask who I'd recommend for an *ad hoc* task force he's setting up to study the parking situation. I recommended you. Could you let his secretary know that you'll do it?"

"Parking task force? Charles, I don't know. I'm on the Curriculum Committee—am about to be late for it, in fact—and on the Appeals Panel and on the Chaplain's Council. And I'm advisor to the yearbook. I don't know how I can add anything else."

"I know you're busy, but I think you'd be really good for this one. I live three blocks away, but you drive in everyday, and you were a commuter student when you were at Benjamin. Besides, you're a thoughtful, logical person who's good at finding solutions to things. You're a natural."

The language was both logical and flattering. He could feel himself slipping into another time commitment. And here he was stacked two deep with waiting students and a Curriculum Committee meeting scheduled for the basement of the Library in three minutes. Oh well, he'd find the time somehow. Parking did need some attention on this campus.

Faculty Governance: The Hidden Component of Workload

When Adam Newprof was first driving down the interstate toward the College of Port St. Julian, he had never heard the expression "faculty governance." His images of a workday were of morning lectures and afternoon labs, of stretches of paper grading, of impromptu sessions with young men and women starving for insights, of spare-time research hours. He had known these teacher-scholar activities would be interrupted now and again by faculty meetings, of course, but he would never have guessed at the total hours to be devoured by the variety of "governance" activities. He is now in his third year at Port St. Julian, and he knows the reality. The first year fooled him. Being new to the faculty, he wasn't on any committees that first fall—and a good thing it was, considering how little sleep he got just making sure he was ready for the next day's classes. But the following March he was elected to the Admissions Committee and the Curriculum Committee, and by Christmas of his second year it dawned on him that committee hours were adding up to the equivalent of another class to teach.

Newprof is beginning to understand that there is not, as we noted in Chapter 1, really any such career as "teaching," and that his actual career is being a college faculty member, with all the dimensions of that job that one discovers only after signing up. Teaching will remain his first love, his abiding reason for being here, but his time will be claimed, too, by the work of creating and maintaining the circumstances in which that teaching is done. Faculty governance is mostly a matter of committees. It is not the favorite work of most faculty members, but especially on the small-college campus, nearly everyone gets involved.

There is no other workplace that resembles very closely the college campus. In a typical American corporation or factory, while employee concerns may be heard and even solicited, the primary responsibility for—and authority over—the workplace rests with company administrators. This is far less true in academe. Because the central enterprise is academic in nature, and because the scope of baccalaureate education is so multifarious (involving in a typical liberal arts college a general education curriculum plus twenty-five to fifty major programs plus a variety of minors and concentrations), it is obvious that no president, dean, or other administrator is qualified to do all the planning, set all the standards, and make all the decisions that shape the enterprise and keep it strong. Let us acknowledge as well that faculty by constitution are less than amenable to having the enterprise "managed" by others. So, while the existence of organizational charts and heads of departments and deans and vice presidents may give the appearance of a "corporate" structure, the college at its core is governed by the faculty.

Liberal arts college governance, like the liberal arts college curriculum, varies a great deal in detail from campus to campus, while maintaining an essential similarity. In decades past it was typical for monthly faculty meetings to be chaired by the president or the dean of the college, but a growing number of colleges now elect a faculty moderator to preside. On some campuses this person—perhaps with the title Faculty Moderator or Speaker of the Faculty—strictly presides over meetings; on others he or she may be a more formal liaison with the administration. The Moderator, in some cases, may be an *ex officio* member of all standing committees of the faculty, and in other cases, may chair a kind of executive committee of the faculty.

The business of the faculty—the setting of academic policies, the approval of courses and programs to be offered, resolutions that express formal faculty positions on issues—is typically conducted in a setting much like a small town meeting. Committees that have done the detailed work on a given matter bring reports and proposals to what is essentially a committee of the whole. Final disposition of proposals, which may be amended on the floor of the faculty meeting, is decided by democratic vote. In larger colleges, instead of functioning as a committee of the whole, a faculty may delegate to an elected senate the authority to conduct official faculty business.

While formal faculty business gets transacted at these monthly meetings, and while these may occasionally be interesting and even exciting, it is in the committees that the individual faculty member finds copious quantities of his or her time being consumed. There is, of course, no universal committee structure for all campuses, but because the work of governance tends to divide along rather natural lines, one is likely to find a list something like that shown in Table 8.1.

Strictly speaking, the committees in Table 8.1 should be called standing committees. It is this collection that attends to the assortment of ongoing, routine matters in the faculty's purview. In addition, each campus is sure to accrue over time a miscellany of *ad hoc* committees, task forces, advisory groups, and the like that are created to handle (a) matters outside the recognized core of permanent governance concerns (e.g., general education, international studies, honors program); (b) issues that need concentrated study beyond that deemed possible or desirable in a standing committee (e.g., parking, college calendar, employee benefits); or (c) assignments of a transient nature (e.g., presidential search). Committee or task force, standing or *ad hoc*, this kind of group campus-citizenship activity lays its claim to significant chunks of faculty time.

Committee Service: Opportunity and Danger

Adam Newprof has slipped deeply into the work of college service in his first three years. Although still a relatively junior faculty member, he is already in a position to help shape circumstances outside his own classrooms and laboratories and to help solve problems that are campus-wide in scope. More hours are being spent in committee work this year than he had expected, and the *ad hoc* parking committee that President Fitzgeorge is creating will add to

Table 8.1
Typical Faculty Committees

Commitee	Typical Functions
Faculty Executive Committee	• Coordinate faculty governance activities • Advise administration on faculty matters • Seek improvements in policies and practices • Coordinate handbook revision
Faculty Personnel Committee	• Review and recommend faculty for tenure and promotion • Propose policies for evaluation and workload • Propose policies for appointments and reappointments • Propose policies for leaves and retirement
Curriculum Committee	• Review proposals for new courses, majors, and concentrations • Review proposals for course and program deletions • Propose degree requirements
Academic Standards Committee	• Propose policies for maintaining academic standards • Review grading standards • Propose admissions and scholarship standards • Act on appeals for exceptions to academic policies
Faculty Research & Development Committee	• Promote scholarship and creative activities in the faculty • Promote activities for improving teaching • Act on proposals for funding of teaching-related projects • Act on proposals for funding of scholarly/creative projects
Library Committee	• Propose policies relating to the Library • Propose department funding for books and periodicals • Monitor Library staffing and budgeting against standards
Budget Advisory Committee	• Review institutional resource and expenditure matters • Review budget proposals against institutional goals and plans • Recommend budgets to the administration
Student Life Committee	• Advise Dean of Students on co-curricular matters • Propose policies and procedures relating to student life • Allocate funds for student activities • Maintain oversight of student organizations
Grievance Committee	• Hear faculty complaints of violation of college policy

that number. The College of Port St. Julian has set no restrictions on committee service, and his department chair has not given him any particular advice regarding either the extent of or the approach to such service. If he gets off to a good start as a committee worker, it will be strictly through luck, or perhaps out of unusually incisive judgment.

Considering how much of the faculty member's career is spent sitting around committee tables, it makes good sense to reflect at the outset on how best to approach this responsibility along with all the others. Committee work can indeed represent opportunity for the new faculty member, but it can also be fraught with danger for the unwary neophyte. Being alert to both the opportunities and the dangers can save considerable time and frustration.

Henry Rosovsky, Harvard's former Dean of the Faculty of Arts and Sciences, hints at the all-too-frequent flavor of committee work in his book, *The University: An Owner's Manual:*

> The desire to participate is great, but self-governance comes only at a high price: it requires much time, knowledge, commitment, and a lot of what the Germans call *Sitzfleisch*....[T]hey sit on innumerable committees...spending hours in fruitless and inconsequential debates. Perhaps the total number of hours used is not all that large, but the cumulative effects are considerable.[1]

There are ways of making the most of committee time, both for yourself and in the interest of good faculty governance. No matter what you as a newcomer to campus may find to be the established *modus operandi,* you can both (a) quickly become an influential force in governance affairs, and (b) see that your committee hours intrude minimally on the rest of your work. These are the guiding principles for committee work that I would commend to the new faculty member:

- ✦ Do your homework.
- ✦ Don't be bashful.
- ✦ Help keep the train on the track.
- ✦ Decide when to say no—and do it!

Let's look at each of these in turn.

It is amazing what an edge one can have in a group enterprise simply by doing a little homework. You will discover early on that most committee members are faithful in attendance, but that they devote little or no time to issues on the agenda except during meeting times. There is a strong tendency to consider it to be the responsibility of the committee chair—but no one else—to think about things between meetings. It is far better to set aside maybe half an hour between times to review the agenda, minutes of past meetings, and other relevant materials, and to make a few notes to take back to the next meeting.

---

[1] Henry Rosovsky, *The University: An Owner's Manual* (New York, NY: W.W. Norton, 1990), p. 277.

Prominent among the notes should be your own ideas about possible solutions to problems before the committee, disposition of items on its agenda, and/or initiatives that it might profitably take. With this modest amount of preparation, you will find it much easier not only to participate, but to become a leader in committee work—and thus in setting directions. You will also contribute significantly to the efficiency with which the group operates.

Some new faculty members will not need the admonishment, "Don't be bashful," in committee meetings, but most will. Recalling that the majority of faculty, especially those in liberal arts colleges, are by nature introverts, their inclination to keep quiet until very sure of their position comes as no surprise. Whereas extroverts think by speaking, introverts think before speaking. Add to this the proclivity of the newcomer to defer to those seen as more senior or as inside an established circle, and you have a near guarantee that new-faculty membership will be marked by reticence and minimal impact. This is not, however, an inevitable state of affairs. The new faculty member who comes in mindful of what is probable needs simply to resolve to change the probability. Particularly when he or she has done the pertinent homework and has jotted down ideas ahead of time, it becomes easier even for the introvert—the thinking through done in advance—to jump into the discussion, and even to play a major role in the very first year of service. I don't advocate this, please be assured, as a means of getting attention for oneself, but rather as a means of making the most valuable possible contribution to the committee's work.

Helping keep the train on the track is without question more of a challenge than either doing homework or being bold. Indeed, a great many of the hours spent in committee activity are spent "off track," in what Rosovsky calls "fruitless and inconsequential debates." By "off track" I mean that committee discussion is prone to meander rather than to move purposefully toward conclusion. In part this traces to the lack of homework done by most members between meetings, and thus to the use of scheduled committee time for "thinking out loud," an activity that seldom proceeds in a straight line and often takes the group off on tangents. Even more thinking out loud takes place when either the chair or several members are extroverts for whom a committee meeting serves an important social function.

So what can you, neither chair nor insider, do to help keep things directed? You will have begun simply by committing to homework and not being shy about supplying ideas, as suggested above. Putting well-considered, pertinent proposals on the table will automatically direct conversation and business flow. But beyond proposals for solutions to problems, you should weigh, too, processes for focusing committee attention effectively and efficiently on the issues to be resolved. An entire committee thinking out loud may lead eventually to group consensus, or it may lead to agreement whether there is true consensus or not, depending on the dynamics in the group. One process that you might suggest the committee use to determine the degree of group accord—and to push the train back onto the track—is that of employing written opinions. When there has been a reasonable amount of discussion on some matter—say, whether a new course being proposed to the Curriculum Committee rates high, medium, or low in furthering the curriculum goals of the college—each committee member is asked to write down an individual opinion on a piece of paper and pass it to the chair. The chair then lists the results on the board for all to see; whether there is consensus becomes immediately clear. That question settled, the next one can be taken up. You might also suggest, in a similar vein, that debates about priorities be brought to closure by having members give individual ratings or rankings to the several competing items—say competing requests for end-of-year funds—then using the group averages to arrive at committee recommendations for priorities in spending. On other occasions it may become clear that a small subcommittee would deal more productively with a task—say constructing a policy to govern applications for sabbaticals—than would the whole committee; if so, you should quickly suggest that assignment be made. You may be surprised at how useful strategically-timed proposals for processes of closure can be in moving the group along, reducing the effects of unhealthy group dynamics (such as domineering personalities), and coming to sound conclusions. You may also be surprised at how welcome your ideas for keeping the train on the track turn out to be.

The fourth principle in the list, "Decide when to say no—and do it!", should probably be the first as you start out. Had Adam Newprof been forewarned in the first year that the calls for college service would grow so relentlessly, he might well have drawn a line at a point that would have averted the sense of overload that he is beginning to feel on too many afternoons. On almost every college campus you will hear grousing about the time spent on committees, task forces, panels and the like. Usually the diagnosis is "too many committees," but a more accurate description of the problem is that there are too many committees per faculty member, i.e., that individuals have said yes too often to calls on their time. While it may be natural to attribute the overextension to external sources ("They keep asking me"), the personal problem gets solved only if the person feeling overextended acts to solve it. Even the new faculty member, who wants to come across as cooperative and energetic, and who is conscious of the need to establish an impressive record during the pre-tenure period, *can* say no.

A good start in college service—and in committee service particularly—means setting a reasonable limit early on—and sticking to it. What is "reasonable" will vary with the person; some people can handle a little more than others. But a good rule of thumb is to limit your membership to no more than one standing committee and one other group that has regularly scheduled meetings. A second good rule is to take a "committee sabbatical"—a total break from committee work—about every fourth year. Faculty governance is important, and every faculty member needs to accept a share in it. But every afternoon expended in or ravaged by a committee meeting is an afternoon out of the library or laboratory or studio, an afternoon unavailable for working with students, an afternoon when no papers get graded. If you are pressured into saying yes out of concern for "the record," don't forget that the record of teaching and scholarship will turn out to be far more critical than the list of committees to which one has given time. You have unquestioned obligations as a campus citizen; just keep a sensible limit on your total commitments.

Departmental Service

The new faculty member will be a citizen not only of the college, but also of an academic department or division. And just as with college citizenship, there will also be citizenship duties within the department.

Adam Newprof has, for example, accepted responsibility for routine instrument repair in his department. The college is too small to warrant its hiring a full-time repair technician, so Newprof gets the assignment. There are other service assignments in the department: coordination of textbook orders, responsibility for the departmental reading room, supervision of student assistants, and maintenance and display of graduate school materials. Charles Noble, the department chair, has divided these up as equitably as possible among the members of the department.

There is not a great deal of new advice to give here. There is a load to be shared beyond the teaching duties of a department, and a good start in departmental service will include accepting your share of the extra-curricular chores. At the same time, one is well advised here as in college service generally to set some limits, to say no when it needs to be said. Doing homework is no less important in departmental business than in college committees, and speaking up in departmental meetings is just as beneficial to the new faculty member as is speaking up in committees.

Community Service

There is more variation in expectations from college to college with regard to service by the faculty member in the community external to the campus than with regard to service in the college and department. And whereas there are some obvious benefits to the new faculty member from a strong start in teaching, scholarship, and campus citizenship, it is harder to make the case for devoting significant time to community service, except in terms of local institutional expectations.

A very high premium is placed on community citizenship at some colleges. Their handbooks will state that, as part of the requirements for tenure, an expectation that the faculty member will be habitually active in community projects and organizations. These colleges see their missions as including serious outreach into the larger community and see their faculty as a prime means of accomplishing this outreach. They will encourage membership in civic clubs, work as a volunteer, or involvement in local organization scouting. In many church-related colleges, involvement in church work will be expected of the new faculty member.

At a larger number of colleges, "community service" is interpreted to mean extending one's professional expertise in assistance to organizations and institutions in the external community. For example, a history professor might speak to a local history society on some topic of expertise; or a political scientist might appear at a civic club meeting to provide an analysis of a recent election outcome; or a biologist might assist public high school students with science fair projects. Most colleges maintain a Speakers Bureau, and new faculty from all disciplines will be recruited for inclusion in the roster of college speakers available to groups in the community.

It is without question valuable to the external reputation of your college if you share your expertise with the larger community. It is also "good for you" (as my mother might say) to get out of the ivory tower once in a while, and to spend time doing public things with non-college groups. Some faculty very much enjoy such involvement and indulge in it extensively. But honest counsel here leads me to caution once more against overextension.

Community service by one definition or the other is ubiquitous in faculty handbook statements about tenure and promotion. The fact is, however, that relatively few department chairs or deans weigh this contribution heavily when evaluating faculty.[2] Contributions to the outside community will always be seen as a plus for a faculty member, but it is rare indeed for someone not to be tenured in a liberal arts college because of community involvement insufficient to meet institutional standards. Still, if you are starting your career as a faculty member at a college that does place high value on community or public service, it will obviously behoove you to attend to this aspect of your responsibilities from the outset.

Student Advising

Adam Newprof in his third year as a faculty member has student advising competing for time with all his other duties. The role of faculty member as advisor is a very clear and and welcome one for him; Doc Paradigm did that job well back at Benjamin College, leaving Newprof with deep conviction about its importance. He wonders now whether Doc had some secret solution to time management that enabled him to sit relaxed with one student in his cluttered office, map out schedules, and answer questions, while other duties called. If there is such magic, Newprof wishes he knew it.

Colleges differ in the degree to which they involve faculty in student advising. The new faculty member in a liberal arts college can, however, expect to

[2] In a 1977 survey, for example, a majority of department chairs said community service was a minor factor in faculty evaluation and 30% said it was not a factor at all. See John A. Centra, *How Universities Evaluate Faculty Performance: A Survey of Department Heads*. GREB Research Report No. 75-5bR (Princeton, NJ: Educational Testing Service, 1979).

be called on to serve as advisor at some time or other. At most liberal arts colleges the advisor role is quite prominent. A few of them have shifted the advising of freshmen and undeclared majors to a professional advising staff, and some others now use a select group of faculty volunteers for this purpose. Responsibility for the advising of majors is nearly always shared by departmental faculty, although in departments with a small number of majors the chair may act as advisor for all of them. Even if the practices at your college should somehow exempt you from formal advising duties, you may be sure that there will be calls for informal advising, many occasions when students will ask for advice about courses and their sequencing, and come to you with questions about academic planning and problems whether you are their official advisor or not.

It is common for the beginning faculty member to assume with student advising, as with teaching, that the sole requirement for serving well as advisor is knowledge. The faculty advisor should certainly know what he or she is talking about, but a good start requires far more. I would recommend to the new faculty member the following guiding principles for student advising:

+ Know your advisees.
+ Practice patience.
+ Do your homework.
+ Establish your availability.
+ Be prepared for the personal.

Let's look briefly at each of these.

Advising will be most effectively accomplished when the advisor knows the advisee. This knowledge will consist first of a thorough familiarity with the student's academic ability, aspirations and record. What are the advisee's SAT scores and high school GPA? Is this student aiming for law school or medical school? How far along the path toward satisfaction of major and general education requirements has the student come? How much is left to be done? How strong is this student's academic record? Has the student been on the dean's list or placed on academic warning? But there are valid questions, too, about the student as a person that should not be overlooked. Is the student an extrovert or introvert, sensing or intuitive type, thinking or feeling type, perceiving or judging type?[3] Based on personality preferences, what advantages does the student have for functioning in an academic environment, and what difficulties can be expected? Does the student have special problems that threaten to complicate academic performance? Good advice doesn't come pre-packaged; it needs to be decided with full cognizance of the person who is to receive it.

---

[3] For a reminder about the meaning of these terms in MBTI typology, please refer back to Chapter 6.

Good advising takes patience. Colleges that have shifted freshman advising away from faculty to professional staff members have been prompted in part by the recognition that many faculty members, perhaps a preponderance, find it a great challenge to deal with students who really don't know what they want to do—and most freshmen don't know. Even juniors often don't know. A good start as advisor will include a resolution to accept that fact, and to practice patience. It will require patience. When asked about the area of intended major, incoming freshmen list "undecided" more often than anything else. Even after choosing a major it is common to see changes of mind about that choice, not just once, but three or four times. Faculty advisors want advisees to come into a schedule-planning session with their goals clearly defined and some course preferences in mind. Sometimes that happens, but more commonly the advisee is uncertain about academic goals and passive about course selection. It can help to remind oneself that the typical student compared to the typical faculty advisor is far less mature, is a very different personality type, and has scant experience on which to base decisions about major and course choices. The realistic advisor will, when each advisee comes in for an advising conference, take a deep breath and set about helping the student think things through. Your longer-term aim should be to encourage movement to greater maturity, clearer vision, and independence. But in the nearer term be prepared to encounter ambivalence and resolved to practice forbearance.

Homework is as critical to good advising as to committee and departmental service. You will want to be ready, when each advisee appears in your door, to speak with authority about major and degree requirements, about the student's academic progress, and about what options make sense at this point. A thorough knowledge of the college catalog is definitely a prerequisite for giving academic advice. You will need to become completely familiar with the catalog at the beginning, and to review it often, especially just before each "advising season." No less important is to keep a file folder for each advisee, and to review its contents carefully prior to the advising session. The folder should contain basic information from the admissions or registrar's office, the results of any testing (IQ, SAT, career aptitude, personality), course and grade records, any correspondence between you and the student (and sometimes his or her parents), and notes you have made during advising conferences. You will also need to acquire knowledge of academic support services available to the student (tutoring, learning skills labs, untimed testing, diagnostic testing), as well as knowledge of how to get help with career planning and placement. You may discover that your college provides advisors with an advising handbook that makes much of this homework easier.

Academic advising is a seasonal business. There is usually a week or ten days programmed late in each term when advisors and advisees meet to plan a schedule for the following term; these are intense periods for an advisor with very many advisees. But there will also be occasions throughout a term when a student has hit some snag and needs advice on how to handle the situation. For both types of advising, occasional and regular, it is good to make certain your advisees know of your availability. At the initial advisement meeting, it helps to give the advisee an "advising syllabus" that sets forth your guidelines for the advisor-advisee relationship, makes note of schedule-planning and/or preregistration periods in the term—and makes clear what your office hours are and how to schedule conferences at other times. The student should not be led to presume that you are "on call," but does need to find you accessible and know how to take advantage of your availability.

The typical liberal arts college faculty member (a rational T-type in the MBTI system) will probably find it logical that someone setting out to serve as advisor should know the intricacies of the catalog, should be well acquainted with the student's academic history, and should be reasonably available to advisees. The teacher is apt to see the advisor-advisee association aimed strictly at planning sensible course schedules and handling related academic problems that may arise. That same faculty member is, however, far less likely to feel comfortable when an advisee shows up with a problem that is personal. That preference notwithstanding, you need to be prepared for the personal. That is not to say that you should feel obliged to play therapist. Indeed, it can be dangerous to slip into that role unless your training prepares you for it. What you should determine to do is (a) to listen attentively and sympathetically, and (b) to direct them to a qualified psychological counselor for assistance that it is beyond your ability. The line between academic advising and personal counseling is always a fuzzy one. Students bring to college with them a multiplicity of personal concerns that may distract them from their studies and complicate the learning process. They are unlikely to distinguish between "advising" and "counseling," and they may well be hurt and alienated by the advisor who is too blunt in making the distinction for them. I know of no magic formula for determining when a personal problem needs attention by a counselor and when a sympathetic ear and a word of encouragement will suffice. But as you assume your responsibility as advisor, you need to be alert to the ways in which the academic and the personal become intertwined, and to create your own guidelines for referring students to a counselor.

Time Spent in Service Activities

At several points in this chapter I have implied that faculty spend a substantial part of each work week in service activities. You may even have sensed a certain quicksand quality to college service, especially where committee work is concerned. It may be useful to have some idea about what kind of service time investment is common in liberal arts colleges. The 1989 Higher Education Research Institute (HERI) faculty survey referred to in earlier chapters again gives us this picture.[4]

---

[4] Survey results are published annually by the Higher Education Research Institute, UCLA Graduate School of Education.

Nearly all (95.5%) four-year college faculty members are involved in college committee work. A large majority (71%) reported spending one to four hours per week in all such activities, another 20% say they spend five-eight hours, and 4.4% spend more than eight hours a week. Graph 8.1 shows the complete distribution. The Carnegie Foundation survey of 1989 showed that 78% of liberal arts college faculty (compared with 26% in research universities and 64% in comprehensive colleges) feel college service to be either very important or fairly important in getting tenure.[5]

As with committee service, nearly all (98.3%) four-year college faculty in the HERI survey reported devoting time to student advising. A majority (53%) say they spend one to four hours per week, nearly a third more (32.5%) report spending five-eight hours, and 13% spend more than eight hours per week. The complete distribution of time is shown in Graph 8.2 below. In the Carnegie Foundation survey cited above, 49% of liberal arts college faculty (compared with 9% in research universities and 30% in comprehensive colleges) feel that student advising is important or fairly important to getting tenure at their institutions.

Service activities do, in fact, constitute a significant time investment for faculty, and a "hidden component" of workload for new faculty, who tend to expect to concentrate on being teacher-scholars. The total hours may, in fact, understate the interference that service activities represent, particularly where scholarship is concerned, in that they tend to interrupt periods that would otherwise be unbroken blocks of time that are so valuable to research, writing, and creativity. Still, this work of the faculty-citizen is vital to the life of the college, and the new faculty member should enter into it ready to make constructive contributions.

---

[5] Ernest L. Boyer, *The Condition of the Professoriate: Attitudes and Trends* (Princeton, NJ: The Carnegie Foundation for the Advancement of Teaching, 1989).

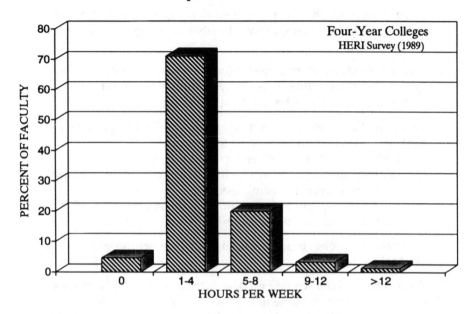

Graph 8.1
Time Spent in Committee Work

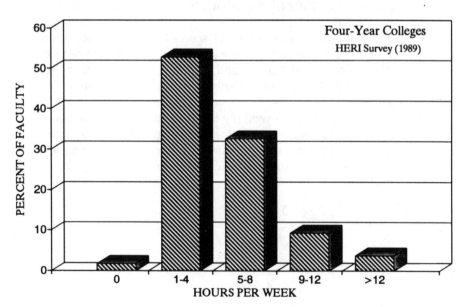

Graph 8.2
Time Spent in Advising

For Discussion

1. In what ways are the prospects of working as a committee member at your college appealing to you? In what ways are you reluctant to get involved?

2. Which committees from Table 8.1 (or the actual list from your faculty handbook) have functions that you think you would find most interesting? Why? Which seem least interesting?

3. When treating community service as part of faculty performance evaluation, what arguments occur to you for:
   (a) considering active membership in civic clubs?
   (b) limiting consideration to activities where the faculty member's academic expertise is being used?
   (c) considering volunteer work done in the community, whether related to one's academic expertise or not?

4. In what ways does student advising offer opportunities to extend your role as teacher?

5. As an advisor, how would you deal with the following situations:
   (a) When planning a schedule, an advisee asks you to recommend a section of freshman English with an instructor who "won't be too hard."
   (b) An advisee says she won't sign up for a course you have suggested because her friends tell her the professor practices sexual harassment.
   (c) A freshman advisee whose SAT scores and high school record are quite good is failing three courses at midterm. When you talk to him, he starts crying and reports that his parents are getting divorced. "I don't even feel like living," he says, "much less studying."
   (d) A distraught junior is working twenty hours a week and taking a full load of courses, including one advanced painting course with studio hours. A month into the fall term he is having serious difficulty managing everything, and comes to you for advice.

The Individual
in the Organization

England is the paradise of individuality, eccentricity, heresy, anomalies, hobbies, and humors.

George Santayana
Soliloquies in England and Later Soliloquies

*A*dam Newprof left the faculty meeting feeling irritable and uneasy. He knew why. It was the motion that Walter Gauge had brought from the Academic Standards Committee, and that had passed by a bare majority.

Maggie Morrow caught up to him as he left the auditorium. "Well, you got out in a hurry, Adam. Why such a rush? You have a pile of papers waiting for you?"

"Oh—hi, Maggie. Sure, there are always papers waiting, but that's not the aggravation of the afternoon."

"Hey! I like that alliteration. So—what *is* the aggravation of the afternoon?" She walked with him, briefcase in hand, toward the new Faber Science Center that had just opened for the fall term a month ago.

"Oh, that silly motion from Academic Standards. I still can't believe it."

"The motion about how much final exams have to count? *That's* got you upset? Why? Do you think thirty percent is too much?"

He turned his head to see whether she was being facetious. She wasn't.

"My gosh, Maggie! That's not the point. The point is that nobody—nobody—has the right to say how much a faculty member will count any grade, final exam or otherwise. Good grief! Surely you don't...."

"I guess I didn't see it as a matter of principle. There are plenty of other faculty policies that we're obliged to follow, why not one more? Hey, come on. Let's go over to College Street and get a cup of Pete's coffee. That'll fix you up."

He shook his head. "No thanks. Marty Fresch is working on his senior seminar, and I told him I'd help him pick out some slides after the faculty meeting. I'll see you tomorrow."

He took the elevator up to the third floor of Faber Hall and unlocked his office door.

"Adam!" Charles Noble was coming up the hall.

"Hi, Charles. You must have escaped the faculty meeting before I did."

"May I come in for a minute?"

"Oh—sure." Newprof turned on the office light and invited Noble in with a wave of his hand. "Want to sit down?"

The department head took the visitor's chair, and Newprof took the swivel chair behind his desk. The office smelled of new floor tile, nothing at all like the offices he, Noble, and Tommy Venable had left behind in the ancient Main Building. Adam thought he detected some strain in Charles Noble's face, and assumed that Charles, like he, was concerned about the Academic Standards final exam policy.

"So what do we do, Charles?"

"You know about Dean Pennington's decision already? Did Tommy tell you?"

"Dean Pennington? No, I was thinking about the final exam policy the faculty just passed. What did the dean decide that's bothering you?"

"She said no to Kelvin."

Newprof's jaw dropped. Claude Kelvin was the department's unanimous choice for appointment to the new assistant professor position being added for next year. He was so obviously the best of the three candidates interviewed that Adam couldn't believe what he was hearing.

"She said no?"

Noble nodded. "She acknowledges that his *vitae* is strong, but she said there was something that her intuition told her to be wary of when she interviewed him on campus. She called a colleague at Old South University, somebody not on his reference list, to see if her hunch was right. This person told her, as the dean put it, to be sure to hire him—if we wanted trouble."

"Meaning what?"

"Apparently he's not easy to get along with. Something of a prima donna, according to the dean's source."

Newprof shook his head in dismay. "I sure didn't see any sign of that on the interview. He seemed confident enough, but he was polite and pleasant. And he already has four publications before getting out of graduate school. And the other two candidates—well, they just weren't as impressive. You know that. Charles, I think we should challenge this."

The department head rubbed his jaw and dropped his eyes. He seemed tired. Adam was too. First the faculty vote and now this. He hadn't had a day this depressing in his three-plus years at the College of Port St. Julian.

The Faculty Personality

Adam Newprof had imagined an autonomous life. Instead he has just had two successive reminders that he is an individual living within an organization. His very strong convictions on two issues have run smack up against organizational walls, one faculty governance and the other administrative, and he is smarting from the impact. As a college faculty member, he enjoys what is probably the most independent occupation available. Yet there *are* limits to his independence. Now and then his will is thwarted.

College faculty as a group cherish autonomy perhaps more than any single thing. This is another point where MBTI typology can give useful insight. We need to avoid over-generalization here, of course. The title above, "The Faculty Personality," implies that there is a single faculty "type," which is obviously not the case. We do nevertheless find certain MBTI preferences highly concentrated in the college faculty ranks, as indicated back in Chapter 6. We find more introverts (I) than extroverts (E), more intuitives (N) than sensing types (S), more thinking types (T) than feeling types (F), and more judging types (J) than perceiving types (P). In the general population, by contrast, there are three times as many E's as I's, three times as many S's as N's, about equal numbers of T's and F's, and about the same number of J's as P's.[1] If your liberal arts college is typical, a typing of the entire faculty will show more INTJ's than any other single type. The distribution will be uneven across departments, but INTJ—a type found in only 1% of the general population—will be the most common type of college teacher. Clearly, higher education does not attract all personality types equally. Indeed, it is successful in concentrating in the ranks of college faculty a personality type that is very rarely encountered in the general population.

Here is Isabel Briggs Myers's summary description of the INTJ type:

> [The INTJ] has a very original mind and a great amount of drive which he uses only when it pleases him. In fields which appeal to his imagination he has a fine power to organize a job or piece of work and carry it through with or without

---

[1] Note that for pre-college teachers, the picture is different: More E's than I's, more S's than N's, and more F's than T's; J's still outnumber P's here, as for college teachers. See Gordon Lawrence, *People Types & Tiger Stripes: A Practical Guide to Learning Styles* (Gainesville, FL: Center for Applications of Psychological Type, 1982), p. 21.

the help of others. He is always skeptical, critical and independent, generally determined, and often stubborn. Can never be driven, seldom led.[2]

Little wonder, reading that description, that college faculty members are so capable of taking charge of a course, organizing it, and orchestrating its movement toward an envisioned outcome. No wonder either that they are so able as scholars; analysis of complex situations, design of incisive means of intellectual inquiry, and synthesis from vast collections of information ferreted out of diverse sources all come naturally to them. At the same time, one detects in the description clues that an INTJ—a strongly individualistic personality— might not ever come to feel entirely comfortable as part of an organization.

You may not be an INTJ in the Myers-Briggs scheme. The chances are very good nonetheless that the desire for autonomy was an important motive in your selection of the faculty career. If so, INTJ or not, it will help to be alert to a natural resistance to any aspects of your college as an organization that constrains you as an individual. A good start will require that you anticipate this resistance and decide how to deal with it. Over the years a great deal of energy can be conserved for your most serious work as teacher-scholar by deciding early on how fundamentally important fighting the organizational limitations will be to your sense of personal dignity. Let me suggest that, while it is good to resist unjustified encroachments on your individuality and academic freedom, an objective consideration of what is at stake when you bristle instinctively, as Newprof is doing, at some act of faculty governance or administrative ruling will lead to a conclusion that honor and academic freedom are very seldom endangered. Let me suggest, in fact, that the truly autonomous individual is the one who draws sensible lines by reasoned choice rather than by instinct.

"I Heard it Through the Grapevine"

The faculty lounge at the College of Port St. Julian is located in a room previously used for storage. Its brick walls are painted white. In the summer a noisy air conditioner roars away in the only window in the room. The furniture is of the mixed salvage variety: a shabby, overstuffed vinyl sofa; a worn, brocade-covered wingback chair donated by a trustee; two well-scratched Queen Annes from some dining set; three wooden folding chairs; a blond oak, modern Danish coffee table. It houses the faculty mail boxes. It is not an elegant room, but it is comfortable enough, and it is a much more important place than it looks.

Adam Newprof spends probably three hours of every busy week there. Partly that is out of the habit he formed when his office was right next door to the lounge; partly it is because he is a serious coffee drinker, and there is a cof-

---

[2] Isabel Briggs Myers, *The Myers-Briggs Type Indicator* (Palo Alto, CA: Consulting Psychologists Press, 1962), p. 71.

fee maker in the lounge on a little side table between the sofa and the faculty mailboxes. But as much as anything, he retreats to the lounge about once a morning because he values the chance to get away from his responsibilities for a few minutes, and to enjoy the camaraderie that always permeates a place where peers can gather and converse with coffee cups in hand.

Although this is Newprof's fourth year as a college faculty member, and the faculty lounge gathering has been a regular part of all four years, he has not yet recognized that what goes on under the guise of relaxed peer-group conversation is actually a key element in an important system of informal campus communication: the grapevine. He has yet to discern that the campus working environment is greatly influenced by what the grapevine is carrying in a given week, and that a large number of presuppositions that underlie attitudes and actions—even his own—grow out of grapevine tendrils.

A faculty member starting out on a new campus does well to be mindful of the potential, and usually invidious, effects of grapevine information. A good start as an individual in an academic organization will require recognition of the existence of the grapevine, sensitivity and insight into its workings, and vigilance against getting caught up in its serpentine twistings.

Staying out of the grapevine snare, even for someone alerted to the danger, is not as easy as it may at first seem. This informal information vine sprouts in the soil of human nature. It thrives in every human organization because nearly all of us are naturally receptive to what it brings us, and we in turn provide just the nutrients that power its growth.

If you should care to do an interesting experiment, one that can help with insights into what is meant by "the soil of human nature," let me suggest the following. During your first term on campus, visit the faculty lounge at least twice a week. Take a notebook along, and as unobtrusively as possible, jot down a few observations. Specifically: (1) Note who is there, (2) Note the topics of conversation and estimate the time spent on each, (3) Note the general tenor of the conversations, and (4) At the end of the term, analyze your notes. In all likelihood, you will not need to do step (4), for the picture will emerge well before midterm.

Unless your new campus is a very rare one, your notes will show that: (1) Not nearly all faculty use the lounge; perhaps a quarter will show up for coffee and conversation at one time or another, but the "regular customers" will consist of a group of maybe fifteen percent of the whole faculty, (2) The conversation will include the expected topics generated from the morning headlines and TV news shows, but a large percentage of the time will be taken up by talk about people on campus rather than about ideas, and (3) There will be a fair amount of amiable interchange, but the tenor of conversation will be negative more than it is positive: laments, complaints, grousing, criticisms, hand-wringing.

Those new faculty familiar with transactional analysis, or who have read Eric Berne's book *Games People Play*,[3] will recognize—will, in fact, anticipate— what the faculty lounge notebook reveals. The interchanges (transactions) that are the building material of lounge conversation come in a variety of identifiable patterns that Berne categorizes as rituals (e.g., greetings), operations (e.g., an honest request for and delivery of information or reassurance), pastimes (e.g., cocktail party topical conversation), or games. The common principal purpose of games is not to share information, but rather to reinforce the self-esteem of the individuals engaged in the game. *Simple* pastimes are primarily intended to structure (otherwise awkwardly spent) time in some social setting; they may be innocuous or even efficacious, but their effects can also be damaging. Berne gives this description of a "game":

> [A game] is a recurring set of transactions, often repetitious, superficially plausible, with a concealed motivation; or, more colloquially, a series of moves with a snare, or "gimmick."[4]

For those not familiar with transactional analysis and game-playing, I provide two examples of games often played on a college campus (as in all organizations), using Berne's titles for them.

If It Weren't for Him/Her. This is a three-handed (or more) game, involving the instigator, a reciprocator, and an absent third party.[5] In its most common campus form, the game begins when the instigator opens by suggesting that the third party—perhaps a colleague, perhaps an administrator, perhaps a student—is responsible for impeding the instigator in accomplishing some goal. The reciprocator becomes a player expressing acceptance of this claim, and giving some reinforcing response. The goal of the game is to gain either reassurance about or vindication for failure to accomplish the goal.

Ain't It Awful? This seems on the surface to be a "two-handed" (or more) game, but in fact, "[i]t is actually three-handed, the ace being held by the often shadowy figure called `They.'"[6] The instigator opens by bemoaning a condition to which he or she has been made subject; lazy students, inadequate library holdings, low pay, heavy workload are all good potential issues on a college campus. The reciprocator keeps the game going with assenting responses, and perhaps with augmenting examples. The payoff is the provoking of sympathy, which, especially if the reciprocator is a colleague from the same campus, can be enthusiastically mutual.

---

[3] Eric Berne, *Games People Play* (New York, NY: Grove Press, 1964).

[4] Berne, p. 48.

[5] Berne sees "If It Weren't for Him" technically as a "pastime" variation on the game, "If It Weren't for You." The latter is primarily a marital game in which the husband (or wife) holds the wife (or husband) responsible for some failure or shortcoming of his (or her) own.

[6] Berne, p. 111. Berne mentions "Water Cooler" and "Coffee Break" as organizational pastime versions of this game, with the essential theme being, "Look what they're doing to us now."

Take the following fictitious example of a coffee-break conversation.

Joe: Let me get to that coffee pot! After two hours of lecturing, my throat needs some refreshment. These summer school courses are killers. I'm teaching two courses this summer—both with huge classes, naturally—and it's a grind.

Sue: I know what you mean. And you're absolutely right about the class size. Last summer my course had over thirty-five students. That's too many for anybody to teach when classes meet every day.

Joe: There's no good reason that our classes should be so large. It's just another way of squeezing as much profit as possible out of every faculty member.

Sue: That point is underscored when you look at the pay. Do you know of any other college that pays so poorly for summer school teaching?

Joe: No four-year college. Our departmental secretary makes more on a per-week basis than I made last summer, and she didn't even finish college.

Sue: By the way, I don't suppose there's any chance of getting that piece on the Aztecs done this fall, the one you had planned to do this summer?

Joe: Are you kidding? I got stuck with that new course on rural sociology this fall. No way to get serious writing done when you're preparing a new course. I don't know why I had to get that assignment. But then, when you're understaffed as we are, there aren't enough people to take on the new courses.

Sue: And we're definitely understaffed. We've needed a new department member for two years.

Joe: Large classes in the summer, poor summer salaries—if I had realized how many ways faculty would be exploited, I'd have thought seriously about some other profession.

Joe and Sue are playing "Ain't It Awful." On the surface the conversation could be taken as an exchange of sincere concerns about genuinely onerous working conditions. But the primary underlying motive is to evoke feelings of sympathy, in this case mutual sympathy, through verbal transactions that imply abuses by others. When Joe opens with the lament about summer school classes, Sue recognizes the game at once and accepts her role spontaneously. Both are teaching summer school voluntarily, and both knew in advance what size classes they would have; a brand new faculty member, overhearing their conversation, would be likely to misunderstand this fact and to infer rather unfriendly conditions for teaching on this campus.

The ultimate end of such game-playing is not information exchange, or even "communication" as we usually mean the word, but rather a means of providing what Berne calls "strokes" for the game-player, a means of satisfying "recognition-hunger."[7] These transactions nevertheless affect very much the participants' sense of what is true. For example, suppose someone says, while playing "If It Weren't for Him," "My department chair is such a number cruncher that I'd bet anything that all he uses to judge teaching effectiveness is student ratings." The listener is quite apt to walk away with the *sense* that the chair in question is someone who uses numbers in an insensitive and probably inappropriate way, even when making judgments about something as complex as teaching effectiveness. The game-player didn't actually *assert* that, but in the listener's mind the impression is very likely to lodge. And although the primary intent of the game instigator was not to damage the reputation of the department chair, but merely to raise the relative stature of the instigator, reputational damage does get done. It's something like the effect that military commanders call "collateral damage" in war time.

It is also the xylem and phloem of the grapevine. The conventional campus wisdom about what is true at any given time is very much shaped by suggestions, implications, conjectures, and distortions that are offered in the context of game-playing. Even when there is ostensible *information* being offered, it often comes as a line in a game, and may well not be supported by clear evidence. Gossip and rumor flourish on the grapevine, based on evidence or not.

You should not take any of what is said in this section as a discouragement from frequenting the lounge on your campus. Not at all. This community center can be a good place to meet colleagues from other departments, and to enjoy the fellowship of others with similar interests and concerns. On a good day you may pick up an idea that will help you with a teaching problem, or go back to your department intellectually catalyzed by a colleague's incisive comments on some issue. But you will start with a distinct advantage if you are aware of the more usual, natural flow.

Berne holds up "game-free" relationships as the ideal for adult human beings. You will not likely find your faculty lounge to reflect that ideal state for a large percentage of the time it is in use. Still, you would do well to claim that ideal for yourself and to pursue it with some seriousness. You will want to stay attentive especially to the potential effects of lounge conversation on your

---

[7] Berne is suggesting by this term that we look after infancy for symbolic substitutes for the physical intimacy usually bestowed on us—and vital to our development and health as—infants. Put another way, we settle for substitute stroking. See pages 13-15 of *Games People Play*.

conclusions about what is true, and thus (a) on your decisions about how to act, and (b) on your morale. Is the president a person who cares about the educational mission of the college, or an insensitive manager who cannot be trusted with priority setting? Is the dean someone who is fair-minded and open, or a person who plays favorites and listens only to a few sycophants? Are there glaring and persistent salary inequities? Is Professor Jones getting away with sexual harassment of students? Does the student assistant in whom you have placed so much trust have a drug-abuse problem? These are the kinds of things that the grapevine will bring you, and you must be prepared to sort them out for yourself.

The grapevine is not, of course, a faculty lounge house plant. Indeed, even when a campus lacks a lounge, its counterpart becomes a corner of a snack bar, a booth in a nearby restaurant, or some other convenient gathering spot. I have concentrated on the lounge because the seeds of the vine are so often dropped there first, and because it is easy to understand the origins, impetus, and implications of the informal information system of the campus by looking at what goes on in the lounge. But the grapevine twists its way through every department and office on a campus, and its roots can be very difficult to locate.

The Administrative Structure

If your start as a faculty member is similar to mine, one of the discoveries of the first year will be that the campus population is divided up rather differently than it seemed from student memory to be. When I was a student, from freshman year through graduate school, it was my unexamined impression that most people on campus were students, the next largest group was the faculty, and there were a few other assorted non-teaching staff members. But not many were in this third group. It came as something of a surprise to learn that in reality the non-teaching-to-teaching ratio on a typical liberal arts college roster tends to be about two-to-one. Until I became an administrator myself, some sixteen years after that first year of teaching, with responsibility for providing a wide range of support and services for students and faculty, I never quite accepted the need for so many staff members to be employed by a college where the primary mission is teaching.

To be sure, there can be excesses in the hiring of staff as in anything else, and there are American campuses where this has happened, particularly during the 1980s. But the simple fact is that to get the job of teaching done effectively as we enter the twenty-first century requires far more than having a teacher sit on one end of a log and a student on the other. There will probably be more staff on your new campus than you expected, some of whom you will come to count on for substantial support in your work as teacher-scholar. It can be helpful (a) to have a good understanding of how a college organizes staff to accomplish tasks that need doing, and (b) to get acquainted personally with as many staff members as possible.

The typical administrative organization of a liberal arts college is shown in outline form in Table 9.1. Because it so common to miss the connection of the responsibilities of non-teaching staff to the teaching mission of the college, I have shown in the extreme right-hand column how this connection (in the ideal) is made. There is quite a bit of information in this table, and you are encouraged to read and reflect on all of it whenever you get the feeling that your college may suffer from "proliferation of administrators." It may. But even a cursory inspection of Table 9.1 suggests strongly that for all these things to get done, the college personnel roster cannot be short.

You may have been provided with an organizational chart for your new college, one showing the president in a box at the top, and lines branching down to increasingly numerous boxes underneath. This kind of chart is typical for corporate hierarchies, and many people who have never lived on a college campus assume that organizational relationships in higher education parallel those in corporations. (Indeed, this is but one of several invalid assumptions of similarities between colleges and universities on the one hand and business organizations on the other.) For staff members the parallel is close. And as a faculty member, you will have a "supervisor" (department or division head), who also has a supervisor (dean or academic vice president), who also has a supervisor (president), who reports to a board. But how faculty members actually relate to those immediately "above" them in the organizational chart differs significantly from how employees of a corporation relate to their supervisors.[8] As a faculty member, you will be part of what is sometimes called a professional bureaucracy—which means a bureaucracy of professionals. In this type of organization, which includes "universities, general hospitals, school systems, public accounting firms, social-work agencies, and craft production firms," the organization relies "on the skills and knowledge of [its] operating professionals to function."[9] Henry Mintzberg describes the difference this way:

> [T]he Professional Bureaucracy is a highly democratic structure, at least for the professionals at the operating core. In fact, not only do the professionals control their own work, but they also seek collective control of the administrative decisions that affect them—decisions, for example, to hire colleagues, to promote them, and to distribute resources....Some of the administrative work the operating professionals do themselves.[10]

---

[8] It is a curious fact that faculty members have often been known to object to the label "employee," when applied to themselves. Perhaps this attitude illustrates as well as anything else that faculty believe they should be doing "their own" work rather than work assigned by an "employer."

[9] Henry Mintzberg, *Structure in Fives: Designing Effective Organizations* (Englewood Cliffs, NJ: Prentice-Hall, 1983), p. 189.

[10] Mintzberg, p. 197.

Table 9.1
Typical Administrative Organization of College Staff

	Administrative Area	Primary Responsibilities	Connection to Teaching Mission
Internal Focus	**Academic Affairs**	• Teaching • Academic advising • Learning skills • Tutoring • Library and media support • Academic record-keeping • Computer support • Support for research • Faculty recruitment • Faculty development	• Provides the instruction • Provides direct support for classroom activities • Provides supplementary support for student learning • Assures that there are faculty to do the teaching
	Student Affairs	• Residential life • Student government • Student publications • Co-curricular programs • Personal counseling • Health services • Career development • Athletic programs	• Provides a student living environment conducive to learning • Provides extra- and co-curricular experiences that contribute to goals for student learning • Assists students in staying physically and emotionally healthy in the interest of effective learning
	Business Affairs	• Collection of fees • Management of financial resources • Accounting • Personnel matters • Building & grounds construction, repairs, and maintenance • Operation of auxiliary enterprises (bookstore, snack bar, etc.) • Management information	• Provides for a fiscally sound college with its resources focused on teaching and learning • Assures a physical environment supportive of teaching & learning • Prepares paychecks and manages employee benefits for faculty and support staff
External Focus	**Admissions Services**	• Recruiting students • Operation of financial aid system	• Assures that the college has sufficient new students to be taught • Assures a match between new-student quality and academic expectations of the college
	Resource Development	• Solicitation of external funds • College publications • Alumni relations • Parent relations • Trustee relations • Media relations • Press releases	• Provides funds from external sources to supplement funding for academic programs • Provides supplemental external funding to bring in qualified students • Enhances reputation of the college with a view to attracting able students and more benefactors

The consequence is that the faculty member has much more autonomy than, say, an assembly-line worker, not only because the work is inherently different, but also because the faculty member controls the work environment much more than the industrial worker can.

There are several ways in which the typical business executive would see the college, this example of a professional bureaucracy, as strange. In a college it is harder to introduce change, to make sure that needs are met that can be addressed effectively only through close coordination across departmental or faculty-staff lines, and to correct problems of performance. Much of the difference between corporation and college traces to the fact that:

> [P]rofessionals in these structures do not generally consider themselves part of a team. To many, the organization is almost incidental, a convenient place to practice their skills. They are loyal to their profession, not to the place where they happen to practice it. But the organization has need for loyalty, too—to support its own strategies, to staff its administrative committees, to see it through conflicts with the professional association. Cooperation, as we saw earlier, is crucial to the functioning of the administrative structure. Yet, as we also saw, professionals resist it furiously. Professors hate to show up for curriculum meetings; they simply do not wish to be dependent on each other.[11]

As a long-time denizen of the college campus, I would take issue only with the sweeping generalization about missing loyalty; I have observed many professors in small liberal arts colleges, and even in larger universities, who demonstrate an abiding loyalty. It is, however, strictly to an ideal of liberal education and of the institution that delivers it, not to the figures temporarily responsible for its administration.

Working with Administrators

As a faculty member, you will not interact directly with every staff member every day, nor will your interactions with all those within your sphere of contact be of the same nature. You will, however, be regularly in contact with non-teaching staff members, and your relationship with and attitude toward them will matter to both your work as teacher-scholar and to your feeling of satisfaction about your work place.

Determination to enjoy a good start in your new profession as faculty member will result in looking for ways to work productively with administrative staff. The following simple guidelines for working with administrators can help.

✦ Acknowledge their legitimate roles in the college.
✦ Get to know them as people.
✦ Learn to speak their language.
✦ Cultivate trust.

---

[11] Mintzberg, pp. 208-209.

Let's consider each of these in more detail.

The professional bureaucracy, Mintzberg points out, is comprised of "collections of individuals who come together to draw on common resources and support services but otherwise want to be left alone."[12] If, as a faculty member, you should assert that all administrators are there to provide resources and support, you would be technically correct, but you would also be missing something. The provision of resources and support should be for *student learning*, not for faculty themselves, and that primary obligation accords administrators certain legitimate spheres of responsibility and authority that deserve to be recognized by faculty members—even though exercise of their legitimate roles may limit the autonomy of the faculty. For example, the administrative creation in Business Affairs of certain purchasing procedures may chafe the faculty member who doesn't want to be bothered with them, but over the long haul (assuming Business Affairs has rational procedures) the financial well-being of the college is strengthened by having the procedures, and healthier finances means more money to be spent on things that enhance learning. Or to go back to the Adam Newprof story at the beginning of this chapter, a dean's decision not to hire someone whom she is truly convinced will not be a good faculty member may irritate a department member, but it is her responsibility to make that kind of judgment, and if it is sound, student learning will ultimately be advanced by it. Granted, there are administrators who push the bounds of their authority; there are those who confuse the collegiate organization with the corporate organization; there are those who need reminding what "the business of the business" really is. But it is important when dealing with administrators, just as with any other group, not to fall into stereotyping. In my experience, the vast majority of college administrative staff members are clear on the mission of their college and as dedicated as the faculty to the accomplishment of that mission. The good-start faculty member who is able to accept the legitimate roles of staff members in enhancing student learning will have a career that is free of the frustration that some people who teach feel continuously when they bump into boundaries set by those in the organization who don't teach.

It always helps to get to know administrators as people. I remember well the first week after I moved into the administration building on a campus where I had served as a faculty member for seventeen years. It was a distinct surprise to discover the behavior of former colleagues toward me changing so abruptly. I recall thinking that, for some of those colleagues, it was as if I had one Monday morning been transformed into a kind of alien in their eyes. But administrators are, in fact, human beings. My counsel for the new faculty member is to approach them that way, and to get personally acquainted as early as you can with those in the best position to assist you in your work. By "personally acquainted" I don't mean to pursue a close friendship; that may be

---

[12] Mintzberg, p. 207.

neither possible nor desirable in many cases. Rather, take time to learn something about them beyond their function in the organization. Look for the personal qualities that set each apart. When you have a concern with something that falls into the administrative realm, go and talk with the relevant staff member face-to-face, one person to another; don't use memos—or worse still, just fume. If you do this, you will quickly discover what benefits can accrue. While you are learning the administrative staff as people, they will also be learning you. It is out of this contact that trust gets built, and when you have a problem, you will find yourself with willing collaborators in its solution.

As you seek a good working relationship with administrators, include in your approach a willingness to learn their language. For some decades now, a common criticism of Americans has been that they are disinclined to learn the languages of other cultures. Something of the same phenomenon can be observed in most faculty interactions with staff members. There are two aspects of "administrative language" that I would point to here. First, just as each academic discipline has its own specialized vocabulary, so do administrative areas of a college. It is useful for the new faculty member to become acquainted with these vocabularies, both in the interest of understanding the people who work in these areas and in the interest of conveying faculty concerns to them. Communication obviously depends on the mutual use of words that can be comprehended. For instance, if you can talk intelligently about the impact of "endowment earnings" or "mandatory transfers" or the "E&G budget" with someone from the business office, you gain credibility as you gain information. Or, when you understand what "conversion rate" and "yield rate" mean to admissions people, you gain insights into factors affecting the quality of the students you will be teaching. As a second aspect, I would entreat new faculty, especially those from the humanities and arts, where the mathematical *quadrivium* tends not to be a favorite aspect of the curriculum, to be open to the language of management information as it is within your power to be. There is a powerful inclination on the part of some faculty members not only to eschew learning this language, but also to reject out of hand any information that is expressed quantitatively—except for grades and salaries! If you're talking with the dean about teaching loads, the conversation is much more productive if you know the significance of "student-faculty ratios" and "full-time equivalent students." These are mathematically- defined concepts, yet they reflect significant realities for the faculty member. Granted, quantitative information can be misused by administrators, but so can anecdotal information. Indeed, the latter is probably more open to misuse than the former, in that it is commonly used to argue from the specific to the general. Moreover, with a little effort, the open-minded faculty member will be in a far better position to form opinions and make decisions by a modest expertise in the use of management information data. This is an area where any innate chauvinism that springs from one's academic discipline should be set aside in the interest of both better communication and wider knowledge.

As a faculty member, I recall deploring the great waste I saw in the chronic conflict between faculty and administration. Now, as an administrator myself, I still see the waste, but I confess to having a different, less simplistic interpretation of its sources. Or in a sense, there is a *very* simple interpretation: faculty members and administrators need to trust one another more. Professor Lewis "By" Barnes of Harvard University has a trust-mistrust paradigm that he uses in teaching organizational behavior. Every human interaction begins, he says, with one of two assumptions: trust or mistrust. Out of the starting assumption comes certain expectations; out of the expectations comes certain behavior; out of the behavior comes reinforcement; the reinforcement determines the type of involvement practiced; and the type of involvement encourages more trust or mistrust. Schematically, these are the possibilities:

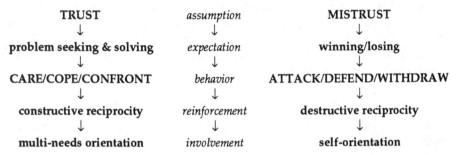

TRUST	*assumption*	MISTRUST
↓	↓	↓
problem seeking & solving	*expectation*	**winning/losing**
↓	↓	↓
CARE/COPE/CONFRONT	*behavior*	**ATTACK/DEFEND/WITHDRAW**
↓	↓	↓
constructive reciprocity	*reinforcement*	**destructive reciprocity**
↓	↓	↓
multi-needs orientation	*involvement*	**self-orientation**

As you begin your residency on a new college campus, you have a choice between Barnes's two assumptions. If you choose trust, you will be expecting something very different from your relationship with others on campus, including the administrative staff, from what those choosing mistrust will be expecting. The waste mentioned above is the waste of friction, the waste of vital energy used up in attacking, defending and withdrawing. How much more profitable—and how much more pleasant to come to work in the morning—when you expect to be engaged in mutual problem-solving with administrators and colleagues alike.

Shortly after I moved to the administration building, I received anonymously in the campus mail a copy of an article entitled "Swimming with Sharks."[13] There was a list of rules for swimming, the first of which was "Assume that all unidentified fish are sharks." It really isn't necessary to survival or safety to live by that rule on a college campus. Certainly, if anyone, administrator or colleague or anyone else, proves untrustworthy, we are fools to trust that person. But until that demonstration is unambiguous, we can choose trust. In doing so we opt for collaboration over conflict, we encourage trust in others, and we supply a powerful glue for strengthening the institution. Good administrators are no more

---

[13] I have lost this article and have been unable to find the reference, so I am unable to report the author or publication in which this article appeared.

the natural enemy of faculty than good teachers are the natural enemy of students. Indeed, if both are truly committed to the mission of the college and to practicing good will, there will never be a need to look around for sharks.

As a college dean, it has been my practice to work closely with first-year faculty. Not only do I meet with them frequently as part of a first-year orientation program, but I also approach them individually to talk about any concerns or problems that I may have detected; I also have lunch or breakfast with each one sometime during the year in an effort to get better acquainted and to offer help where it may be desired. It has been interesting to see how these new faculty members react to my initiatives. Often I get expressions of obviously sincere appreciation, sometimes coupled with surprise, for being alert to their needs and feelings. But in a few cases, I have heard indirectly that someone has wondered out loud what my motives were in all this—and even that a senior faculty member has warned them to be suspicious that the dean might be out to co-opt them! That kind of instinctive suspicion is something you, as good-start faculty member, should be wary of. When the choice is yours, assume good motives. Assume trust.

Faculty Governance: Collegial Constraints

We dealt rather thoroughly with faculty governance as a workload issue back in Chapter 8. Here I will address governance briefly as it impacts on the individual faculty member's sense of being appropriately free as a professional. Chances are that you will begin your work as faculty member with greater awareness of the administrative apparatus than of the organized faculty as a potential source of limitations on your independence. The fact is, as a random review of faculty handbooks will illustrate, it is quite common for faculties to construct systems of committees and policies that have the effect of creating an added layer of administration with which its individual members must contend.

Adam Newprof, at the beginning of this chapter, has encountered a fairly extreme instance, in which the faculty's Academic Standards Committee has legislated what percent of the course grade each faculty member must count the final exam. Clearly, this policy, despite its having been voted in by a majority of the faculty, is deciding a matter that most teachers would take to be up to one's own personal and professional judgment. Newprof will have to decide whether to conform to the policy, ignore it, or try to get it changed. Extreme though this example is, it comes from a real experience, and it does not exhaust the possibilities. Other faculty-set policies may determine the office hours you keep, how your course syllabi are organized, how you treat student absences from class, and a large variety of other practices that instinct tells you should be your decision as teacher.

Frustrating though it can be, organization of a faculty for purposes of governance is necessary for purposes of maintaining standards in a multiplicity of areas (curriculum, grading, honors, tenure and promotion), protecting rights and interests (faculty and student), advising on administrative policies, and allocating equitably certain college resources (e.g., travel funds, faculty research funds, and sabbaticals). When you become convinced that in the pursuit of these legitimate ends, means are being considered that transgress your sense of propriety, it will be up to you to argue against them in the places where arguing counts. Your argument may be made in writing to the chair of whatever committee is proposing a policy you wish to challenge, or it may be made in person. The argument will be strongest if you focus on the principle in danger of being violated. In the conversation between Adam Newprof and Maggie Morrow, it is not, obviously, whether the "right" percentage for the final exam is 30% or some other portion, but rather whether the majority of the faculty can rightly set *any* percentage for the dissenting minority.

In your first year as a faculty member at a new college, you will probably feel reluctant to contest motions from committees and to confront faculty leaders. We talked about that back in Chapter 8. Modesty is, to be sure, a virtue; but when you practice excess reticence, you forego opportunities to keep within bounds organizational encroachment into what should be your individual bailiwick. Just as you collaborate with colleagues to solve problems and set academic directions, you should determine to work with them to protect important principles.

Summing Up

The challenge of coming to feel comfortable as an individual in the organization that is a college may well prove to be more difficult for you over time than gaining confidence as a teacher or self-assurance as a scholar. Colleges, while more democratic than corporations are, still place limits on those who work within their walls, even on the individual faculty professionals at their core. Still, taken in the context of other options, the college campus comes closer to being that "paradise of individuality, eccentricity, heresy, anomalies, hobbies, and humors" than any place this side of Santayana's England.

Be prepared for the limitations. As an individual limited by the organization you will be subject to accountability of various sorts: performance evaluations, student evaluations, faculty policies, Board of Trustee policies, departmental policies and procedures, accounting procedures, purchasing procedures, travel regulations, committee rulings, tenure and promotion reviews, and decisions by department chairs, deans, and presidents. So be prepared. But keep in mind, too, that the life of a faculty member is still the most autonomous professional life available in America today.

Your success as a faculty member will rest ultimately in the degree to which you become expert as a teacher and scholar. But your *happiness* as a faculty member will rest on that realization of expertise *plus* your ability to adjust to life in the campus association of students, faculty colleagues *and* administrators. If you doubt that, look around you at the faculty you find on your new campus. Among them will be those senior members who are still able teachers, but whose attitudes are tinged with bitterness borne of years of resentment at being separated from pure freedom by policies, processes, and decisions not of their own devising. But among them, too, will be those senior members who have worked within the system of faculty governance and administrative organization, who have understood that "having their own way all the time" just wasn't a realistic or even theoretically possible aspiration, who have decided to stay free of the tangles of the campus grapevine, and who feel generally good about what they have been able to accomplish over the years by working in a spirit of collaboration with all campus constituencies.

My good-start counsel is that, even as you work at mastering your chosen profession of teaching, and as you commit yourself to growth as a scholar, you also try mightily for the autonomy that can come only from making enlightened choices about working within the system. You may decide that the system needs to change, and that's fine. But just as in a democracy, there will be avenues within the system itself for bringing about needed change. Decide to use these avenues—faculty legislation and administrative processes, yes, but often just honest conversation—and not let years of unnecessary accumulated rancor deprive you of the satisfactions that should come from the life of teacher-scholar. Approached wisely, you will find that the college can be a friendly organization—even for the most individualistic of all personality types!

For Discussion

1. Discuss how the following staff members might be seen as supporting the teaching mission (or advancing the cause of student learning) in a college.
   (a) the manager of the college bookstore
   (b) a member of the grounds crew
   (c) the assistant dean responsible for faculty development programs
   (d) the Director of Financial Aid
   (e) the Director of Athletics
   (f) the Director of Planned Giving
   (g) the President

2. Which of the following matters do you feel are appropriate for decision by faculty vote? Which are not? Why?
   (a) whether every instructor gives a comprehensive final exam in every course

(b) what fraction of the final grade in each course is determined by the final exam

(c) what minimum office hours are to be kept by faculty

(d) what attendance policy will be followed by faculty

(e) what system will be used by faculty for relating numerical and letter grades

(f) what grade-point average is required for graduation

3. Adam Newprof has just returned to his office from the faculty lounge. While there he heard Dr. Cathy Charisma, Chair of Foreign Languages, tell Dr. Walter Gauge, Professor of Classics, something she had "on good authority." The president had, she learned, called in Dr. Bob Bigbucks, Chair of Business Administration, for a "conference on salaries" later this week. As they talked, Charisma and Gauge agreed that only one interpretation was possible: the administration was preparing to do a big market adjustment in Business salaries. Everyone knew, Gauge pointed out, that next year's budgets would be tighter than usual, so the only way Business could get big salary improvements would be at the expense of faculty in other departments. Newprof, who feels that he has really knocked himself out this year, is totally dismayed.

How would you advise Adam Newprof? If Charisma and Gauge had been sensitive to the morale of Newprof, how might they have handled this situation differently?

4. Consider the coffee-break conversation between Joe and Sue given in this chapter as an example of the "Ain't-It-Awful" game. Suggest how Sue might have responded had she wanted to discourage game-playing and to transform their exchange into a mature conversation between adults.

Taking Charge of Your Life:
The Management of Time and Stress

For thogh we slepe or wake, or rome, or ride,
Ay fleeth the tyme, it wyl no man abyde.
Chaucer
The Wife of Bath's Tale
The Canterbury Tales

*T*t was Saturday afternoon. Specifically, it was the last Saturday afternoon in March. In Port St. Julian late March is full-flowered springtime, and the campus of the College of Port St. Julian is a garden. All around the Science Center, azaleas were in flamboyant bloom. Inside the Science Center, up on the third floor, Adam Newprof, halfway through a set of freshman chemistry test papers, was oblivious to the season and the flowers.

With the red pen he slashed two final X's, then scrawled a note at the bottom of the test paper lying before him. He was figuring the grade that would go on the front page, when he sensed that he was not alone. His eyes looked up, but his head didn't move.

"Hi there, Dr. Newprof." The cheery voice in the doorway interrupted the suspended calculations.

"Maggie! Where did you come from?" Newprof straightened, arched his aching back, and with his free hand rubbed at his tense neck muscles.

"From a terrific bike ride," Maggie Morrow answered. "Down by East Point Park and the seawall, and up past the marina, and then across town on Patriot Street. It's a great day out there. You should take advantage of it." She entered the office and plopped down in the visitor's chair across from him.

"Are you kidding?" He waved at the paper-cluttered desk. "Just look at all this."

"So what do you expect to find on a professor's desk? You should see mine. Well—you *have* seen mine. Not two square inches of wood showing on any day."

He leaned back wearily in his chair. She was a gem. He never ceased to be amazed at how much more relaxed she was than he, even when they faced exactly the same situations.

"Look," she went on, "I've come in here on a mission. You're going out walking with me."

"Hey, come on, Maggie," he demurred. "You know I'd like to, but I simply have too much to do."

"What do you have, a dozen more papers? You can finish those tomorrow. It's a gorgeous, balmy Saturday out there, and you've got to go on a walk with me."

He shook his head. "It's not just the papers. When I finish these, I have to spend some time analyzing the data that Jenny Liu and I collected in the lab yesterday. We're doing an Academy of Science presentation in a few weeks, and this last experiment is critical. And I promised Bobby Vegas I'd get his med school recommendation letter done this weekend, and Charles Noble that I'd review the texts we're considering for next year's freshman course."

Maggie wrinkled up her nose. "Ahh, you old...."

"No, seriously, Maggie. If there was any way at all to escape this cell, I'd be out like a shot. You know that."

He was jealous of Maggie Morrow. She always made it look easy. How did she do it? She was already recognized as an outstanding teacher, she was forever being elected or appointed to something, yet she seemed so much less tense and harried than he, Adam, usually felt. What was her secret?

"So—what about tomorrow? Will you go out to the zoo with me tomorrow? If you don't make some time for yourself soon, you're going to miss spring altogether."

"Sunday? I don't know. It's my turn to teach Sunday School in the morning. Then I'm doing a brand new lecture on orbital symmetry in Advanced Organic this term, and I had planned to use Sunday afternoon to work that up. It's going to take some time."

Maggie pushed up out of her chair. "Okay, Dr. Newprof, I've had enough. We're making a date for tomorrow afternoon at two o'clock. I'm coming by and dragging you out of your apartment, if I have to. No more excuses. After our visit to the zoo, we'll talk about how you can reclaim your life."

Adam watched her stride down the hall toward the elevator. Then she was gone. He rose and went to the window, aware of the pain in his lower back and a dull headache coming on. It was, he realized as the pinks and reds of azaleas caught his eye, indeed springtime in the world outside the Science Center. *Reclaim your life,* Maggie Morrow had said. As if it were a matter of choice.

He turned away from the window, depressed now by the glimpse of a waning day that he had no chance of enjoying. Not only was his work list too long; he had also forgotten to mail his mother a birthday card, and he had missed the barbershop for a second Saturday. He looked wistfully at the stack of test papers, chewed at the remainder of a fingernail, then began rummaging through his desk drawer for an aspirin.

The Nature and Sources of Faculty Stress

Just as he hadn't anticipated needing any kind of guide to the profession of college faculty member, Adam Newprof had no inkling that he would, in the fourth year of that profession, need help "reclaiming his life," as Maggie Morrow had put it. He had come to the College of Port St. Julian fully expecting to work hard, but hard work was nothing new. All through his school years his teachers had praised him for his industry. During college he worked as a lab assistant, took eighteen hours of course work per term, and graduated second in his class. During the graduate school years he had kept late hours in the laboratory and library, and would often forego for the sake of research the Saturday football games that friends wouldn't think about missing. Even in the Army, he had come back to the lab at night and worked on projects on his own time. He had been entirely prepared to work beyond the eight-hour day of a factory worker or industrial chemist. He had not, however, expected to drive to work most mornings with acid indigestion and a vague dread of the day.

Newprof, sitting in his office on this spring Saturday, has not taken stock of the situation in any analytical way, but if he did, these are some of the items he would flag as contributing to his present anxious feelings about his circumstances as a Port St. Julian faculty member: (1) He has a mental inventory of tasks that need doing and a sense of how much time they will take, and he fears that new items are being added to the list faster than he can check old ones off; (2) His organic chemistry class isn't going well this term; he has had two pre-med majors who continually challenge his method of grading, and who have created in the rest of the class, Adam suspects, a conviction that Newprof is unfair; (3) The Board of Trustees has been late announcing salary increases for next year, and the grapevine says that raises will be minimal at best; (4) Old President Fitzgeorge retired after last year's spring term, and was replaced over the summer with a former Navy admiral without experience in academe. The new president is prone to making surprise administrative announcements that Fitzgeorge would never have made without consulting the faculty; and (5) Leisure activities and even personal chores have been essentially pushed out of his week.

Stress, the name we give to what Newprof is feeling, is no stranger to college campuses. The common image of the college professor tends to be of a tweedy character who spends languid afternoons in a book-lined office that smells of pipe smoke and shows up for lectures a few times each week. The reality can too often approximate the scene described above for Adam Newprof—or something worse. In delineating faculty responsibilities, faculty handbooks inevitably identify those three discrete aspects of the job: teaching, scholarship, and service. These are indeed the ingredients, but they are seldom discrete. The real academic life encourages no neat structure for the workday, no uncluttered space carved out for each of the three defined performance areas. Teaching, scholarship, and service can come to seem always in competition for the same limited hours. The classes themselves follow a fixed schedule, to be sure, but the lecture preparations, committee meetings, interruptions by students, writing projects, paper grading, and departmental tasks can become a cacophony of calls for time and attention, no one of which the faculty member feels able to answer adequately before the next call comes. What the non-faculty member is inclined to see as a highly flexible, minimally demanding workday too often proves a workday that is open-ended, and therefore endless, for the faculty member who has not come to terms with it.

Stress is not, of course, a mere state of mind. A kind of physiological relic, the stress reaction once readied our ancestors for physical action. The primitive hunter needed not simply slightly greater wit than prey and foe, but swift augmentation of energy as well. The same physicochemical system that supplied bursts of adrenaline and blood sugar to the spear-flinger and charging warrior functions unerringly in the modern faculty member responding to a lazy student or launching into a last-minute lecture preparation. The chemistry is unchanged. At least the chemistry of *provocation* is unchanged. Deep inside the brain the hypothalamus clicks on, activating neurotransmitters that signal distress to the pituitary gland, the brain stem, and the spinal column. The pituitary in turn stimulates the adrenal cortex, and the brain stem and spinal column the interior of the adrenal glands. Into the bloodstream come chemical effluents, cortisol from the adrenal cortex, and adrenaline (or epinephrine) and norepinephrine from the adrenal glands. Blood sugar levels climb. The heart speeds up. The blood pressure elevates. The muscles tense. The senses become more acute. Gastric acid is expelled. The whole body is energized for fight or flight.[1] The professor darting from class to committee

---

[1] The phrase "fight or flight" comes from Dr. Walter Cannon, a pioneer psychologist in the study of stress. Considering how humans evolved with a mechanism for facing sudden change that is so deleterious to so many modern people, Cannon wrote: "But fear and aggressive feeling, as anticipatory responses to critical situations, make ready for action and thereby they have had great survival values." Walter B. Cannon, *Bodily Changes in Pain, Hunger, Fear, and Rage*, 2nd edition (New York, NY: Appleton Publishing, 1929), p. 27.

meeting becomes, biochemically speaking, the hunter whirling about to confront a saber-toothed tiger.

But the biochemistry of the aroused professor differs markedly thereafter from that of the aroused hunter-warrior. The psychophysiological systems of the two work the same way, but the former lacks the means of the latter for discharging the extra energy generated to meet the stressful situation. Both are mobilized for vigorous muscular action, but the professor flings no spear, climbs no tree, charges no adversary. When the stress has an intellectual rather than a physical focus, the stress response with all its physiological ramifications becomes maladaptive. And in a day when one is constantly jumping from one intellectual problem to another, turning again and again to face new, albeit non-muscular challenges, the hypothalamus keeps clicking, the cortisol and catecholamines (adrenaline and norepinephrine) keep pumping, and the faculty member experiences sustained periods without relief.

The long-term consequences can be notably injurious not merely to morale, but to physical health as well. Hypertension, coronary artery disease, headaches, peptic ulcers, arthritis, immunological disorders, and even cancer can, research suggests, be products of sustained stress.[2] Faculty members are as susceptible to these consequences as anyone else. Indeed, given the fact that those who choose the college faculty profession tend to be especially conscientious high achievers, who set ambitious goals for themselves and are chronically overcommitted, it might be expected that as a group they are outstanding candidates for this list of stress-related health problems. Peter Seldin begins a chapter on academic stress with this paragraph:

> It takes only a few minutes of conversation with college or university professors around the country to realize that academic stress is a national phenomenon. An eastern professor refers to his university as a "stress factory." A midwestern faculty member insists that the words *stress* and *academic* are redundant. A professor at a West Coast university reports that her stress level is several notches higher than it was when she worked in industry.[3]

Long-term well-being, physical as well as mental, in an environment so charged with stress, can become imperiled. Over time, personal lives can be ravaged. Careers can be derailed.

The look at Adam Newprof on a tense, lost Saturday, and the foregoing review of the dangers of and prospects for stress are not offered here to dismay the early-career faculty member. Quite the contrary. If you are a good-start faculty member, you will want to understand how stress works, to be keenly attuned to the major sources of stress and intent on dealing with them

---

[2] See David Holmes, *Abnormal Psychology* (New York, NY: HarperCollins, 1991), Chapter 18, for a rather thorough discussion at the layman's level of the stress-illness connection.

[3] Peter Seldin, "Research Findings on Causes of Academic Stress," in Peter Seldin, editor, *Coping with Faculty Stress* (San Francisco, CA: Jossey-Bass, 1987), p. 13.

effectively. In *Coping with Faculty Stress*, Peter Seldin identifies the following specific major sources of stress among college and university professors:

✦ Inadequate participation in institutional planning and governance
✦ Too many tasks, too little time
✦ Low pay and poor working conditions
✦ Inadequate faculty recognition and reward
✦ Unrealized career expectations and goals
✦ Unsatisfactory interactions

At first blush these may seem to be sources over which the individual faculty member has little control. We shall examine that proposition below, but let me say here that Maggie Morrow's suggestion that Adam Newprof might reclaim his life is not at all an absurd idea. And the earlier he decides to do that, the more satisfying—and saner—his career will prove to be.

Coping with Stress

Robert Veninga and James Spradley, in their book *The Work/Stress Connection*, describe "The Honeymoon stage" of a job this way:

> [D]uring this phase, we develop habits of dealing with stress. If successful, the honeymoon period can go on and on. However, if the strategies we develop are ineffective, the burnout process begins in earnest. Most important, we have missed an opportunity to equip ourselves to deal with unforeseen stress that can erupt at any time from our job, family, or the wider world.
>
> Some people become almost invulnerable to stress during this period and sail along for years, perhaps for the rest of their lives, no matter how rough the seas.[4]

If you are a brand new faculty member, you are in The Honeymoon stage of your job. You are feeling enthusiastic, idealistic, eager for the challenge, energized. All things are possible. If you would like to sail along that way for years, even the rest of your life, no matter how rough the seas, this chapter could be the most important in *Good Start*.

The management of time and stress is a neglected topic in faculty orientation and faculty development programs. Where these programs are part of campus practice, teaching is, naturally, treated extensively, with attention given to pedagogy, to student-teacher interactions, to testing and grading— to all those things covered in Chapter 6 of this book. Pointers are given on getting started as a scholar, and groups may be invited to discuss the proper role of research in a liberal arts college or how to keep teaching and scholarship connected. And in faculty lounges you will hear much to confirm the omnipresent sense of time-shortage and high tension. But it is almost as if the

---

[4] Robert L. Veninga and James P. Spradley, *The Work/Stress Connection* (Boston, MA: Little, Brown, and Company, 1981), p. 41.

prospects for *coping*, for fighting back against the genetic disadvantage of the stress reaction and the myriad encroachments on faculty time, are so dismal that campuses do just as well to capitulate and get on with other, more promising endeavors. I would argue that the stakes are too high to capitulate. I would argue that anyone at the start of what is intended to be a long, satisfying career as an effective teacher or scholar will be obliged to minimize to the threat of stress to those worthy aspirations. As Veninga and Spradley indicate, if during The Honeymoon stage "the strategies we develop [for coping with stress] are ineffective, the burnout process begins..." But the faculty member who is successful at this stage—the good-start faculty member—can "become almost invulnerable to stress..."

Becoming invulnerable is not, granted, equally easy for all. Take Erika and Luisa. Erika and Luisa are twin daughters of family friends, a German professor and his wife. The girls are so identical to the eye that almost everyone confuses them. But how differently they respond to the pressures of life! Faced with the same kindergarten coloring assignment one December, Erika grabbed a crayon and started right in; but Luisa surveyed the picture of the big Christmas tree covered with all those stars, tentatively began coloring one star, then burst into tears, wailing, "It's just too *much!*" From the beginning, as all parents know, we are different individuals, variably equipped to deal with the world. "Type A" and "Type B"[5] are the labels we most often identify the intense Luisa type and the relaxed Erika type. And all of us in academe are well aware of which is more highly concentrated in the conscientious, high-achieving faculty ranks of every good liberal arts college.

Adam Newprof is a Type A. On this Saturday, as on nearly every day, he feels that *it's just too much.* How will Maggie Morrow go about converting him from the Luisa type to an easy-going Erika? She won't, of course. But there *are* ways, short of a "personality transplant," to help Newprof save himself from a predicament omnipresent on college campuses. Exactly how Maggie means to approach the challenge, I can't say; but let me suggest to the early-career faculty member the following guidelines for coping with stress.

- ✦ Be a Master, not a Victim.
- ✦ Take control of your time.
- ✦ Stay alert to the sources, mechanism, and symptoms of stress.
- ✦ Set realistic expectations.
- ✦ Choose the better interpretation.
- ✦ Remember your muscles.

[5] Terms coined by two cardiologists upon observing that so many of their patients shared certain personality traits: overcommitment, powerful sense of time urgency, competitiveness, concern over achievement, hostility, aggressiveness. See M. Friedman and R. H. Rosenman, "Association of Specific Overt Behavior Pattern with Blood and Cardiovascular Findings: Blood Cholesterol Level, Blood Clotting Time, Incidence of Arcus Senilis and Clinical Coronary Artery Disease," *Journal of the American Medical Association 169*, 1286 (1959).

♦ Release the pressure.
♦ Get enough rest.
♦ Be a Master, not a Victim.

Stress is an inescapable feature of the academic life—and of every other. There is no magic potion for banishing it. There is no magic formula for managing it. But there is a key. That's why the list above begins and ends with the same sentence: Be a Master, not a Victim. It is a call for an outlook without which you can do none of the other things on the list. If you think of yourself as being in control, you will react to the stressful situations that come along in a totally different way than someone who sees himself or herself as a victim. Richard N. Bolles describes the latter person as having the "Victim Mentality," which he sums up this way:

> My life is essentially at the mercy of vast powerful forces...*out there* and beyond my control. Therefore I am the victim of, and at the mercy of...

He goes on to provide a long list of forces "out there" from which the reader may identify those in one's own life. Just as in game-playing (see Chapter 9), this Victim Mentality serves its purpose. As Bolles puts it,

> The Victim Mentality ultimately discharges you from any responsibility for your life, since clearly what is happening to you is not your fault.[6]

It accomplishes little to be absolved from "fault," to have whining justified. What is infinitely more valuable is the certainty that you have accepted the responsibility for your own life, and that you are taking initiatives to deal with whatever comes your way. Teaching load, conflict with students or administrators, too many papers to grade—whatever the stressor, there is nearly always something you can do to change the situation (examples follow below). And even in the case where you truly cannot change the external circumstance, you will stay healthier in mind and body by choosing a mature internal reaction to it. The call to be a master is not a call to pretend that life is free from outside forces and events that threaten and test you, but rather an invitation to see yourself as able to respond productively to those forces and events.

Perhaps it is in the sense that there is just too little time for it all that the faculty member, new or seasoned, is most apt to feel like a victim. The counsel to take control of your time may well evoke some response like "Fat chance!" from the harried professor in the middle of a typically crowded week. But if you accept that the call to be a Master, not a Victim, is the *key* to stress control, the *test* of effective stress control is surely whether you feel successful at time management. This item on our list is so important that we will devote the following section of this chapter to it alone. At this point, let me note simply that you can hope to feel in control only if you *are*. This means taking very specific actions rather than being buffeted about by the circumstances of the day.

Because the stress reaction is a natural part of being human, built firmly into human physiology, we cannot escape it, nor can we build a behavioral path around it. With the very best success at seeing ourselves as Masters, getting control of our time, and accomplishing the rest of the list laid out above, at every provocation the hypothalamus will click on, the neurotransmitters will communicate, and the biochemistry will begin. We are not always even conscious that we are under stress. Working on a new lecture or finishing up an article for publication may be activities that you very much *enjoy*. Beginning work at a new college, starting a whole new career, may be very exciting and fulfilling. But stress does not require either alarm or depression; the stress reaction works in positive situations just as certainly as in negative ones. Coping requires being alert to all the sources, the mechanism, and the symptoms of stress. You will make the best use of your coping strategies when you are mindful of how stress originates, how it is working—and *that* it is working. Your body gives you clues. Rapid heartbeat, headaches, queasiness, chronic fatigue, tense muscles, heartburn, insomnia, even itching, can be signals in a kind of early-warning system. They can be telling you to let up, to take a break. If you find yourself buying Maalox and aspirin with some frequency, even if you don't *feel* "stressed out," don't ignore the warning.

In their national Faculty Stress Research Project of 1984, Walter Gmelch and co-workers found that the number one stressor for faculty was "imposing excessively high self-expectations."[7] That should come as no surprise. Once more: Who aims for a professorship? It is typically the conscientious, driven, high achiever. The ex-student who was depressed over a B+. In faculty orientation programs I have noted that no amount of clarity about standards for tenure suffices to relax the most driven in a new faculty cohort; their goals, and usually their accomplishments, always exceed any formal institutional expectations. Yet it is rare indeed to find recognition that the stress they experience is coming even in part from self-imposed expectations. In teaching, in scholarship, in service, the extra-conscientious faculty member is inevitably trying to do more—and feeling vaguely victimized. Have you taken into account the change in environment from research university to liberal arts college? Does the exam have to be all-essay, and so take twice as long to grade? Must you say yes to taking on a fourth committee assignment? Is it essential that the research project you're working on be of Nobel Prize quality before you try to publish it? In short, have you set realistic expectations for yourself? Take soundings from time to time; ask a senior faculty member, your chair, or the dean about the goals that you have in mind. Setting high standards is

[7] W. H. Gmelch, N. P. Lovrich, and P. K. Wilke, "Stress in Academe: A National Perspective," *Research in Higher Education 20*, (1984), p. 477.

laudable, but setting yourself up for unnecessary tension and disappointment is simply bad judgment. Should you sign a contract to co-author a book on medical ethics? Should you take ten extra students into your Shakespeare class? Should you come up next year for promotion to associate professor? These may or may not be things that make sense, given your particular situation, and it is wise to seek timely guidance in deciding. Over the long haul, if the expectations you set are excessive, you will likely become either (a) passive, feeling hopeless and giving up, or (b) aggressive, feeling hostile and blaming others. Here's a much more profitable response:

> "I'm going to do the best I can at what I'm doing. But I'm not going to kill myself. I'm going to take all that energy expended in worry over not meeting my goals and put it into activities that bring some rewards."[8]

If you can determine early in your career that you will keep your expectations in the realistic range, and will follow through with that resolution, you will have made a mighty and pivotal contribution to the management—or more exactly, the prevention—of stress.

As suggested in the chapter on the individual in the organization, new faculty members (and others) can be affected in their morale and decision-making by what they pick up from the college grapevine. Hearing over coffee that only administrators will receive travel money next year is an unsettling way to begin the workday. Indeed, such grapevine "information," valid or not, can be a prime source of faculty stress. The information may be far from being hard fact, but it has its effect. Another type of quasi-fact comes to us from the interpretations we place on the words, actions, or inactions of others. The department chair said, "Your seminar was fine." Did that mean that she thought it could be better? More students signed up for Professor Black's section of English Literature than for mine. Does that mean that I don't have as good a reputation as a teacher? The dean asked me to have lunch with him. Is there a problem that I don't know about? In each of these situations, the faculty member's interpretation will be crucial in determining just how much of a stressor the "information" proves to be. There is a choice. It's the old "half full, half empty" dilemma. When there are such choices, stress will be reduced by your decision to choose the better interpretation. If you keep a log of the number of times in one week that these kinds of equivocal situations present themselves, you will see the potential for cumulative contribution to your stress. Yet every campus has in abundance faculty who are fretting over what might—but also might *not*—be bad news, slights, criticisms, or disrespect. The tendency to take the negative interpretation can lead to hard feelings between faculty colleagues, to deep distrust between faculty members and administrators, and to needless corrosive tension. You do have a choice. Why not opt for the better interpretation? You will be saving yourself superfluous stress.

---

[8] Veninga and Spradley, p. 97.

Recognizing the stress reaction as a preparation for physical action, it follows that one way to relieve it is through physical exercise. A number of industrial organizations have recognized the efficacious results of exercise, and some have even installed gyms and scheduled exercise programs. Many hotels now provide exercise rooms for traveling executives and others seeking to relieve stress. You will be doing yourself a great favor if you develop the habit from the beginning of including regular physical exercise in every day. It may be a pick-up game of basketball, a brisk walk, or jogging. Whatever the form, remember your muscles. Not only will you feel better at the end of the day, but you will also discover that your work hours are more productive.

Exercise is one way that you can release the pressure of a stressful day. There are other, less physical outlets that may be less obvious to you, but can totally change the feel of a hectic day or week. Here are some examples:

◆ Engage in hobbies—painting, music, crafts, fly casting.
◆ Use lunch hours to escape—off-campus lunches with no shop talk, chess or bridge with friends, reading a novel.
◆ Give yourself treats—an unscheduled movie, dinner out with your spouse, an unplanned purchase.
◆ Commit yourself to non-academic involvements—church work, volunteer work, activism, politics.
◆ Go home early—to get a home chore done, to relax with the newspaper, to take a nap.

These are all escape measures, actions you can take to break out of the stress trap, and they work. You may feel guilty at first at the mere thought of "neglecting" your work for such indulgences; most faculty members probably will. But once you accept that the release of pent-up pressure helps you work more efficiently, and then have actually experienced the fruits of such practices, you will need no further convincing.

Finally, there is the matter of rest. It is all too common to find that in the first year of life as a faculty member, sleep and rest are severely curtailed. After a long day on campus, you are likely to leave the office with a briefcase stuffed with papers or with lectures to prepare—and a full evening of work before you. The night is well along before you get to bed. And before your system has recovered from the stress of the day before, the alarm is going off and it is time to start another day. You need rest to work well. It girds you for everything you take on, both personal and professional. Getting enough of it is a crucial part of time management, which is squarely in your hands. More about that in the next section.

Managing Your Time

The management of time is obviously so intimately intertwined with the management of stress that the two can be separated only artificially, as I have done in this chapter. Your time is your life. If Maggie Morrow is successful at helping Adam Newprof reclaim his life, the evidence for it will not be that on a given Saturday she will find a laid-back Type-B rather than an uptight Type-A Adam in his office; the proof will be that on Saturdays and every other day he is controlling his time, acting rather than reacting, and living a *whole*, balanced life. Should Adam accept Maggie's invitation for Sunday, and should that be the beginning of a serious life-reclamation project, he will find few role models in the ranks of senior faculty at Port St. Julian College. He will find outstanding teachers from whom he can learn, dedicated and accomplished scholars to inspire him, and faculty leaders whose statesmanship can serve as a worthy paradigm for the new college citizen. But the odds of discovering an older colleague who is living the balanced life, a model time manager, so to speak, are small indeed. What he is more likely to find are people totally immersed in the job and displaying collectively nearly every symptom of stress. Mary Deane Sorcinelli and Marshall Gregory describe the situation this way:

> Academic careers are not merely work. Like other careers, they tend to become a way of life. The problem is that careers tend to become the whole life, and that a whole life defined this narrowly creates tensions.[9]

Time management calls for a conscious definition of life. The earlier you set out to arrive at your definition, the easier it will prove to do it. And the earlier you do it, the more years you will enjoy of career satisfaction—and a full personal life. As with the management of stress, there is no magic formula, but there are some guidelines for time management that I would offer to the new faculty member:

+ Be a Master, not a Victim.
+ Start the day sanely.
+ Organize your day, your week, your year.
+ Keep a good balance.
+ Limit your work hours.
+ Retreat when you need to.
+ Schedule enough rest.

"Time management," though the phrase has the sound of something mechanical, maybe even gimmicky, is really a mental attitude more than a "system." That's why still again you see a list that begins with the exhortation to be a Master, not a Victim. It is vital to begin your effort to claim your life by believing that you can, by rejecting the notion that shortages of time come principally from what others do. Others will, no question about it, move into

---

[9] Mary Deane Sorcinelli and Marshall W. Gregory, "Faculty Stress: The Tension Between Career Demands and 'Having It All,'" in Peter Seldin, editor, *Coping with Faculty Stress* (San Francisco, CA: Jossey-Bass, 1987), p. 44.

your day with every imaginable sort of encroachment—but only to the extent that you invite and/or permit such claims on your time. Teaching, scholarship, and citizenship activities will collide —but only if you allow them to do so. Your collection of professional responsibilities can deprive you of time for personal activities and family life—but not out of some natural law beyond your power to arrest. Success with controlling time, as with coping with stress, begins with a firm rejection of the victim mentality and an optimistic acceptance of personal responsibility.

Let's begin the plan for managing time at the beginning of the day. If you start the workday sanely, you will find that the rest of the day is easier to deal with. Veninga and Spradley say, "The most important two-hour period in your day is prior to starting work. During that period you set the tone for the day." If you are taking time for breakfast with the family, followed by a leisurely cup of coffee over the morning newspaper, that isn't bad. If you take a twenty-minute walk, that's even better. The point is to reach your office having controlled your day for the first two hours, and to have brought to work with you a sense of calmness and accomplishment. Some of the most productive people I have known have also been the most relaxed, and they have almost always been early risers, people who got up at 4:30 or 5:00 a.m. and read, wrote, and/or exercised before breakfast. Not every one can do this, but those who can seem to profit from it. On the other hand, those who reach the campus in a rush, with a fast-food sausage biscuit in one hand, tend to stay in a stew all day. Let me suggest that, if you are at present a late riser who leaves home in a hurry, you reset your alarm and try a week-long experiment in lifestyle change. Give yourself two good hours before work and see how it affects the rest of the day.

Claiming a sane two-hour start-up period gives you a good beginning on organizing your day. You may, however, find it easier to imagine achieving a slow-paced early morning than a full day that follows your plan. But organization is possible—and necessary, if you mean to use time management to reduce stress. It should begin with a determination of what you are organizing for, a summary of your goals for the day. It doesn't work to stop with a vague mental list; you need to get it down in writing. Using a distinctively-colored note pad that you keep in sight on your desk can be a useful approach. List-writing is a point where the earlier admonition to set realistic expectations for yourself should be practiced resolutely. Your daily list should be doable, or you will simply add to the stress you feel. Some people draw a line near the bottom of the page, write their "must" goals above the line, and their "maybe" or "if-there's-time" items below the line. Use a daily calendar now to organize the day; I suggest one with hours and quarter hours marked off. With a pencil, block off and label times to be used in accomplishing your goals, beginning with the fixed periods. The overall organizing process, from goal-setting to completed calendar, might look something like this:

✦ Write down a realistic list of *goals* for the day.
✦ Block out *fixed periods* (classes, scheduled office hours, committee meetings).
✦ Block out periods for *research and scholarship* (if you're doing research on the particular day).
✦ Block out *do-not-disturb office hours* (for lecture preparation, paper grading, correspondence, writing). Use an answering machine, if necessary, to keep even phone calls from intruding. *Protect this time.*
✦ Block out *"free" time* (short periods during the work day used at your discretion: exercise, coffee breaks, personal errands, and the like).
✦ Block out *personal time* (longer periods, usually after your day on campus, for household chores, family activities, leisure activities).

Each daily plan should be put into finished form at the end of the preceding day, and should fit into an overall plan for the week, which in turn should be moving you toward the completion of goals for the term and year. In setting goals for yearly accomplishments, if at all possible, protect your summers for research and other projects where extended periods of time are valuable, and for additional personal and family time; no other profession allows you such an advantage, but you have to decide whether to capitalize on it. To help you get extended time blocks during an academic term, ask your department chair to schedule your courses in ways that don't chop every day into small pieces.

Let me acknowledge that the notion of imposing structure on the workday will not appeal equally to everyone.[10] One attraction of the academic life for many of us was, after all, the *absence* of excessive structure. The fact is though that without a fairly explicit plan—one that *you* have created, and one that can vary greatly from day to day—a vacuum is created into which will surely come rushing a myriad of intrusions to claim the day you meant to call your own.

As you organize, then follow through on your plan, you will profit significantly from a serious effort to keep a good balance. Even when it's your plan, you will be tempted to skimp on some areas and over-emphasize others in a way that ultimately has consequences. Assess your calendar carefully at least once each week and ask pointed questions. Are work and personal life kept in proportion? Is there enough physical activity to relieve the stress of a life with a mental focus? Is there a good balance among teaching, scholarship, and service? Is the plan contributing to your long-term goals? All of us who are long-time academic veterans have known people who fell victim to practicing excess in each of these three areas of responsibility. One department chair, for example, came to me one fall after I had begun deaning, to lament, "I just don't know how I can do any more." She went on to describe the very real sense of overload she was feeling, and I arranged for an extra course release in the

---

[10] Recall the MBTI (Myers-Briggs type indicator) preferences discussed in Chapter 6.

spring term. When I reviewed her annual activity report later that year, I discovered that she had taken on eighteen (yes, 18!) significant service activities—standing committees, *ad hoc* task forces, search committees, and the like—in the previous two terms. Another faculty member, after his promotion to full professor, complained at one point that the very late hours he was spending on his research had put a strain on his marriage; a year later he was divorced and depressed. And teaching, too, has taken its toll. Every faculty member will occasionally be late leaving the office, or have to postpone a planned trip to the library, because a student needed help that couldn't be delayed. But a repeating pattern of that sort is indicative of problems, and inevitably causes problems in some other area, either personal life or career. It is not, in fact, uncommon to discover that "total dedication to teaching" is a convenient (albeit unconscious) technique for avoiding other activities, personal or professional, that one dreads. Other teaching practices that consume inordinate amounts of time needed elsewhere have to do with subjective versus objective testing, numbers of graded assignments during a term, and invitations for students to call you at home.[11] Balance is important, and imbalance comes with a price—that *you* have to pay.

You address the need for balance, too, when you limit your work hours. To any seasoned faculty members reading this, who didn't become successful time managers earlier on, that assertion may seem absurd. If you are inclined to agree, why not try an experiment? Try scheduling over a two-week span a reasonable hour for leaving campus—and leaving your briefcase behind. *Do no night work.* Use your do-not-disturb office hours for what would otherwise have been evening homework for you. Note each day any unfinished work remaining. At the end of the two weeks compare the amount of unfinished work with the amount that remained to be done when your briefcase went home every night. I would wager that you will find (a) that at least as much work is getting finished, and (b) that the quality of your time at home is greatly enhanced.[12] Similarly, you should protect your weekends. There will occasionally be a Parents' Weekend or some similar activity to take you to campus; now and then it is sensible, too, to take a Saturday morning to clean up a cluttered desk. Otherwise, you are consuming hours that can provide a vital restorative period for you and healthy involvement with your family and friends.

Sometimes, despite your best efforts at organizing the day, the interruptions are just interminable. Even the do-not-disturb sign is ignored. In the face of such obstacles to claiming your day and getting the items on your list checked off, abandon your office. Retreat when you need to. You should find

---

[11] This is *not* an argument for decreasing standards or refusing help when it's needed; it *is* an argument for sensible practices.

[12] It took me far too many years to discover these facts for myself. Someone should have told me in the beginning.

an alternate place to write, read, or grade, a place where you will not be easily
found. The most obvious location is the college library, in a remote carrel or
study room. Another approach is to block off a morning or afternoon (but *not*
an evening) now and then to hole up at home until a project is finished. The
occasional Saturday morning mentioned in the paragraph above can serve the
same purpose. The obvious point is to get your work done as pleasantly as
possible, and with the least amount of stress.

Few people want to become so highly organized that they actually block
out a period and label it "rest." Even so, as suggested in the previous section,
your time management falls short unless you schedule enough rest. I won't
elaborate again here on the reasons, but I will underscore the need to be conscious of the foundational value of rest, and the vital importance of organizing
your days, weeks, and years with ample opportunity for it.

Two Final Words

This chapter has set forth a number of guidelines for managing time and
stress. As we end it, I want to add two final words that are really corollaries of
the admonition to set realistic expectations. I save them for the end of this
chapter because I think they bear special reflection. Here they are:

- ✦ Don't despair when you get off track.
- ✦ Don't hold out for "cosmic justice."

Guidelines aren't magic formulas, and no matter how committed you
might be to subscribing to them, there will be hours and days when you just
can't stick to them. Don't despair when this happens and you get off track.
Obviously it isn't always possible to kick a visitor out of your office just when
the schedule says it's time for a do-not-disturb hour. And it isn't always possible to claim that two-hour sane beginning for a day, or to leave the office on
time to come home. But even if you are able to follow the guidelines for 80%
of the time, they can be transforming. Do your best, but don't let occasional
inability to stay totally faithful to a set of guidelines intended to relieve stress,
wind up adding to your stress! Keep in mind that you're a human being. Staying in reasonable control of your life 80% of the time isn't bad.

Faculty members, arguably more than any group, tend to yearn for what I
often call "cosmic justice." I use that term to refer to the justice that would be
meted out by some omniscient, perfectly fair judge. Stress can often be traced
to what may be called an "expectation gap," the distance separating what the
individual privately expects from what actually comes to pass. Justice gets
measured across that gap. And when one party expects an action or decision
that takes perfectly into account every possible variable that an omniscient
cosmic judge could consider, disappointment—and stress—are absolutely
assured. Bruce Partin, chair of the fine arts department at Roanoke College,

talks about "unilateral contracts" in describing the intense level to which private expectations can build.[13] Is my salary appropriate? Will I be named department chair? Will I get the class schedule I asked for? Will I get the teaching award? If you can determine now that you won't set "unilateral contracts," that you won't hold out for "cosmic justice," but will settle for honest efforts at equity and fairness, you can eliminate at the outset a corrosive that can otherwise eat away needlessly at your happiness for a full career.

For Discussion

1. Suggest specific steps that Adam Newprof might take, as he rejects the "Victim Mentality" and takes charge of his life, when faced with the following stressful situations.

   (a) The new College of Port St. Julian president, Marshall Takecharge, has proposed increasing the teaching load for science faculty from twelve to fifteen contact hours per week, which will add to an already overcrowded workweek for Newprof.

   (b) Newprof has an organic chemistry class this term that is becoming increasingly hostile toward him. He strongly suspects that two pre-med "grade-grubbers" are spreading the word in the class that their professor is unfair in his grading.

   (c) With tests to give and grade, committee meetings to attend, classes to meet, lectures to prepare, and lab reports to read, Newprof hasn't been to a movie in a month, washed his car in three months, or visited his parents since Christmas.

2. From conversations you have heard, what would you say are currently the top three sources of stress for faculty at your college? How might principles in this chapter be used in addressing them?

3. The suggestions to "organize your day" will be inherently easier to follow for some faculty than others. Recalling the MBTI typology in Chapter 6, speculate on the relative ease in following this advice for these types: INTJ, ESTJ, ENFP.

4. If you were a dean or department chair hoping to influence new faculty to protect summers for research, writing, and personal lives, what measures would you take?

---

[13] Bruce L. Partin, "The Unilateral Contract: A Faculty Morale Nightmare," *The Department Chair,* Vol. 2, No.2, (1991).

11

Promotion and Tenure

"*H*ey, professors!" Pete Makropolos's teeth flashed like piano keys under his salt-and-pepper moustache. "What's this they're telling me? You getting married?"

Adam Newprof closed the door behind him and followed Maggie Morrow to their usual booth by the window. Both were beaming. Pete had heard their news already.

"They told you right, Pete. She said yes. Coming up the week after graduation."

Makropolos came over to their booth, wiping his hands on his apron. "Hey, terrific! Tell you what. In honor of the occasion, the coffee's on me this morning. Wait—I'll do even better. Free danish. What the heck? How often do two of my best customers set the date?"

He was back shortly with the coffee and two cheese danish. Maggie smiled up at him.

"You're coming to the wedding, aren't you, Pete?"

"You bet. You send an invitation, I'll be there in my best outfit. Count on it. Now, I'll leave you to make your honeymoon plans while I wait on those other customers coming in. Don't do anything to embarrass me, lovers."

Adam sipped the strong coffee and savored its flavor along with the face across the table that had become so much a part of his life in Port St. Julian. They had been through a lot together, he and Maggie Morrow. They had come into the College of Port St. Julian together nearly four years ago. They had helped each other learn to teach. They had worked long hours together on the task force that proposed the new general education curriculum. She had encouraged him to send off his first paper to the *Journal of the American Chemical Society*, and he had pestered her until she submitted some of her poems for inclusion in an anthology of Southern poetry. But the biggest test they would share in the upcoming fall term.

"Are you nervous?" she asked him.

"About the tenure review next fall?"

"No! About the wedding, you crumb. Surely you're not thinking about tenure when your wedding is only a month away. Do you want to provoke a divorce before we're even married?"

He smiled and shook his head. "Sorry, Maggie. It's on my mind these days, I have to admit. I apologize."

"I should hope so. Come on now, Adam. Why on earth are you so uncertain about that tenure review? I can't think of anyone else who should breeze through so easily. Just relax. Look at me. I'll be up in the fall too, and you don't see me worrying, do you?"

"Okay, so I'm not entirely rational about this. That's how I'm built."

"Well, *be* rational, for goodness sake. There's not a chance in the world that you'll be turned down for tenure. Look at the record, Mr. Scientist."

"It's not the record that makes me nervous. I guess it's knowing that seven people from other departments will be sitting down around a table and assessing the record through their own eyes. After all, people do have axes to grind sometimes, and they do make mistakes."

"Look, I'm tired of seeing you fret about this thing. You've earned tenure and you'll get it. And so will I. Now, get your mind on to something *really* important. Do I need to offer suggestions?"

Adam laughed. "No. You do not. But when you're an old tenured full professor and I'm digging ditches, you'll remember this conversation."

Accountability and Recognition

Adam Newprof is not alone. In my own work with new faculty and in reports that I hear from other institutions, there is no single issue that causes more anxiety than the matter of tenure. They worry over their teaching, they struggle to get a program of scholarship underway, they fret over getting elected to faculty committees, but more than any of those they are apprehensive about measuring up at tenure time.

The tenure review is the definitive "accountability test" faced by faculty members, but there are two other types of accountability to which faculty at most colleges are subject: performance evaluation and promotion in rank. In a growing number of colleges there is also a midterm review scheduled for a point about halfway through the probationary period before tenure, and a post-tenure review as well at intervals up to retirement. We have looked already in the previous chapter about the tendency of faculty to feel especially averse to scrutiny by others. They have endured exam after exam over years as undergraduates and graduate students; they have had dissertations that had to pass muster with committees of scholars; but it is as if, having been subject to meeting the standards of others for so long, they are ready to be free of examination forever. Ready or not, accountability is a part of the professional picture for faculty members, and it will be for you. As you think about a good start in this profession, I would like to convince you that evaluations of all three varieties can be minimally painful, and can even be helpful.

Performance[1] evaluation has assumed an increasing prominence in academe as external accrediting agencies have come to require it. Where local systems have been fully developed, untenured faculty are generally evaluated by their department or division heads (or occasionally, when the faculty is not too large, by the dean) on an annual basis; the annual evaluation is continued for tenured faculty at a number of colleges, but at others it moves to a two-, three-, or five-year frequency. The approaches taken vary widely, ranging from a brief narrative paragraph to a rather detailed rating form coupled with a fairly extensive narrative and a face-to-face discussion between evaluator and faculty member. Whatever the approach, the performance areas examined are standard: teaching, scholarship, and service.[2] In the best systems, the evaluation will not result merely in an overall rating or label for the quality of work done, but will include specific citations of accomplishments of note, plus specific recommendations for improvement in each area.

For people who are themselves constantly engaged in evaluating others (students), faculty are not only unenthusiastic about being evaluated themselves, they are also susceptible to being "wounded" by any appraisal that finds them to be less than perfect. That is not a criticism, but an observation. I suspect strongly that this sensitivity stems again from the type of people who choose the faculty profession, characteristically very conscientious people who invest themselves totally in their work and identify with it personally to a degree approached, perhaps, only by artists. It should not be surprising that they do not take readily to any deep probing into performance.

Yet there can be abundant benefits in the performance evaluation, especially for those on the road to tenure. I would urge strongly that the good-start faculty member determine not to be wounded by or defensive about evaluation findings, but rather to extract those benefits that can come only from regular examination of how things are going. For example, your department chair

---

[1] "Performance" is another one of those words that most faculty members find mildly disagreeable. It is nonetheless the usual label for this type of evaluation.

[2] The exact labels vary; "research" or "professional development" may replace "scholarship," for example, and "citizenship" may replace "service."

might, at the end of your first year of teaching, recommend that you give more attention to course organization. One reaction[3] would be to bristle at the suggestion that your courses were lacking in organization, to reject the advice, and to feel depressed at this criticism of your work as a teacher. Another—wiser, I would say—reaction would be to examine the chair's reasons for feeling that some improvement in organization might be needed, and if you found those reasons compelling, to decide to make the organization better the next time around. The second reaction should lead to more effective teaching, and if that is your aim, both you and your students will have profited. The non-defensive faculty member will establish a good feedback system and will gain a sense that things are going better and better with each year. What better way can one approach the tenure decision? The sage evaluator—like a good teacher—will emphasize that it's okay not to be perfect; it's only when one fails to acknowledge and learn from one's mistakes that the offense becomes serious.

The accrediting agencies have left us with little choice as to whether or not colleges will conduct performance evaluations of faculty. But even if they had, I would argue for having them. After all, if the faculty are doing the most important work of the college, do we not have an obligation to ask regularly and seriously how well it is being done?

Indeed, well before any official evaluation of your performance (or if you happen to be at a college where no formal process is in place), it is smart to do a self-assessment of how things are going. It isn't hard to do, and it can help you face the "real" evaluation with much greater confidence. You will want to begin by gathering whatever kinds of information your evaluator will be using later on as evidence of your performance.[4] With this material before you, use either the evaluation forms of your college (if forms are used) or the standards set forth in your faculty handbook to see what aspects of performance you need to examine with special care. Appraise the record *candidly* item by item, actually rating yourself, if there is a form. In addition, it can be helpful, despite the redundancy, to write out three sets of "pluses and minuses," one each for teaching, scholarship, and service. This extra step forces you to think coherently about how the whole picture is likely to appear to the evaluator. The sole object of this exercise is not, of course, just to estimate early on what is probably going to happen at evaluation time; instead, an important

---

[3] And perhaps the predictable one for an INTJ personality, which finds it difficult to accept the judgment and leadership of others in any circumstance!

[4] Although we are living in a period when the notion of "evidence" is not universally accepted, you can be sure that a college that uses formal evaluations will expect the evaluator to have some sound basis of deciding on the quality of performance. You may want to refer back to Chapters 6 and 7 to see what typical evidence is used to establish the quality of teaching and scholarship.

goal should be to identify for yourself what needs attention so that you can attend to it right away.[5]

To acquire some guidance as to what features of performance tend to matter most, along with the criteria on your particular campus, you might wish to inspect the following list of factors taken from Peter Seldin's 1988 survey of liberal arts college deans:[6]

Factor	% Saying Major Factor in Overall Performance Evaluation
Classroom teaching	99.8%
Student advising	64.4%
Campus committee work	54.1%
Length of service in rank	43.9%
Research	38.8%
Publication	29.4%
Personal attributes	29.4%
Activity in professional societies	24.9%
Public service	19.5%
Supervision of graduate study	2.8%
Supervision of honors program	2.4%
Consultation	2.4%
Competing job offers	1.8%

While there is a tendency to see evaluation as primarily intended to discover and correct deficiencies, and even the above paragraphs may have that tone, it is also through evaluation that we are able to recognize faculty accomplishments. The most obvious example of this recognition is when someone is promoted in rank, but at performance evaluation time, too, it is just as essential to underscore successes and strengths as to point out shortcomings. Even when the evaluator is sensitive to this recognition function of evaluation, the perfectionist faculty member being evaluated is very apt to be deaf to the praise, hearing only the din of criticism. There is potential for development in both approval and observations about imperfections. I would urge the good-start faculty member to be open to the praise and learn from it too. Don't presume that the chair is just being polite or trying to soften the criticism with a dash of applause. Pay attention to what the chair feels is working for you. Those things that the chair finds praise-worthy at performance evaluation time, a personnel committee, the dean, and the president are likely to find as good evidence for tenure and promotion.

---

[5] The counterpart in student learning is for the student to self-test before the real test comes around.

[6] Peter Seldin, "How Colleges Evaluate Faculty," *AAHE Bulletin 41* (1989).

The Road to Tenure and Promotion

There is surely no status more coveted by faculty who don't have it and no academic custom more resented by the general public than tenure. The vast majority of liberal arts colleges offer tenure, books have been written on the subject,[7] and yet there is a great deal of irrationality with regard to tenure both inside and outside of academe. Primarily intended to guarantee academic freedom, both faculty and non-faculty too often take tenure to be instead a guarantor of lifetime employment. The precise perquisites provided by tenure are actually set, not by a universally accepted definition, but by the Board of Trustees of the individual college. Looking for the "lowest common denominator," we find that the essential provision of tenure is *a guarantee that a faculty member will not be discharged without cause.* "Cause" is established by means of a list of conditions specified in the faculty handbook. These usually include failure to perform required duties (either out of neglect or because of physical or mental incapacity), violation of a stipulated moral code, program reduction or elimination, or institutional financial exigency. Further, while the college can usually sever its ties with an untenured faculty member simply by deciding not to renew that person's annual contract,[8] dismissal of a tenured faculty member requires that the faculty member's case can be heard formally, usually by a faculty committee. Whatever the public view, and whatever faculty handbooks may have to say about it, tenure does, in fact, almost always mean assurance of a permanent appointment. No wonder so many workers in other "industries" envy the tenured faculty member!

Promotion in rank receives far less attention than does tenure, even though promotion normally carries with it an increase in salary, while the bestowing of tenure often does not. There is frequent debate among faculty as to whether promotion or tenure should require a higher level of demonstrated performance. There is even a literature on "tenurability *vs* promotability."[9] The debate seems to be fueled by confusion between the relative benefits of each *status* on the one hand, and the significance of each *decision* on the other. Clearly, job security is more valuable to most faculty than is a modest salary increase, which leads some faculty and administrators to conclude that tenure should be "harder to get" than promotion from assistant to associate professor. But when we look at what is being decided in each instance, the argument

---

[7] See, for example, Commission on Academic Tenure in Higher Education, *Faculty Tenure* (San Francisco, CA: Jossey-Bass , 1973).

[8] Individual colleges may well provide more protection than this for the untenured faculty member, but if so, it is done at the discretion of the college rather than because of some "industry standard."

[9] See, for example, Y. S. Lincoln, "The Structure of Promotion and Tenure Decisions in Institutions of Higher Education: A Policy Analysis," *The Review of Higher Education 6* (1983), pp. 217-231.

goes the other way. A decision to tenure is a decision to "bet the future" on someone, i.e., a judgment that this person is of a quality—as teacher, scholar, and citizen—that shows promise for future achievements. A decision to promote, on the other hand, is a judgment that someone has achieved enough of significance to earn the special recognition represented by advancement in rank. Looked at this way, promotion, unlike tenure, is public acknowledgment of *meritorious accomplishment*. It is not uncommon to find colleges avoiding debate of this kind by having the decisions about tenure and promotion to associate professor coincide. In any event, the same evaluation factors are nearly always involved in the two types of decisions, whatever their relative timing.

The following results of a 1987 U.S. Department of Education survey of department chairs in four-year private colleges will give some idea of the relative importance being attached to various factors at tenure time.

Factor	% Saying "Very Important" in Granting Tenure
Teaching quality	96%
Highest degree	75%
Fit with department or institution	56%
Institutional activities or service	54%
Fit with student body	49%
Quality of research	22%
Quality of publications	19%
Reputation in professional field	19%
Community or professional service	19%
Affirmative action considerations	16%
Number of publications	10%
Reputation of candidate's graduate school	6%
Ability to obtain outside funding	0%

As reported in *The Department Chair*, Vol. 1, No. 1, 1990

That background provided, how should you, as a good-start faculty member, approach this matter of tenure and promotion? Let me respond to that with a personal account. I can recall when I was a young professor in an old college expressing to a departmental colleague who was some thirty years older my apprehension about tenure. Looking slightly bemused, he said, "Oh, don't worry about it. It'll happen in due time." It struck me that he was being rather nonchalant about a matter that I considered most serious, maybe even central. I thought to myself that he could afford to be casual. He was tenured so long before that it was ancient history, and he had been a full professor since I was a first grader. Indeed, he had been a dean by the time I got to college. His career was no longer in question. Mine still was. The following year, my third as a faculty member, I received a letter from the president telling me that the trustees had awarded me tenure and promoted me to Associate

Professor. No evaluation. No committee to meet with. No interrogation by the department chairman. Just a decision that allowed me to relax.

Academe has changed since those days. Tenure and promotion are always preceded by formal evaluation processes, and the "stress index" has trended upward, I suspect, because we have made everything so formal. Still, I would argue that my older colleague gave good advice when he said, "Relax." It's the same advice that I gave to students in my classes over the years when they were worried about tests and grades early in a course. And aren't the situations—passing a course and achieving tenure or promotion—rather similar? Why do students in a college course feel such high anxiety? Is it because they believe themselves incapable of mastering the subject? I think not. Their greatest fear is surely that the professor will deal with them arbitrarily and capriciously, ask them tricky questions, count off too many points, and give them too little time to finish an assignment.

What do faculty fear? How many worry that they are incapable of being good enough at their jobs to pass muster? Few, I suspect. I would contend that faculty, like their students, worry most about arbitrariness and capriciousness. Will I get caught on a technicality? Will I fail with the Faculty Personnel Committee, the dean, or the president because they don't like me? Will the "judges" become so preoccupied with a few minor shortcomings that they ignore my valuable contributions?

A major responsibility of every college, I believe, is to lower the "stress index" of its faculty just as much as possible by making utterly clear statements about expectations. The most common approach to relieving anxiety about tenure and promotion has been to create sections of faculty handbooks that are couched in all sorts of legal terms intended not to provide clarification but rather protection in the (likely?) event that, when decision time comes around, the committee or administration might try to shoot down the deserving faculty member. I would like to suggest that such a prospect is no more likely than the prospect of a professor flunking a student just for the fun of it. And that, in turn, is no more reasonable than a doctor rejoicing when a patient dies. The strategy for reducing stress, I would maintain, should lie in clear messages rather than crafty prose.

To that end, I would opt for language something like the following.

> To be endorsed for tenure, the faculty member must have served the requisite probationary period and must have demonstrated:
> 1. evidence of solid competence as a teacher
> 2. dedication to and evidence of active scholarship
> 3. active involvement in college service
> 4. good fit for faculty membership in light of the purpose of the college, and his or her demonstrated ability to work effectively with colleagues
>
> To be endorsed for promotion the faculty member must have served

the requisite time in rank and have demonstrated the same qualities as are described for tenure above, with evidence of competence in all and noteworthy accomplishments in one or more of the three performance areas.

I think anyone who reads that statement, faculty member or administrator, will understand what it means. Handbook language never stops with anything so simple, of course. Lawyerly purposes require layers of definitions. Well, what do you *mean*, the lawyer must ask, by "solid competence"? And what exactly constitutes "*active* scholarship"? And what *counts* as "college service"? And (shudder!), "good *fit*," for goodness sake? Come on!

Questions of that ilk are, of course, perfectly understandable in an environment that cultivates analysis and debate, and they are not *bad* questions at all. There is much to be derived from discussions about how we know with reasonable certainty that faculty candidates for tenure and promotion have met the standards set forth above. What kinds of evidence are valid and available? How can I know that I am making good progress toward reaching those standards? It is neither questioning nor precision of language that I'm criticizing, but rather the priority in handbook writing of protection over clear communication. However the handbook on your campus reads, chances are that if you take the statement above as a guide and succeed in meeting its provisions, you will sail through the tenure and promotion reviews that lie ahead for you.

My observation to students who came by to argue over points was that (a) they needed to trust me to do the fairest, most conscientious job possible in evaluating their level of mastery; (b) that if I were such a scoundrel as to grade their work arbitrarily, there was ultimately no real protection; and (c) that my satisfaction as a teacher came from seeing my efforts at teaching them succeed and therefore it was silly to presume that I faked the evidence so as to prove that I had failed to teach. Their focus therefore should be on mastering the subject thoroughly and trusting me to be an authentic teacher, someone who cared about his students and longed earnestly to see them succeed.

My observation to faculty looking toward tenure and promotion differs little from that. The challenge is simply to *be* your best. The challenge is to be competent as a teacher, to remain alive as a scholar, to practice good college citizenship, to work cooperatively with colleagues in support of the mission of the college. For students the counsel might be: *Concentrate on mastery and the grades will take care of themselves.* To athletes it might be: *The best way to win trophies is to be a champion.* Unless we are working with scoundrels, it is what we *are* that will matter, not what we manage to *appear* to be. What I am saying is that the most productive strategy for becoming tenured or promoted is to concentrate on being good at what you do. Administrators and personnel committees want new faculty to succeed. Their success guarantees the corporate success of the college.

Although confident that the statement of expectations given above is unambiguous, I will suggest some additional questions that are worth asking in each faculty performance area to evaluate one's performance.

1. Teaching

- Do course materials (syllabi, handouts, assignments) present intellectual tasks that are appropriately challenging? (What do annual evaluations indicate were the department chair's opinion of the quality of the intellectual tasks?)
- Are student ratings of instruction indicative of a teacher who is effective at communicating and making the learning experience as pleasant as possible? (Do students' ratings of overall effectiveness fall generally at or above college norms?)
- Do standardized test results (when available) indicate that students have a high level of mastery of the subject matter?
- What evidence is there of continuing efforts to improve teaching?

2. Scholarship

- Does the record of paper presentation and publication suggest an ongoing study of some defined area of scholarship and/or creativity?
- What indications are there that the faculty member has scholarly and/or creative works in progress?
- What indications of scholarly accomplishment have been given by the department chair's annual evaluations?
- Is there evidence of continuing active involvement in professional organizations (meeting attendance, officer, panel participant, session chair)?
- Has there been regular involvement of students in research or independent study projects?
- Has support been sought for funding research projects?
- What evidence is there of maintaining currency in the discipline?

3. Service

- Has the faculty member regularly accepted his or her share of "citizenship" duties (committee work, departmental chores, advising students and student organizations, etc.)?
- Has the faculty member occasionally served as a resource person or speaker in the community?
- Has the faculty member had a generally positive impact on campus morale?

4. Fit

- Has the faculty member cooperated with colleagues in solving problems and taking initiatives for progress?

- Has the individual demonstrated a basic understanding of and commitment to the purposes of liberal arts education?
- Has the individual demonstrated support for and sympathy with the statement of purpose of the college?

If Ernest Boyer's proposed "reconsideration" of scholarship (see Chapter 7) comes to be taken seriously, colleges may well reorganize their performance evaluation forms to erase boundaries between what have traditionally been treated as distinct areas. Indeed, it is difficult to see how any significant encouragement can be extended to connect teaching and scholarship or scholarship and service until evaluation instruments can be designed which reflect the overlaps.

You should make certain to take full advantage of each year's performance evaluation by the department chair as you try to assess your progress toward tenure. Ask questions. Insist on clear answers. Ask for advice. Ask for support. Maybe even make up a "test" for yourself based on the standards set forth above. Whatever means you use, be sure you use them regularly; don't wait until the year before the decision is due to start thinking seriously about it.

In case you would like an "instrument" to assist you in your efforts to assess progress toward tenure, one called "Twenty Questions" is supplied on the following pages. It is not a precision instrument, but it can give you a good idea about your own degree of progress.

TWENTY QUESTIONS

An Instrument for Assessing Progress Toward Tenure

Circle the letters on the scoring sheet for the responses that seem to apply best, then refer to the interpretation key on the reverse side of the scoring sheet.

TEACHING

1. **What does the feedback from your colleagues and your department chair suggest about the intellectual tasks you set for your students, the appropriateness of tests and course materials used, and your course organization?**
   a. Very encouraging feedback; nearly everything positive.
   b. Generally encouraging feedback; just a few key items that seem to need attention.
   c. Feedback suggests some significant attention is needed to making improvements.

2. **What do your students' ratings suggest about their reception of your teaching?**
   a. Very reassuring; student ratings have generally been above the college mean.
   b. Generally reassuring; student ratings have generally been very close to the college mean.
   c. I'm concerned; student ratings have mostly been significantly under the college mean.

3. **What do results of departmental or nationally-normed exams suggest about how much your students are learning?**
   a. Very reassuring; students from my classes have achieved generally at high levels.
   b. Generally reassuring; students from my classes have achieved on a par with most.
   c. Somewhat troubling; students from my classes have achieved at generally low levels.

4. **What indications have there been, based on attrition data (withdrawals plus failures), that the students in your courses have profited from your teaching?**
   a. Very encouraging indications; minimal attrition in all courses.
   b. Generally encouraging indications; only modest attrition in my courses compared with departmental norms.
   c. Attrition is high enough to be troubling; worse than is normal in my department.

5. **What do class grades suggest about standards set in your courses?**
   a. Very reassuring; class GPAs have nearly always been in line with the students' GPAs in the other courses they were taking.
   b. Generally reassuring; class GPAs have been generally either a bit higher or lower than the students' GPAs in the other courses they were taking.
   c. Somewhat troubling; class GPAs have often been considerably higher or lower than the students' GPAs in other courses they were taking.

6. **How have you used feedback from colleagues and course/instructor survey data from your students?**
   a. I've tried to look at feedback and student survey data objectively, to continue to do those things that seemed to be working well, and to make changes where they seemed to be needed.
   b. I've considered feedback and survey data and have been either encouraged or discouraged at various times, but haven't deliberately acted on the basis of either.
   c. I have generally ignored feedback and survey data.

7. **How successful do you feel as a teacher at this point?**
   a. Very successful.
   b. Successful, but with aspirations of being even better.
   c. Not especially successful.

SCHOLARSHIP

8. **What have you done about staking out an area of scholarly or creative activity for yourself?**
   a. I have defined clearly for myself an area of scholarly or creative activity, have the literature well in hand, have projects in progress, and have a clear plan for what I will be doing next.
   b. I have identified an area in which to work, am fairly current in the literature, and have specific projects planned.
   c. I have no active scholarly or creative projects underway or imminent.

9. **To what extent have you published papers based on your research or scholarly work?**
   a. Regularly; nearly every year.
   b. Occasionally; about every other year.
   c. Rarely or never; nothing in the past three years.

10. **To what extent have you presented papers based on your research or scholarly work?**
    a. Regularly; nearly every year.

    b. Occasionally; about every other year.

    c. Rarely or never; nothing in the past three years.

11. **What efforts have you made to keep current in your field?**
    a. Have regularly attended workshops and conferences that promised to provide updating in my field; have kept up with the new literature.
    b. Have occasionally attended workshops and conferences that promised to provide updating in my field, have occasionally read relevant new publications.
    c. Have done little reading beyond texts, and have seldom attended workshops or conferences that promised to provide updating in my field.

12. **To what extent have you collaborated with students on research or scholarly projects?**
    a. I have regularly directed students in research or independent study projects in my area of interest.
    b. I have occasionally directed students in research or independent study projects in my area of interest.
    c. I have directed students in research or independent study rarely or not at all.

13. **To what extent have you been involved in professional organizations?**
    a. Leadership position in a professional organization, with regular attendance at its meetings.
    b. Membership in a professional organization, with regular attendance at its meetings.
    c. Inactive in any professional organization; have seldom attended professional meetings.

14. **To what extent have you sought funding for scholarly projects?**
    a. Have regularly sought external and internal grants for projects.
    b. Have regularly sought internal grants for projects.
    c. Have seldom sought either external or internal grants for projects.

CITIZENSHIP

15. **How extensively have you participated in college governance and the associated committee work?**
    a. Quite extensively; I have served regularly on standing or *ad hoc* committees, task forces, study groups, councils, or panels, and have been a source of ideas or leadership for their work.
    b. To a reasonable extent; I have occasionally served on college committees, task forces, groups, councils, or panels, and have accepted assignments in the course of that service.

    c. Not very extensively; I have rarely been involved in college governance and committee work.

16. **How well acquainted are you with colleagues from other departments and with college staff members?**
    a. Very well; I know all the faculty and key staff members by name and have friends outside the department.
    b. Fairly well; I know most everyone in the faculty and several staff members by name.
    c. Not well; I know few people outside my department.

17. **How extensively have you participated in departmental affairs?**
    a. Quite extensively; I have entered regularly into departmental discussions, provided ideas for departmental progress, and volunteered for departmental responsibilities.
    b. To a reasonable extent; I have occasionally entered into departmental discussions and accepted departmental responsibilities.
    c. Not very extensively; I have not been actively involved in departmental meetings, and have usually begged off departmental assignments.

18. **To what extent have you been involved in providing professional expertise to the community?**
    a. Quite extensively; I have regularly given talks to community groups and/or provided them with professional information.
    b. To a reasonable extent; I have occasionally given talks to community groups and/or provided them with professional information.
    c. Rarely or never.

INSTITUTIONAL FIT

19. **How much at home do you feel at the college?**
    a. Very much at home; I am an enthusiastic supporter of the mission of this college, and enjoy working to further its ends.
    b. Comfortable; I generally support the mission of the college and accept my responsibility to further its ends.
    c. Not very much at home; I honestly have problems with some aspects of the mission of the college, and have difficulty working to further its ends.

20. **How compatible do you feel yourself to be with your colleagues?**
    a. Very compatible; we work together well, and I get special satisfaction from being a member of a team.
    b. Compatible enough; we have no major problems working together.
    c. Not very compatible; we often have serious conflict when trying to work together.

SCORING

TEACHING

1.   ....c.........   .b..a......
2.   ....c.........   .b..a......
3.   ....c.........   .b..a......
4.   ....c.........   .b...............................a......................
5.   ....c.........   .b...............................a......................
6.   ....c.........   .b.........................a.........................
7.   ....c.........   .b.........................a.........................

SCHOLARSHIP

8.   ....c.........   .b..a......
9.   ....c.........   .b..a......
10.   ....c.........   .b...............................a......................
11.   ....c.........   .b...............................a......................
12.   ....c.........   .b.........................a.........................
13.   ....c.........   .b.........................a.........................
14.   ....c.........   .b.........................a.........................

CITIZENSHIP

15.   ....c.........   .b..............................a......
16.   ....c.........   .b...............................a......................
17.   ....c.........   .b...............................a......................
18.   ....c.........   .b.........................a.........................

INSTITUTIONAL FIT

19.   ....c.........   .b..............................a......
20.   ....c.........   .b..............................a......

INTERPRETATION OF RESULTS

Examine the pattern of circles on the scoring sheet. The farther to the right the pattern clusters, the more certain the progress toward tenure.

If responses are generally in the "a" zone to the right, you are well on the way to a positive tenure decision, and could serve as a model for others.

If responses are generally in the "b" zone in the center, you are making reasonable progress toward tenure.

If responses are generally in the "c" zone to the left, it is highly unlikely that you will be tenured unless you change the record significantly before time for the decision is made.

Within the "a" and "b" zones, the farther to the right a response lies within the zone, the more significant indicator of "tenurability" that response may be considered to be.

Where *any* response lies in the "c" zone, regardless of the *general* pattern, you should consider what needs to be done to move into the "b" or "a" zones.

For Discussion————————————————

1. One argument that has been made against the formal evaluation of faculty performance is that it turns attention inward on oneself rather than outward on the work to be done. Do you feel that argument has any merit? Speculate on the reasons for the increased practice of formal faculty evaluation despite the risk of encouraging excess self-consciousness in faculty. (Get beyond the external pressure from accrediting agencies, and look for reasons they are exerting pressure, as well as the possible benefits of evaluation.)

2. The institution of tenure is often associated with "academic freedom." What do you understand to be meant by "academic freedom," and what does your faculty handbook have to say about it?

3. A distinction was made in this chapter between "tenurability" and "promotability." What is your own feeling about whether tenure or promotion should require higher standards of accomplishment? Why?

4. Propose questions that might be placed on an evaluation form to assess one's "scholarship of integration," "scholarship of application," and "scholarship of teaching"—three of the four overlapping aspects of scholarship identified by Boyer in *Scholarship Reconsidered*.[10]

---

[10] Ernest L. Boyer, *Scholarship Reconsidered: Priorities of the Professoriate* (Princeton, NJ: The Carnegie Foundation for the Advancement of Teaching, 1990), pp. 24-25.

12

Staying Good

Meet is it changes should control
Our being, lest we rest in ease.
Alfred, Lord Tennyson
Love Thou Thy Land

*T*he dean greeted the young man, but didn't invite him to sit down.

"Come on, Dr. Goodstart. Let's go outside and find a bench. It's too nice a day to sit in this stuffy office."

The older man ushered his visitor past the secretary's desk and across the reception room. They turned right in the hallway, and exited through the large front doors onto the porch of Founder Hall. They paused at the top of the steps between two tall white columns as the dean pointed to a construction project underway across the quad.

"I guess you can see some changes in the new art building since you were here for an interview."

"Sure can," Goodstart answered. "The steel was just going up when I was here in March. I had imagined it would be a very contemporary-looking building, but I can see now how compatible it's going to be with the older buildings. I like that."

"Come on—may I call you Gary? Let's grab that bench down under the big beech tree."

When they had settled in the shade of the beech, the young man pushed his glasses up and surveyed the front campus.

"You know, this campus is even prettier than I remembered it. I think I'm going to like teaching here."

"I think you will, too, Gary. I try not to make premature judgments, but something tells me that you're exactly the kind of person who'll be right at home on the Poplar Cove College faculty."

"I hope so. How many other new faculty are coming in this fall?"

"There'll be, let's see, I guess nine more. Yours is a new position, and five others are. We're still growing, it seems. We had seventy faculty when I came here four years ago. This fall, when your group comes in, we'll have eighty-four."

"That's pretty rapid growth. New buildings, higher enrollment, better students, more faculty, new programs—seems like an exciting time to come to Poplar Cove. Tell me, have you enjoyed being the dean here? I know you must get a lot of satisfaction from all the progress, but you taught for a long time, didn't you?"

The dean nodded and smiled. "Yes I did. Fifteen years. And I miss it still. But administration has its rewards, too."

The younger man shook his head. "I don't think I could *ever* do administration. I want to be in there with the students, helping them learn, helping to—shape—them. Does that sound corny?"

"Not corny at all. That's how you should feel as you start a career as a college faculty member. It's how I felt."

"So—if you don't mind my asking—what made you leave the classroom?

"You know, when I started teaching, I never dreamed of anything else. I thought I'd hone my craft until I was the best teacher there ever was, and that I'd settle down in an office that held a thousand books and dispense wisdom to succeeding generations of eager young minds. I saw teaching as such an—eternal—calling. Stable, constant. But you never know how things will develop. In my fifth year, just after my tenure decision, my department chair told me that he had decided to step down because of health problems, and that he had recommended me as his successor. So halfway through my fifth year I became a department chair. That's when I began to see how much influence for good someone could have doing administrative work. When the deanship here was advertised, I had been a chair for about a decade, and I guess I was at a point in life when calling a few more of the shots appealed to me. Anyway, I applied, got selected, and now I have four years of deaning behind me. Now—so much for my story. Let's talk about you. What can I do to help as you look ahead to next month?"

"Well, this may seem sort of silly, but the reason I asked to see you this morning was to get some advice. I've learned during my years as a student that getting off to a good beginning in a course is a key to success, and I guess I'd just like to hear your ideas about how to get things started off right as a faculty member."

Dean Newprof smiled in quiet satisfaction. This new recruit was a rare find.

After the Start

When driving down that interstate toward Port St. Julian nearly two decades before, Adam Newprof had been focused very much on the immediate future. He had been thinking about moving into his first office, teaching his first classes. What he had known then about the life of a faculty member had been learned through a student's eyes, and necessarily over a very brief snippet of time. The professors who had taught him had had careers before and after he spent time with them, but Newprof never thought of them in that way. Doc Paradigm would always be, for him, a man in his fifties, bald, a pipe clenched between his teeth, forever about to do some research he never got around to, chronically underprepared for lectures, but without equal in caring for and helping his students. Approaching Port St. Julian to start his own career, Newprof had supposed that this old college would become his professional home, that he would enjoy its familiar rhythms year after year after year. He had presumed that the years before—school, college, graduate school, the army hitch—were stages on the way to stability. His thoughts had not been about a "career" at all, but about a life.

If he had been right, there would be no need for this chapter. But a book that sets out to advise faculty members entering the profession would end prematurely if it left its readers with the impression that getting a good start is the whole story. Work in recent years has shown that human development does not end at, say, age twenty-one, but rather that adult life, too, consists of successive predictable stages. And, while there are surely individual differences, even those choosing the faculty life experience these stages. There are, in addition, ways in which the career of a faculty member is unique, and which result in certain changing emphases and preoccupations as the years pass.

A phase which many in the general public—and often even those connected with higher education—*believe* faculty enter is that following the granting of tenure. The conventional wisdom is that a post-tenure sclerosis sets in. There is often talk about "deadwood" as the product of giving a lifelong appointment to a faculty member. After all, doesn't the achievement of job security equate with a major reduction in accountability, and doesn't it stand to reason that a person forgiven accountability will become less productive? Isn't deadwood exactly what one would expect to be created by passage through the portal of tenure? Experience with many faculty members over many years tells me that this conventional wisdom is, in fact, a gross over-generalization; people who care about teaching and scholarship, and who approach their work conscientiously before tenure nearly always retain those characteristics after tenure. But not always. I have rarely seen a sharp transition in attitudes and work habits once tenure has been granted. What I *have* seen is a more gradual transition some years after the tenure decision. But tenure is not the only or even the primary force in the formation of developmental strata in faculty careers.

We will look further shortly at typical developmental phases that have been identified for faculty maturing in their profession. The point to be made here is that a good start, crucial as it is, is not automatic assurance that you will *stay* good throughout your career. As far away as mid-career and later-career may seem as you begin, they will eventually come. Your best assurance of staying a stimulating teacher, a productive scholar, and a good college citizen lies in the development in your early career of attitudes and habits that will stand you in good stead, not just through the tenure decision, but over the long haul.

Faculty Career Phases

We human beings—especially those who are attracted to the life of a faculty member— want to believe that we are unique. And so we are, each of us. But we also share far more than we tend to assume starting out. We would like to believe that our futures are unpredictable, and so they are in their detail. Still, studies of many individual faculty career histories reveal common threads and patterns that the good-start faculty member will want to take fully into account from the beginning. Roger Baldwin, one of the psychologists who has taken a look at the professional development of college faculty, offers this observation:

> Contrary to the popular myth, college and university professors do not reside in an ivory tower. They are subject to the same psychosocial forces as are other adults. Alternating periods of goal seeking and reassessment are common as academics proceed through their careers.[1]

A moment's reflection would probably lead any of us to expect, rather than thirty-five years of homogeneity, times of shifting preoccupation and focus. We would expect, for example, that in the first several years the major concentration would be on teaching, learning to do it well, developing techniques and strategies, gaining confidence; committee work and other service activities would occupy us less. In later years, matured in the teaching craft, we are likely to see a significant shift, with far more involvement in institutional citizenship activities and far less time required to meet our obligation as teacher. Baldwin has identified four rather distinct career stages shared by college faculty. The summary in the following table uses his labels for these stages.

Baldwin's stages cannot be assigned precise lengths, but most faculty members with fifteen or twenty years of experience will quarrel little with their general outline. The aim of the good-start faculty member should not be to defy somehow the predictions of the psychologists, but rather to expect that there will *be* stages, to recognize what is happening when one gets there, and to be

[1] Roger G. Baldwin, "Faculty Career Stages and Implications for Professional Development," in Jack H. Schuster, Daniel W. Wheeler, and Associates, *Enhancing Faculty Careers* (San Francisco, CA: Jossey-Bass, 1990), pp. 23-24.

Faculty Career Stages

Stage	Novice Professor	Early Academic Career	Midcareer	Late Career
Theme	• Getting into the academic world	• Settling down and making a name	• Accepting a career plateau or setting new goals	• Leaving a legacy
Characteristics	• Growth • Feelings of intense pressure	• Mastery of principal faculty roles • Concrete goals • "Make-or-break" feeling	• Productivity • Rewards • Questioning • Feeling of plateauing	• Thoughts of retirement • Paradox: Satisfaction with misgivings
Major Concerns and Activities	• Teaching competence • Starting a program of scholarship • Learning college culture, resources, policies, etc. • Juggling family & career responsibilities	• Refinement of teaching techniques and courses • Notice as a scholar • Involvement in professional organizations • Concern about the future • Service activity	• Desire for senior status in college and discipline • Worry about losing mastery • Heavy service activity • Consideration of shift to administration	• Finishing significant projects • Pride in accomplishments • Concern about losing touch with discipline • Fear of isolation • Sense of being unappreciated
Hazards	• Neglecting family • Being consumed by teaching & neglecting scholarship	• Neglecting family • Overextension • Vague anxiety	• Becoming deadwood • Resenting younger faculty	• Cynicism • Isolation

Adapted from Baldwin (1990)

attentive to the particular hazards of each stage. It may not be possible to defy the stages, to stay forever young as teacher-scholar-citizen, but it *is* possible to stay good through all the stages.

Staying Good as a Teacher

In the earlier years, particularly in the first year, there can be moments of deep pain for the conscientious teacher. For the perfectionist, even one pair of eyes glazing over or one question that is not smoothly fielded can spoil a class period or even a whole day. The skin thickens, however, and skill improves with time. Still, when the craft of teaching has been mastered, and when ultra-sensitivity has been attenuated, there are challenges for the experienced teacher who wants to remain lively and engaging over the years.

As with guidelines given in earlier chapters, we will look at a list of guidelines for staying good as a teacher, then discuss each in a subsequent paragraph. Here is the list:

+ Stay current.
+ Rework your courses regularly.
+ Discuss teaching with colleagues.
+ Stay alert to feedback.
+ Take advantage of faculty development opportunities.

The need to stay current is obvious. Stories abound of those who teach, say, the biology or political science of twenty years ago. No one means to do that, but if one's learning stopped twenty years ago, that will inevitably be the vintage of what is taught. I am not talking here about the type of currency that is needed to remain a contributing scholar, but rather the currency that is required to keep undergraduate course content accurate and properly set in the context of an evolving discipline. This will mean primarily (a) scanning closely the new texts that come out in the field, reading with particular care sections on topics that you are not at present including in your courses and that have not appeared in previous texts; (b) reading reviews of new texts, with an eye for titles you have not seen, treatments of new topics, and approaches to topics that are novel; (c) attending seminars and presentations at professional meetings that concentrate on new developments in the discipline; and (d) reading articles in journals devoted to the teaching of (as opposed to research findings in) the discipline.

The advantages to reworking your courses regularly are nearly as obvious as those of staying current in the field. Considering how much time one puts into the initial development of a course syllabus and lecture notes, the temptation to get multiple-year use out of them is also obvious. Beyond that, there is a certain comfort in working from familiar notes, and lowering the energy level needed for doing the class. If you mean to stay good at teaching, these enticements toward stagnation must, however, be overcome. Whether or not your latest efforts at staying current have turned up important new topics for incorporation or interesting new approaches worth trying, the process of rethinking the organization of things and reflecting on what worked well and less well the last time through will lead to course improvements. And in writing up new notes for your classes, your mind is automatically refreshed, yielding dividends in vitality and interest for your students.

Because most faculty members are introverts, and because teaching tends to be such a solitary occupation, discussion of teaching with others takes place far less frequently on college campuses than would be ideal. Where it does take place, the reports of benefits—and enjoyment—are nearly universal. If you find no such discussion on your campus, I would urge you to get it started yourself. In the simplest case, you may drop into a colleague's office to talk over a problem you are encountering in getting a particular concept across. There is greater profit still in organizing a group of faculty members who are willing to meet now and then to talk about teaching—variations in pedagogy, success and failures, techniques for dealing with difficult concepts, the motivation of students, approaches to testing and grading, and anything else that a group member brings up. This kind of ongoing conversation about teaching keeps you more open to new strategies for helping students learn, reenergizes you regularly for the task of teaching, refocuses you on the central mission of the college—and allows you to assist newer faculty who can profit from your experience as teacher.

Harder to act on than the first three admonitions, is the caution to stay alert to feedback about your teaching. Or more to the point, it seems harder for people to react appropriately to that feedback. Feedback may come from colleagues who are teaching your former students in a higher-level course, from the departmental grapevine, from direct student comments to you, and from student rating data for your courses. There is no lack of feedback. The trick is to be open to what it is telling you. In each case, in the tenth or twentieth year of teaching as in the first, you will need to set aside that natural inclination toward defensiveness, and to analyze as objectively as possible what you are hearing, then to act on your analysis in whatever way seems to be in order. It is important, of course, not to generalize from or overreact to isolated criticisms. One way to assess how generally one student's expressed view may be shared by others is to make habitual use of student ratings done in your courses. In Chapter 6, we looked at the use of those data which express with numerical symbols the general view of each class. It doesn't tell you everything, but it certainly gives valuable insight in many cases. For instance, if you hear a student complaint that you are unwilling to answer questions, and if your college includes an item that reads "This instructor was willing to provide assistance" or "This instructor was open to questions," it is an easy matter to determine whether or not this perception is shared by much of the class. If your college does not provide the results of student ratings in graphical form, I would strongly encourage you to put the data in that form for yourself.[2] (You may wish to refer back to Graph 6.2 for an example with accompanying discussion.) Looking at how results for your courses compare with campus norms each term can help assure that, for the core of normative items included on the campus form, things are staying on track. Where at any point something seems to need attention, you will be dealing with it early.

Faculty development opportunities exist on nearly every campus. Others are offered regionally or nationally. It is easy to think about those that focus on teaching as activities for newer faculty, but their value is at least as great for more senior faculty members. Like the teaching discussion groups recommended above, these not only can provide you with new ideas about and approaches to teaching, but they also furnish stimulation that helps keep your teaching lively until retirement.

Staying Good as a Scholar

The advantages of active scholarship and encouragement for the new faculty member to make a commitment to it were included in Chapter 7. Those who do make that commitment from the beginning usually will not need any special pointers about keeping their efforts fueled as time goes by. There are, however, some guidelines for staying good as a scholar that can stand the liberal arts college faculty member in good stead, when practiced on a continuing basis.

✦ Keep up with the literature.
✦ Keep active in professional societies.
✦ Keep a seminar program going in the department.
✦ Keep something cooking.
✦ Collaborate.

To keep up with the literature as a scholar means something more than "staying current," as that term was used in connection with maintaining good teaching. For purposes of active scholarship, you will want to review the table of contents of principal journals in whatever niche (as we called it in Chapter 7) you have staked out for yourself, then to acquire for your files and read carefully those articles that have relevance. There will also be the occasional monograph that falls within your area of interest, and these should also be obtained (through inter-library loan or otherwise) and read. Once you have developed this habit, the time required to keep up will really not be excessive. There is no one practice that will make a bigger contribution to your sense of "being on top of things" than knowing the latest publications in your area.

---

[2] This is an easy matter with computer packages that create graphs quickly from numerical data. If you are unacquainted with what is available and/or how to use it, your academic computer center or a colleague in another department will be able to give you a hand.

There are multiple ways to keep active in professional societies and multiple ways in which doing so will prove advantageous to the maturing scholar. First, it is vital to attend professional meetings, especially regional and national conferences, at least once each year, and more if time and resources will allow. We often hear laments over the vast number of esoteric papers presented at professional conferences. There is considerable basis for such criticisms, but as someone who has attended many, many such meetings, I can say without hesitation that I have never returned to campus without learning something new, and usually I have brought back an idea of something new to pursue. If you pick your papers thoughtfully, you are certain to enrich your knowledge of the discipline and to realize added stimulation for your own research and inquiry. And at even the most disappointing conference, contact with colleagues from other colleges and universities is still worth a great deal. One way you can improve the quality is to submit a paper yourself from time to time, and to make certain it is presented expertly. You can also be actively involved in professional organizations by service as an officer, a session chair, or a panel member; thereby improving the quality of the organization's activities, gaining the stimulation that comes from such involvement, and gaining as well recognition for yourself and your college.

If it is not happening already, you can initiate a seminar program which will help you, along with your colleagues, to maintain a lively atmosphere in the department. I am thinking here about a program that makes use of departmental faculty, invited speakers, and perhaps senior students to permit a weekly or biweekly forum for the presentation of seminars from the "cutting edge" of the discipline. These can include both the results of research going on in the department and presentations based on the recent literature. Universities with graduate schools will often send speakers from their faculty at no expense to the host department. This is another opportunity for valuable contact with other scholars, which also enhances the department's reputation with regional universities. Whatever the other benefits, you can expect this kind of program to provide the same sort of stimulation that comes from attendance at professional meetings.

"Keep something cooking" is a way of exhorting you to have going always some specific scholarly project. In a liberal arts college, this will not necessarily be a writing project, although writing in a disciplinary field is something most serious scholars will want to do now and then. It may be preparation of a paper or poster session for a national or regional meeting. It may be a research project in the laboratory or library. It may be work on a new textbook, lab manual, or study guide. It may be classroom research. The point is to maintain an active rather than passive posture with respect to your discipline over the years. You will want your students to see you, not as someone who used to be a scholar, but rather as a currently practicing scholar who enjoys learning and creating, whatever his or her age.

Collaboration with both students and peers was recommended in the earlier chapter on scholarship (Chapter 7). Beyond the advantages indicated there for getting significant work done expeditiously, collaboration gives the scholar that extra push to move along with a project that comes from having a partner to prod and to feel responsible for. If students are working with you, you will be meeting with them regularly to give direction, answer questions, and discuss findings. If you are collaborating with a colleague, you will be conferring in a similar fashion, and there will be expectations for your contributions to the project that will keep you on a schedule that could otherwise slide.

Staying Good as a Citizen

In the "Novice Professor" or "Early Academic Career" stages, it is not unusual to hear faculty members worrying out loud about getting elected to a standing committee of the faculty. It is also common to find "Midcareer" faculty members devoting more total time to service activities than to scholarship, and nearly as much time to service as to teaching. By midcareer it can be difficult to remember being anxious about opportunities for getting involved in college service; a few people will, after tenure, even become virtual dropouts from duties of citizenship. However one's feelings about them may evolve, citizenship and service remain as duties for nearly all faculty members, and it is important that one stay good at them through all career stages. I offer these guidelines for staying good as a citizen:

◆ Follow the service guidelines.
◆ Stay active, but avoid overextension.
◆ Practice statesmanship.

In Chapter 8 guidelines were given for committee work (• Do your homework, • Don't be bashful, • Help keep the train on the track, • Decide when to say no—and do it!) and for advising (• Know your advisees, • Practice patience, • Do your homework, • Establish your availability, • Be prepared for the personal). There is no need to elaborate further on these here, but these are principles that will serve at every career stage.

The admonition to stay active, but to avoid overextension is really a call for striking a healthy balance. It is vital for one to stay involved in faculty governance, departmental service, and student advising, both from the individual and institutional viewpoint. It is only by such involvement that the individual faculty member can continue to help shape the work environment. And the experience of the "Midcareer" and "Late Career" faculty member is a valuable asset to the institution. The pitfalls of becoming drawn too deeply into service activities were pointed out in Chapter 8, and the final guideline for committee work (Decide when to say no—and do it!) is aimed in that direction.

The practice of statesmanship should be a goal of every faculty member, but it is in "Midcareer" and "Late Career" that one is likely to have the maturity and stature to be especially effective in this role. It is a role too seldom accepted, so there will be abundant opportunities for any willing good-start faculty member who aspires to become a truly outstanding leader of the faculty. The statesman will set a high priority on the institutional good, will work at building bridges between campus factions, will act as peacemaker when there is faculty-administration friction. Perhaps it is in the section of Chapter 9 that deals with game-playing that we get some insight into the rarity of faculty statesmanship. Perhaps, when a fight is obviously shaping up over, say, salaries, it is human nature that discourages the midcareer faculty member from moderating emotional, faculty-lounge rhetoric and seeking to find some collaborative path that administration and faculty can follow together. It may be that demagoguery is in a sense more "natural" than statesmanship. If so, that only makes the latter practice more laudable. Easy or hard, natural or not, if you aim at statesmanship, your worth to your college—not to the administration of the college, but to the college as a community—will be immense.

Moving to Administration

Adam Newprof, as you have seen, is, after two decades in higher education, doing work he had no inkling towards in the beginning. He has left teaching behind, is no longer active as a chemist, and is instead investing very full days as an administrator. It may not be a service to suggest the possibility to enthusiastic teacher-scholars on the threshold of a career, that a day may come when they will willingly leave the faculty profession for something else. But, as we have seen, there is a point for many faculty members, during what Baldwin calls the midcareer stage, when they begin to ask questions about how they want to spend the years ahead. Most make their passage through that season and stay with their first choice. A few, though, decide to make a change, as Adam Newprof has.

Should you eventually think about a change, you should know that there are ways of testing whether administration is something you would find satisfying. Some colleges include in their faculty development programs opportunity for administrative internships. In this kind of program, the faculty member accepts duties in an administrative office on campus, working there with a full-time administrator for a certain period each week and receiving released-time from teaching. This is a risk-free way of gaining administrative experience and investigating how interesting and satisfying it might prove for you. More common as a means of trying out administration is to accept appointment as a part-time administrator. Most colleges employ such positions as a method of assuring the proper attention to and leadership for such enterprises as honors programs, general education programs, international studies, and the like. Like internships, these appointments allow for continued teaching, but lower the teaching load to give time for the administrative work. A more conspicuous example of part-time administration is the role of department chair. The faculty member who accepts this responsibility gets a somewhat deeper taste of academic management, in that there are typically some personnel responsibilities—hiring, scheduling, evaluation—for department chairs. Finally, some institutions make use of temporary administrative appointments. A typical example is to establish an assistant or associate deanship and appoint faculty to the post for a stated period of time, perhaps three to five years. The position may be full-time or part-time, depending on the preference of the dean, and it usually provides the assistant with rather broad exposure to academic administration. Whether intern, director, coordinator, or assistant dean, some faculty find the experience to be just what they need to help them decide whether or not to make a change in career paths.

Adam Newprof has found a great deal of satisfaction in administration. As he notes, he does miss teaching, but he has found some of the same gratification in working with young faculty members like Gary Goodstart. He has less control over his work day than when he was teaching, and finds far more of his time consumed in responding to others than he had expected. An offsetting compensation is, however, being in a position to shape far more significantly the environment in which teaching and learning go on. While he is no longer in the classroom himself, and although his direct contact with students is limited, he knows that his initiatives and decisions affect students all over the campus.

A price that must often be paid for moving to administration, and one that you should think about carefully, is the necessity for giving up not only teaching, but also one's academic home. It is not uncommon for the first-time experience as an administrator to come at the college where one has taught for some years; that may happen when an assistant or associate deanship or directorship opens up on the campus, and an able faculty member gets drafted into the position. For a deanship or a vice presidency, there are times when an "inside person" is a successful candidate; but at that level the search committee frequently has a kind of "savior syndrome," a longing to find some charismatic, flawless leader who will set all things straight. When this happens, outside candidates are unquestionably at an advantage, so that the midcareer faculty member who aspires to a deanship or vice presidency must give up any romantic notions of leading the college that one loves and calls home, and begin to explore the opportunities on other campuses. Adam Newprof never dreamed of leaving the College of Port St. Julian and taking up a new life at a college six hundred miles from Port St. Julian, at a place that he had, quite frankly, never even heard of before answering an ad in *The Chronicle*. But here he is three states away, at Poplar Cove College, fully recovered from a failed application to be dean at the College of Port St. Julian, and feeling successful in a new place.

Summing Up

You have chosen the best of the professions. After nearly two decades in the classroom and a decade more in college administration, after endless hours of grading papers and disappointing experiences with the faculty grapevine, after vexation with administrators who challenged my autonomy and frustration with faculty who are "never driven and seldom led," I still believe it is the best. Beyond the paper-grading, imperfect administrators, committee hours, and the students' game-playing, there is the unparalleled satisfaction of seeing eyes light up, the pleasure of intellectual pursuit, the priceless opportunity to shape minds and values, that makes being a faculty member a profession without peer.

It is not, however, an easy profession. The hours are long. Students and parents confuse the goal of diploma with the goal of education. The public often seems antipathetic. You never quite succeed as fully as you had hoped. You worry perennially about losing touch with your discipline. Just how easy it turns out to be will surely depend on how you start out. That good start will be critical to every aspect of your career—teaching, scholarship, citizenship, and an understanding of yourself as a developing professional. The theme of time travel in novels and films is longstanding. A popular example from the 1980s was the movie "Back to the Future," in which the protagonist travels back to the 1960s to visit his parents-to-be as teenagers and thereby changes his own future. When he gets back to the future (or to the present with which the film began), he finds it a better place for his going back and tinkering with the past. We think of that kind of story as the most impossible kind of fiction. Yet you, as a new faculty member, have a very similar kind of opportunity to make your future better. You can start now with your creation of the kind of faculty member you want to be next year and twenty years from now.

I have tried in the preceding chapters to suggest concrete ways of excelling in this best of professions. I have no doubt what a difference a good beginning can make. As you build your bookcases, think about how you will build yourself as a professional teacher-scholar. As one who still recalls the naive excitement at the outset, who knows well the evangelist-maestro-mentor-thespian-godship dream, I wish for you—not by accident or serendipity, but out of your own design and determination—a good start.

References

Aleamoni, Lawrence. "Evaluation Myths," *Academic Leader*, October 1985.

American Association of University Professors. *Academe*, March-April 1991.

American Association of University Professors. *Academe*, March-April 1992.

Astin, Alexander W., Korn, William S., Berz, Ellyne R. and Bailey, Robin. *The American Freshman National Norms for 1990.* Los Angeles, CA: Higher Education Research Institute, 1990.

Astin, Alexander W., Korn, William S., and Dey, Eric L. *The American College Teacher, National Norms for the 1989-90 HERI Faculty Survey.* Los Angeles, CA: Higher Education Research Institute, 1991.

Baldwin, Roger G. "Faculty Career Stages and Implications for Professional Development." In Jack H. Schuster, Daniel W. Wheeler, and Associates. *Enhancing Faculty Careers.* San Francisco, CA: Jossey-Bass, 1990.

Belmont Abbey College, Belmont, NC, 1990 catalog.

Bennett, William J. *To Reclaim a Legacy: A Report on the Humanities in Higher Education.* Washington, DC: National Endowment for the Humanities, 1984.

Berne, Eric. *Games People Play.* New York, NY: Grove Press, 1964.

Bolles, Richard N. *Three Boxes of Life and How to Get Out of Them.* Berkeley, CA: Ten Speed Press, 1981.

Bowen, William G. and Sosa, Julie Ann. *Prospects for Faculty in the Arts & Sciences.* Princeton, NJ: Princeton University Press, 1989.

Boyer, Ernest L. *The Condition of the Professoriate: Attitudes and Trends, 1989.* Princeton, NJ: The Carnegie Foundation for the Advancement of Teaching, 1989.

Boyer, Ernest L. *Scholarship Reconsidered: Priorities of the Professoriate.* Princeton, NJ: Princeton University Press, 1990.

Boyer, Ernest L. *A Classification of Institutions of Higher Education.* Princeton, NJ: Princeton University Press, 1987.

Boyer, Ernest L. *College: The Undergraduate Experience in America.* New York, NY: Harper and Row, 1987.

Cannon, Walter B. *Bodily Changes in Pain, Hunger, Fear, and Rage,* 2nd edition. New York, NY: Appleton Publishing, 1929.

Carnegie Foundation for the Advancement of Teaching. "Are Liberal Arts Colleges Really Different?", *Change*, March/April 1990.

Cashin, William E. "Student Ratings of Teaching: A Summary of the Research," IDEA Paper No. 20, Center for Faculty Evaluation & Development, Kansas State University, 1988.

Centra, John A. *How Universities Evaluate Faculty Performance: A Survey of Department Heads*. GREB Research Report No. 75-5bR. Princeton, NJ: Educational Testing Service, 1979.

Centra, John A. "Research Productivity and Teaching Effectiveness," *Research in Higher Education 18*, 379 (1983).

Cohen, P. A. "Effectiveness of Student-Rating Feedback for Improving College Instruction: A Meta-Analysis of Findings," *Research in Higher Education 13*, 321 (1980).

Commission on Academic Tenure in Higher Education. *Faculty Tenure*. San Francisco, CA: Jossey-Bass, 1973.

Copperud, Carol. *The Test Design Handbook*. Englewood Cliffs, NJ: Educational Technology Publications, 1979.

Davis-Van Atta, David, Carrier, Sam C., and Frankfort, Frank. *Educating America's Scientists: The Role of the Research Colleges*. Oberlin, OH: Oberlin College, 1985.

Dressel, Paul L., and Marcus, Dora. *On Teaching and Learning in College*. San Francisco, CA: Jossey-Bass, 1982.

Ebel, Robert L. *Essentials of Educational Measurement*. Englewood Cliffs, NJ: Prentice-Hall, 1986.

Eble, Kenneth E. *The Profane Comedy* . New York, NY: Macmillan, 1962.

Ehrenberg, Ronald G. "The Future of Academic Salaries: Will the 1990s Be a Bust Like the 1970s or a Boom Like the 1980s?", *Academe*, March-April 1991.

Eliot, Charles W. *Educational Reform: Essays and Addresses*. New York, NY: Century Co., 1898.

Featherstone, Joseph. "A Note on Liberal Learning," *Colloquy*, Fall 1988, Michigan State University.

Ferrum College, Ferrum, Virginia, 1990 catalog.

Francis, Carol. "Student Aid: Is it Working Like It Is Supposed To?," *Change*, July/August 1990.

Friedman, M. and Rosenman, R. H. "Association of Specific Overt Behavior Pattern with Blood and Cardiovascular Findings: Blood Cholesterol Level, Blood Clotting Time, Incidence of Arcus Senilis and Clinical Coronary Artery Disease," *Journal of the American Medical Association 169*, 1286 (1959).

Gaff, Jerry G. *New Life for the College Curriculum*. San Francisco, CA: Jossey-Bass, 1991.

Gilman, Daniel C. *University Problems in the United States*. New York, NY: Century Co., 1898.

Gleick, James. *Chaos: Making a New Science*. New York, NY: Viking Press, 1987.

Gmelch, W. H., Lovrich, N. P., and Wilke, P. K. "Stress in Academe: A National Perspective," *Research in Higher Education 20*, 477 (1984).

Harper, William R. *The Prospects of the Small College*. Chicago, IL: University of Chicago Press, 1900.

High School Graduates: Projections by State, 1986 to 2004 . Boulder, CO: Western Interstate Commission for Higher Education, 1987.

Holmes, David. *Abnormal Psychology*. New York, NY: Harper Collins Publishers, 1991.

Jan Krukowski Associates, Inc., with Kane, Parsons & Associates. *Attitudes About the Liberal Arts*. New York, NY: Jan Krukowski Associates, Inc., 1987.

Keirsey, David and Bates, Marilyn. *Please Understand Me*. Del Mar, CA: Prometheus Nemesis Book Company, 1984.

Kimball, Bruce A. *Orators & Philosophers: A History of the Idea of Liberal Education* . New York, NY: Teachers College Press, 1986.

Lawrence, Gordon. *People Types & Tiger Stripes: A Practical Guide to Learning Styles*, 2nd. Ed. Gainesville, FL.: Center for Applications of Psychological Type, 1979.

LeMoyne-Owen College, Memphis, Tennessee, 1990 catalog.

Lincoln, Y. S. "The Structure of Promotion and Tenure Decisions in Institutions of Higher Education: A Policy Analysis," *The Review of Higher Education 6*, 217 (1983).

Lyman, Howard B. *Test Scores and What They Mean*. Englewood Cliffs, NJ: Prentice-Hall, 1986.

Mandell, Richard D. *The Professor Game*. Garden City, NY: Doubleday, 1977.

Miller, Patrick W. and Erickson, Harley E. *Teacher-Written Student Tests: A Guide for Planning, Creating, Administering, and Assessing*. Washington, DC: National Education Association, 1985.

Mills College, Oakland, California, 1990 catalog.

Mintzberg, Henry. *Structure in Fives: Designing Effective Organizations*. Englewood Cliffs, NJ: Prentice-Hall, 1983.

Morrill, Paul Hampton and Speer, Emil R. *The Academic Profession: Teaching in Higher Education*. New York, NY: Human Sciences Press, 1982.

Myers, Isabel Briggs. *The Myers-Briggs Type Indicator*. Palo Alto, CA: Consulting Psychologists Press, 1962.

Myers, Isabel Briggs with Myers, Peter B. *Gifts Differing*. Palo Alto, CA: Consulting Psychologists Press, 1980.

National Research Council Survey of Earned Doctorates, survey results published annually.

National Institute of Education. *Involvement in Learning: Realizing the Potential of American Higher Education*. Washington, DC: U.S. Government Printing Office, 1984.

Newman, Cardinal John Henry. "Discourse IV: Liberal Knowledge Its Own End," *Scope and Nature of University Education*. London: J.M. Dent, 1915.

Partin, Bruce L. "The Unilateral Contract: A Faculty Morale Nightmare," *The Department Chair*, Vol. 2, No.2, 1991.

Pirsig, Robert M. *Zen and the Art of Motorcycle Maintenance*. New York, NY: William Morrow & Company, 1974.

Pollio, Howard R. "What Students Think About and Do During College Lectures," *Teaching-Learning Issues 52*, 1 (1984).

Project on Redefining the Meaning and Purpose of Baccalaureate Degrees. *Integrity in the Curriculum: A Report to the Academic Community*. Washington, DC: Association of American Colleges, 1985.

Provost, Judith A. and Anchors, Scott. *Applications of the Myers-Briggs Type Indicator in Higher Education*. Palo Alto, CA: Consulting Psychologists Press, 1987.

Roanoke College, Salem, Virginia, 1990 catalog.

Rosovsky, Henry. *The University: An Owner's Manual*. New York, NY: W.W. Norton, 1990.

Saint Mary College, Leavenworth, Kansas, 1990 catalog.

Seldin, Peter. "How Colleges Evaluate Professors, 1988 vs. 1983," *AAHE Bulletin 41*, 3 (1989).

Seldin, Peter. "Research Findings on Causes of Academic Stress," in Peter Seldin, editor, *Coping with Faculty Stress*. San Francisco, CA: Jossey-Bass, 1987.

Seldin, Peter. *The Teaching Portfolio: A Practical Guide to Improved Performance and Promotion/Tenure Decisions*. Bolton, MA: Anker Publishing Company, 1991.

Simpson College, Indianola, Iowa, 1990 catalog.

Sorcinelli, Mary Deane and Gregory, Marshall W. "Faculty Stress: The Tension Between Career Demands and 'Having It All,'" in Seldin, Peter, editor, *Coping with Faculty Stress*. San Francisco, CA: Jossey-Bass, 1987.

Study Group on the Conditions of Excellence in American Higher Education, National Institute of Education. *Involvement in Learning: Realizing the Potential of American Higher Education*. Washington, DC: U.S. Government Printing Office, 1984.

Upham, A. H. "The Liberal Arts," *Association of American Colleges Bulletin 16*, 332 (1930).

Veninga, Robert L. and Spradley, James P. *The Work/Stress Connection*. Boston, MA: Little, Brown, 1981.

Weimer, Maryellen. *Improving College Teaching: Strategies for Developing Instructional Effectiveness*. San Francisco, CA: Jossey-Bass, 1990.

Whitehead, Alfred North. *The Aims of Education*. New York, NY: Macmillan, 1929.

Wood, P. "Student and Peer Ratings of College Teaching and Peer Ratings of Research and Service." Paper presented at the annual meeting of the American Educational Research Association, Toronto, March 1978.

Wotruba, T. R. and Wright, P. L. "How to Develop a Teacher-Rating Instrument: A Research Approach," *Journal of Higher Education 46* (6), 653 (1975).

Index